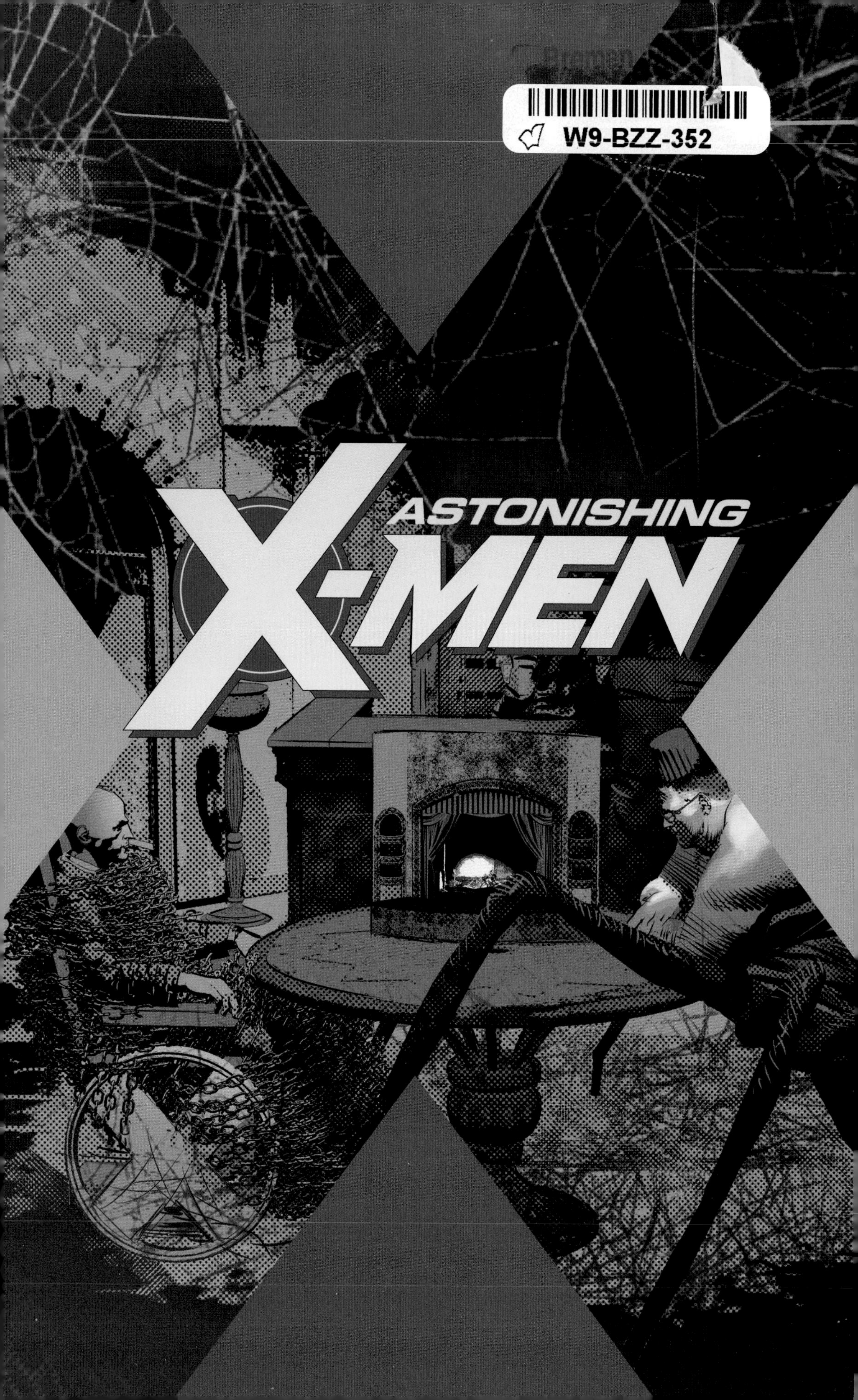
ASTONISHING
X-MEN

ASTONISHING X-MEN BY CHARLES SOULE VOL. 1: LIFE OF X. Contains material originally published in magazine form as ASTONISHING X-MEN #1-6. First printing 2018. ISBN 978-1-302-90850-8. Published by MARVEL WORLDWIDE, INC., a subsidiary of MARVEL ENTERTAINMENT, LLC. OFFICE OF PUBLICATION: 135 West 50th Street, New York, NY 10020. Copyright © 2018 MARVEL No similarity between any of the names, characters, persons, and/or institutions in this magazine with those of any living or dead person or institution is intended, and any such similarity which may exist is purely coincidental. **Printed in the U.S.A.** DAN BUCKLEY, President, Marvel Entertainment; JOE QUESADA, Chief Creative Officer; TOM BREVOORT, SVP of Publishing; DAVID BOGART, SVP of Business Affairs & Operations, Publishing & Partnership; DAVID GABRIEL, SVP of Sales & Marketing, Publishing; JEFF YOUNGQUIST, VP of Production & Special Projects; DAN CARR, Executive Director of Publishing Technology; ALEX MORALES, Director of Publishing Operations; SUSAN CRESPI, Production Manager; STAN LEE, Chairman Emeritus. For information regarding advertising in Marvel Comics or on Marvel.com, please contact Vit DeBellis, Custom Solutions & Integrated Advertising Manager, at vdebellis@marvel.com. For Marvel subscription inquiries, please call 888-511-5480. **Manufactured between 12/29/2017 and 1/30/2018 by LSC COMMUNICATIONS INC., KENDALLVILLE, IN, USA.**

10 9 8 7 6 5 4 3 2 1

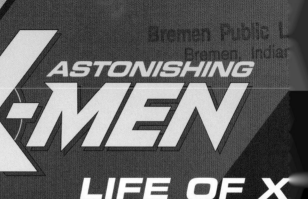

ASTONISHING X-MEN

LIFE OF X

Writer/**CHARLES SOULE**

ISSUE #1

Penciler/**JIM CHEUNG**

Inkers/**MARK MORALES,
GUILLERMO ORTEGO
& WALDEN WONG**

Color Artists/**RICHARD ISANOVE
& RAIN BEREDO**

Cover Art/**JIM CHEUNG
& RICHARD ISANOVE**

ISSUE #2

Artist/**MIKE DEODATO JR.**

Color Artist/**FRANK MARTIN**

Cover Art/**MIKE DEODATO JR.
& MARCELO MAIOLO**

ISSUE #3

Penciler/**ED McGUINNESS**
Inker/**MARK MORALES**
Color Artist/**JASON KEITH**
Cover Art/**ED McGUINNESS,
MARK MORALES
& DAVE McCAIG**

ISSUE #4

Penciler/**CARLOS PACHECO**

Inker/**RAFAEL FONTERIZ**

Color Artist/**RAIN BEREDO**

Cover Art/**CARLOS PACHECO
RAFAEL FONTERIZ
& NOLAN WOODARD**

ISSUE #5

Artist/**RAMON ROSANAS**

Color Artist/**NOLAN WOODARD**

Cover Art/**RAMON ROSANAS
& NOLAN WOODARD**

ISSUE #6

Artist/**MIKE DEL MUNDO**

Color Artists/**MIKE DEL MUNDO
& MARCO D'ALFONSO**

Cover Art/**MIKE DEL MUNDO**

Letterer/**VC's CLAYTON COWLES**

Assistant Editor/**CHRISTINA HARRINGTON**

Editor/**MARK PANICCIA**

X-Men created by Stan Lee & Jack Kirby

Collection Editor/**JENNIFER GRÜNWALD** · Assistant Editor/**CAITLIN O'CONNELL**
Associate Managing Editor/**KATERI WOODY** · Editor, Special Projects/**MARK D. BEAZLEY**
VP Production & Special Projects/**JEFF YOUNGQUIST** · SVP Print, Sales & Marketing/**DAVID GABRIEL**
Book Designer/**JAY BOWEN**

Editor in Chief/**C.B. CEBULSKI** · Chief Creative Officer/**JOE QUESADA**
President/**DAN BUCKLEY** · Executive Producer/**ALAN FINE**

1

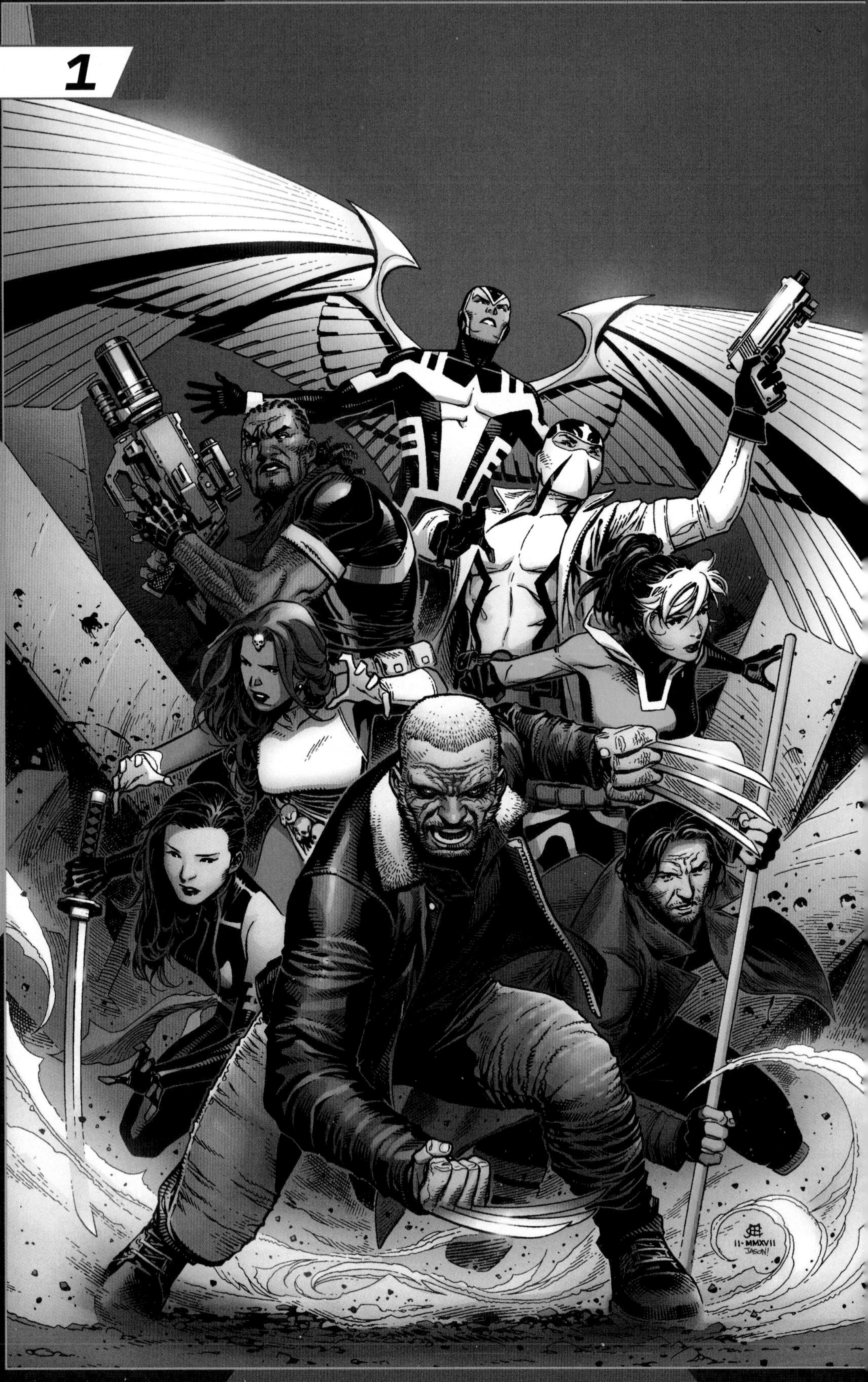
11·MMXVII
JASON!

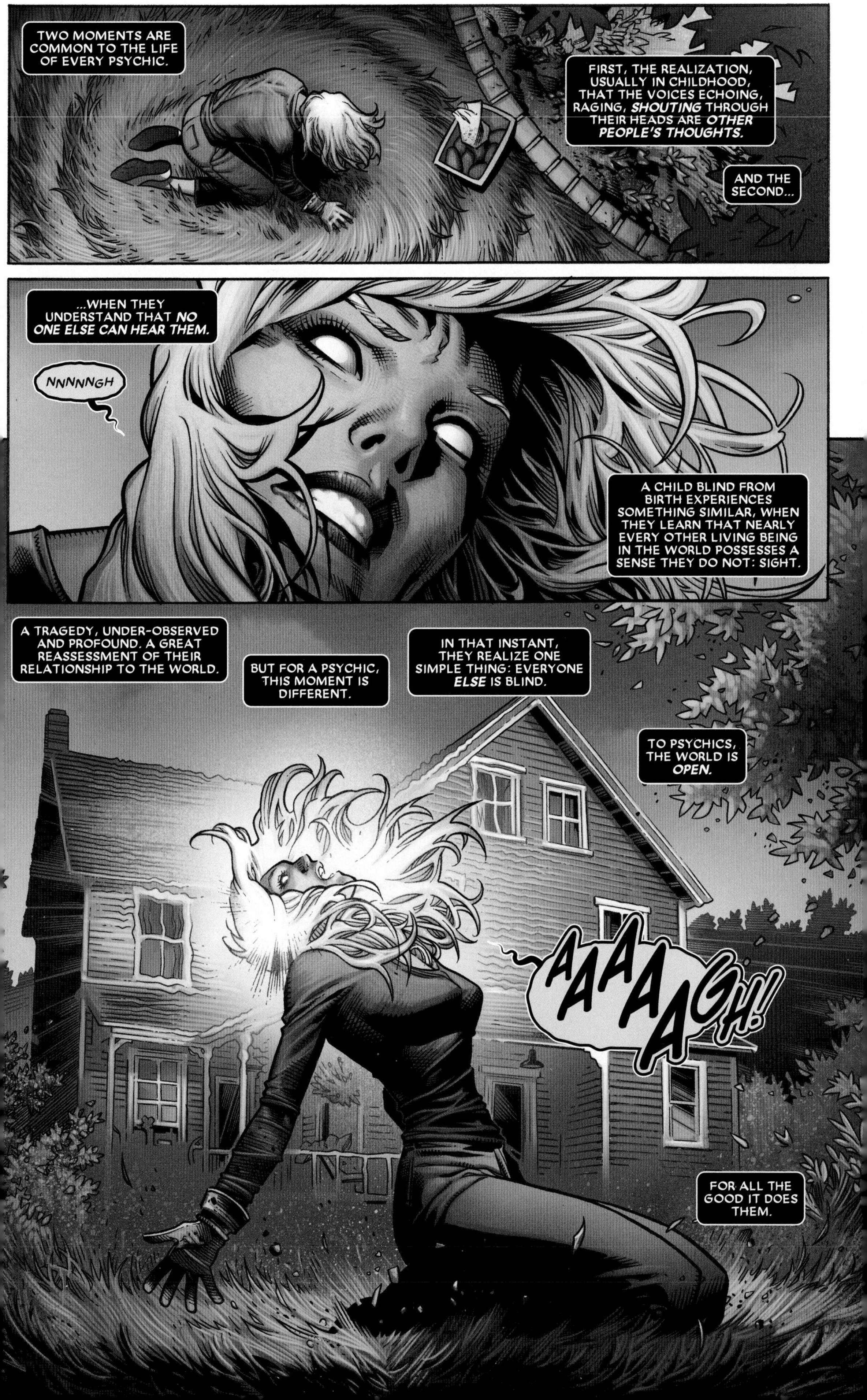
TWO MOMENTS ARE COMMON TO THE LIFE OF EVERY PSYCHIC.
FIRST, THE REALIZATION, USUALLY IN CHILDHOOD, THAT THE VOICES ECHOING, RAGING, *SHOUTING* THROUGH THEIR HEADS ARE *OTHER PEOPLE'S THOUGHTS.*
AND THE SECOND...
...WHEN THEY UNDERSTAND THAT *NO ONE ELSE CAN HEAR THEM.*
NNNNNGH
A CHILD BLIND FROM BIRTH EXPERIENCES SOMETHING SIMILAR, WHEN THEY LEARN THAT NEARLY EVERY OTHER LIVING BEING IN THE WORLD POSSESSES A SENSE THEY DO NOT: SIGHT.
A TRAGEDY, UNDER-OBSERVED AND PROFOUND. A GREAT REASSESSMENT OF THEIR RELATIONSHIP TO THE WORLD.
BUT FOR A PSYCHIC, THIS MOMENT IS DIFFERENT.
IN THAT INSTANT, THEY REALIZE ONE SIMPLE THING: EVERYONE *ELSE* IS BLIND.
TO PSYCHICS, THE WORLD IS *OPEN.*
AAAAAAGH!
FOR ALL THE GOOD IT DOES THEM.

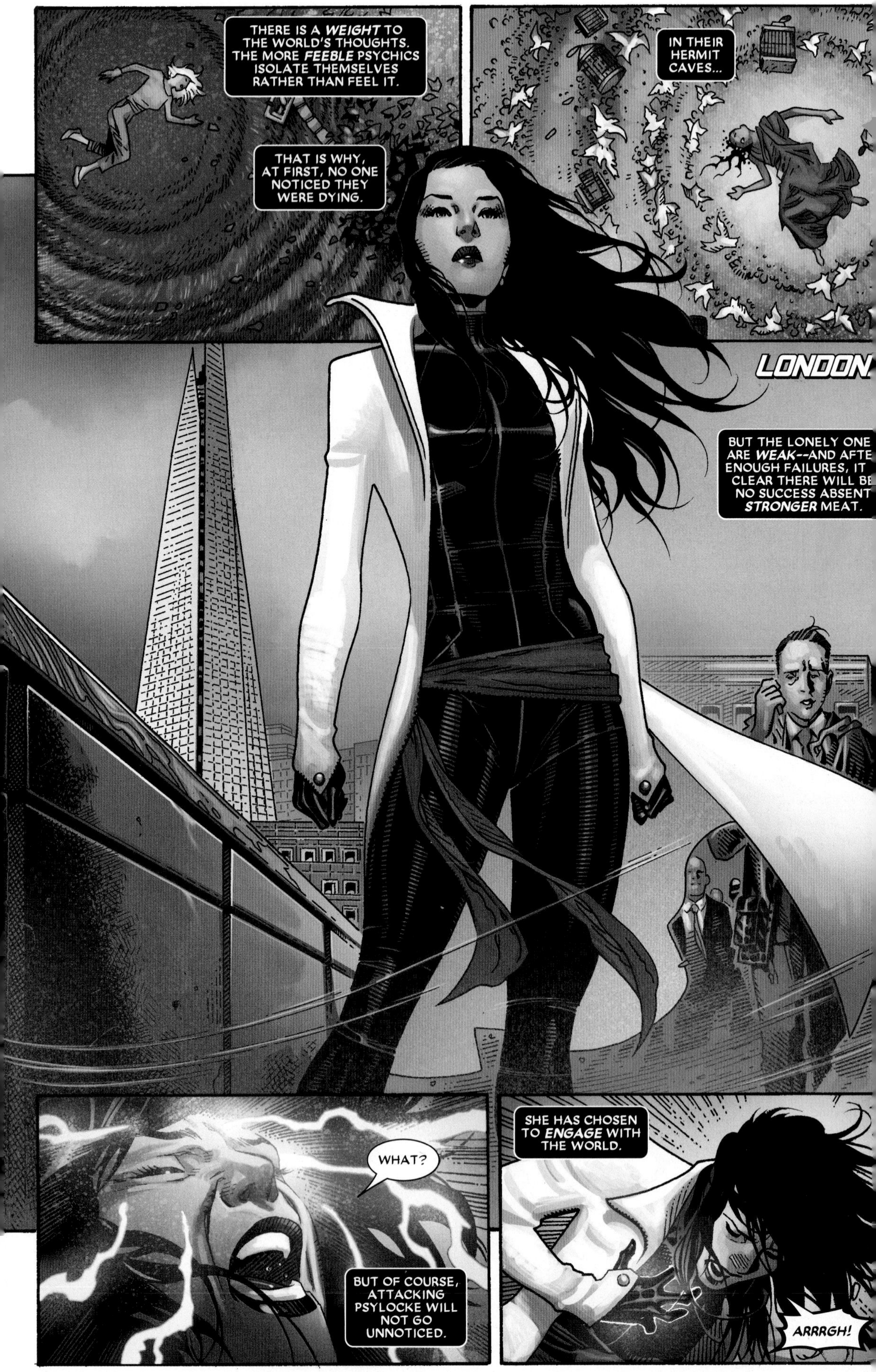
THERE IS A WEIGHT TO THE WORLD'S THOUGHTS. THE MORE FEEBLE PSYCHICS ISOLATE THEMSELVES RATHER THAN FEEL IT.
THAT IS WHY, AT FIRST, NO ONE NOTICED THEY WERE DYING.
IN THEIR HERMIT CAVES...
LONDON
BUT THE LONELY ONE ARE WEAK--AND AFTE ENOUGH FAILURES, IT CLEAR THERE WILL BE NO SUCCESS ABSENT STRONGER MEAT.
WHAT?
BUT OF COURSE, ATTACKING PSYLOCKE WILL NOT GO UNNOTICED.
SHE HAS CHOSEN TO ENGAGE WITH THE WORLD.
ARRRGH!

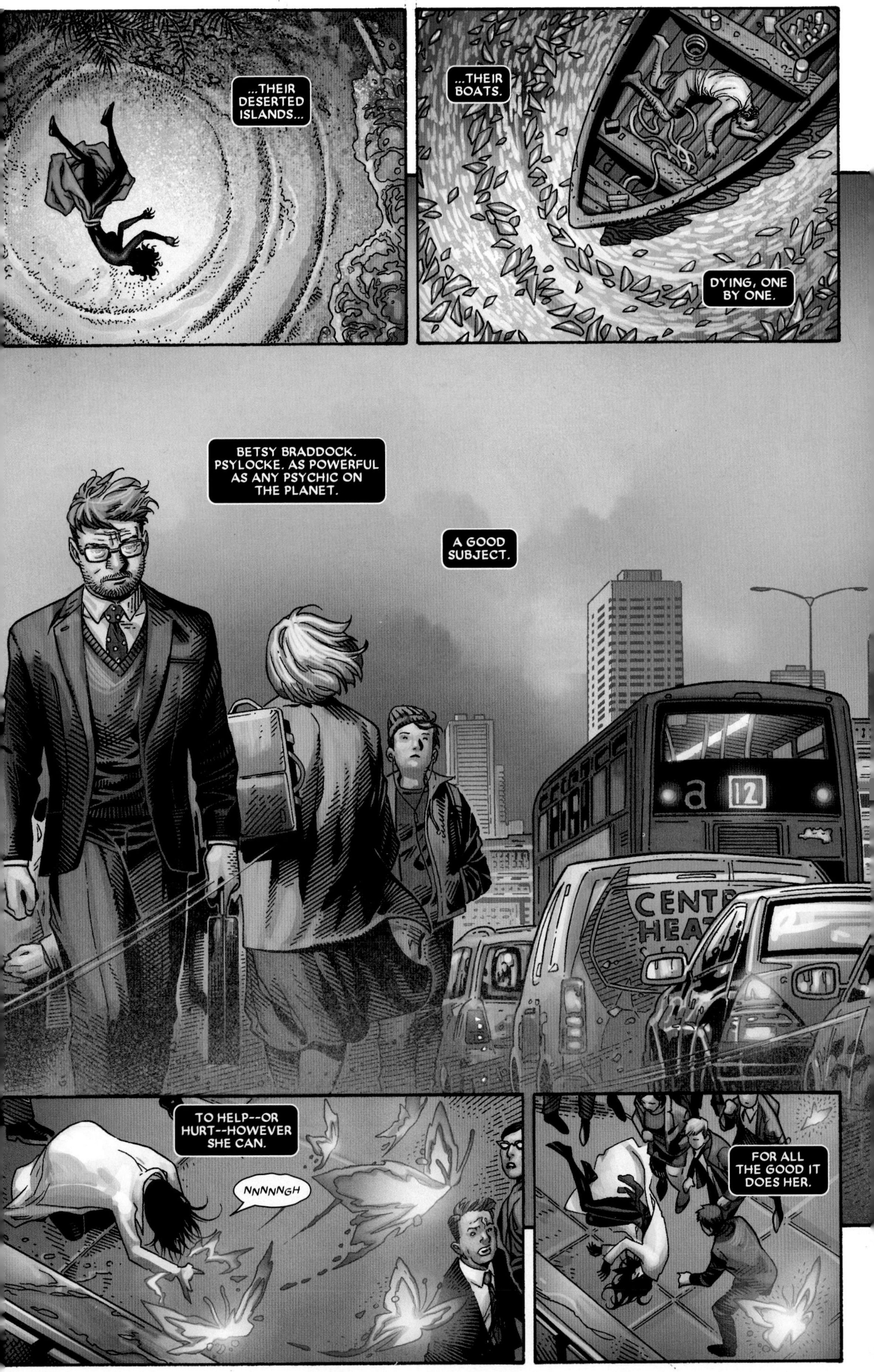
...THEIR DESERTED ISLANDS...
...THEIR BOATS.
DYING, ONE BY ONE.
BETSY BRADDOCK. PSYLOCKE. AS POWERFUL AS ANY PSYCHIC ON THE PLANET.
A GOOD SUBJECT.
CENTR
HEAT
TO HELP--OR HURT--HOWEVER SHE CAN.
NNNNNGH
FOR ALL THE GOOD IT DOES HER.

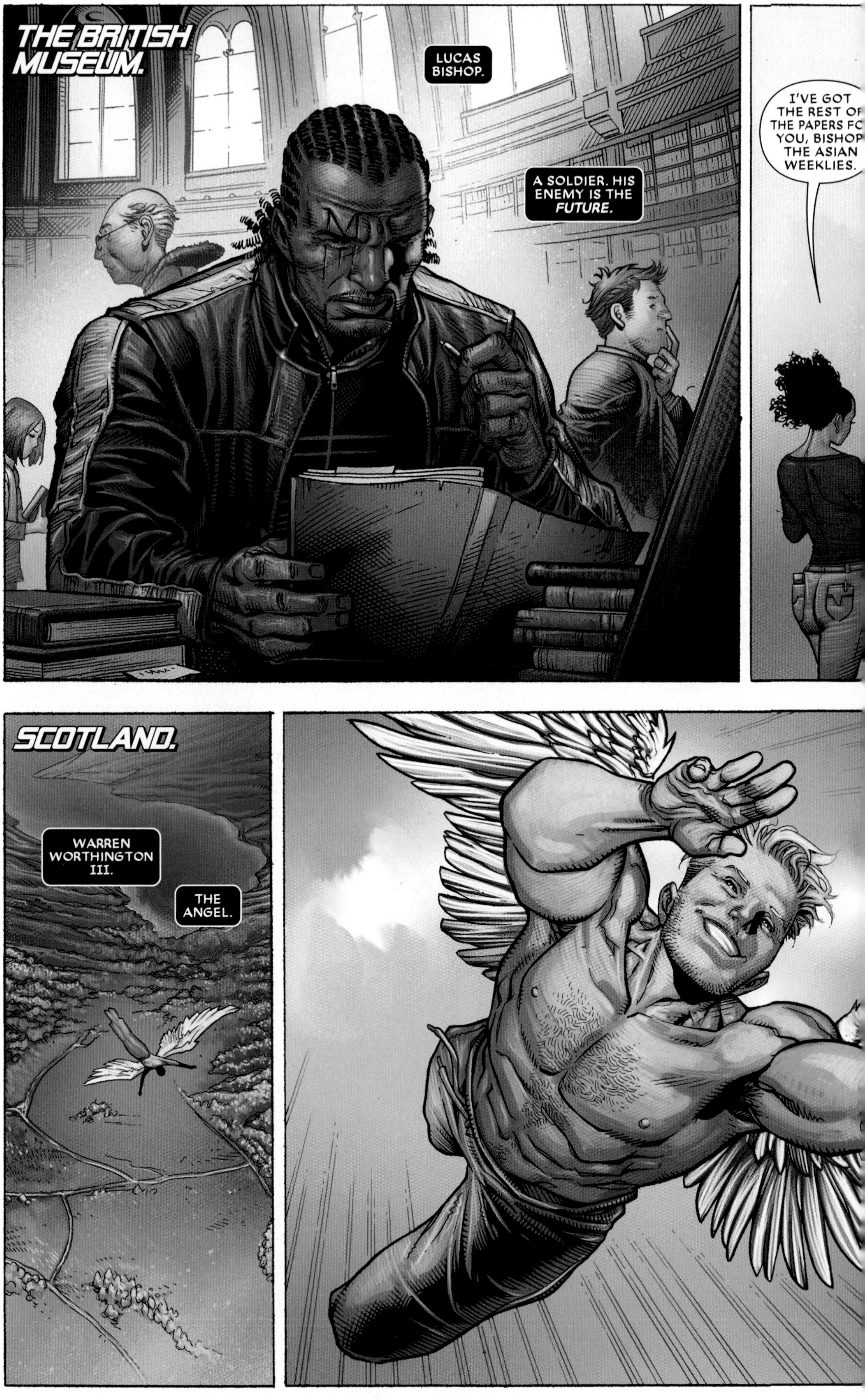
THE BRITISH MUSEUM.
LUCAS BISHOP.
A SOLDIER. HIS ENEMY IS THE *FUTURE.*
I'VE GOT THE REST OF THE PAPERS FO YOU, BISHOP THE ASIAN WEEKLIES.
SCOTLAND.
WARREN WORTHINGTON III.
THE ANGEL.

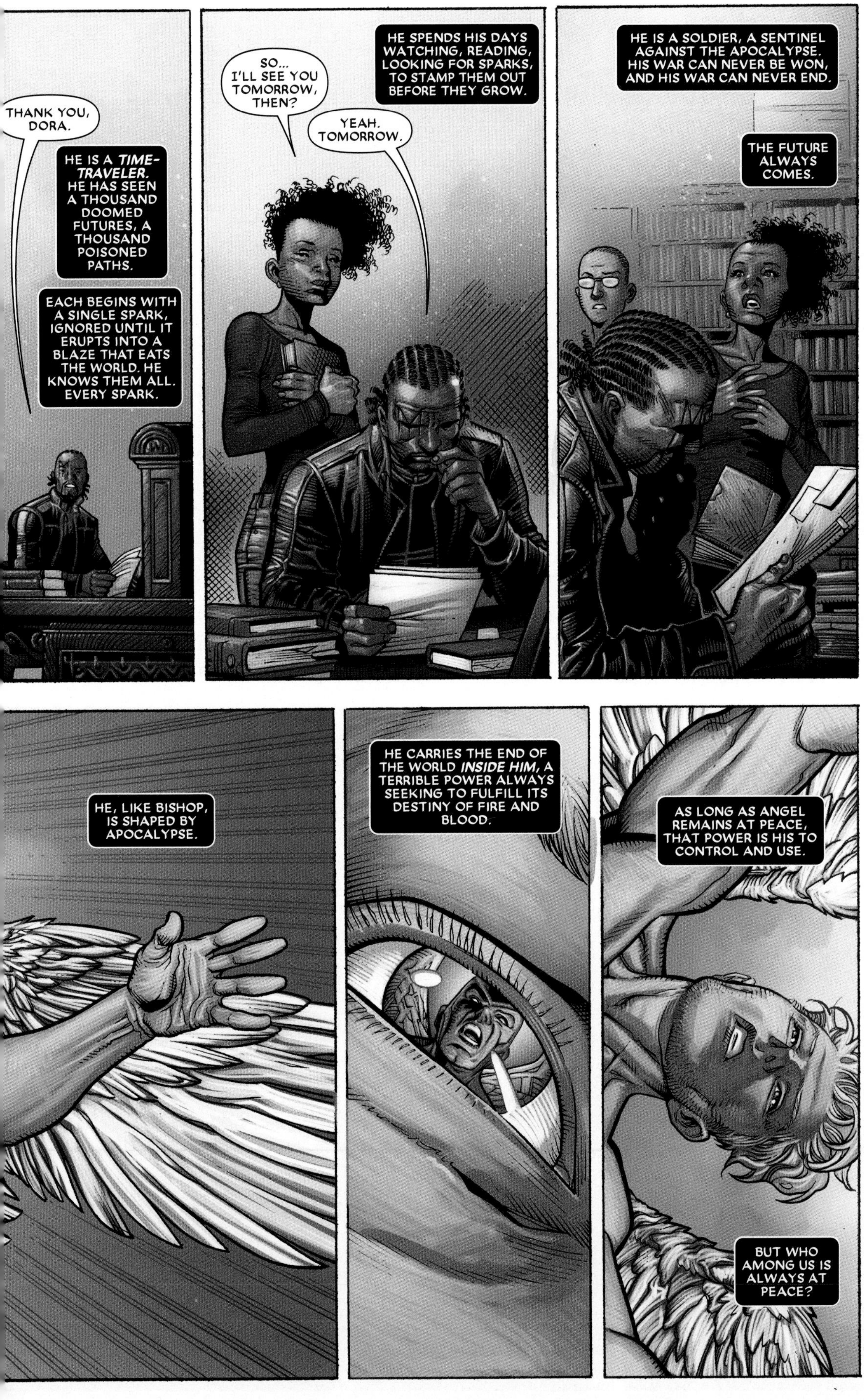

THANK YOU, DORA.
HE IS A *TIME-TRAVELER.* HE HAS SEEN A THOUSAND DOOMED FUTURES, A THOUSAND POISONED PATHS.
EACH BEGINS WITH A SINGLE SPARK, IGNORED UNTIL IT ERUPTS INTO A BLAZE THAT EATS THE WORLD. HE KNOWS THEM ALL. EVERY SPARK.
SO... I'LL SEE YOU TOMORROW, THEN?
HE SPENDS HIS DAYS WATCHING, READING, LOOKING FOR SPARKS, TO STAMP THEM OUT BEFORE THEY GROW.
YEAH. TOMORROW.
HE IS A SOLDIER, A SENTINEL AGAINST THE APOCALYPSE. HIS WAR CAN NEVER BE WON, AND HIS WAR CAN NEVER END.
THE FUTURE ALWAYS COMES.
HE, LIKE BISHOP, IS SHAPED BY APOCALYPSE.
HE CARRIES THE END OF THE WORLD *INSIDE HIM,* A TERRIBLE POWER ALWAYS SEEKING TO FULFILL ITS DESTINY OF FIRE AND BLOOD.
AS LONG AS ANGEL REMAINS AT PEACE, THAT POWER IS HIS TO CONTROL AND USE.
BUT WHO AMONG US IS ALWAYS AT PEACE?

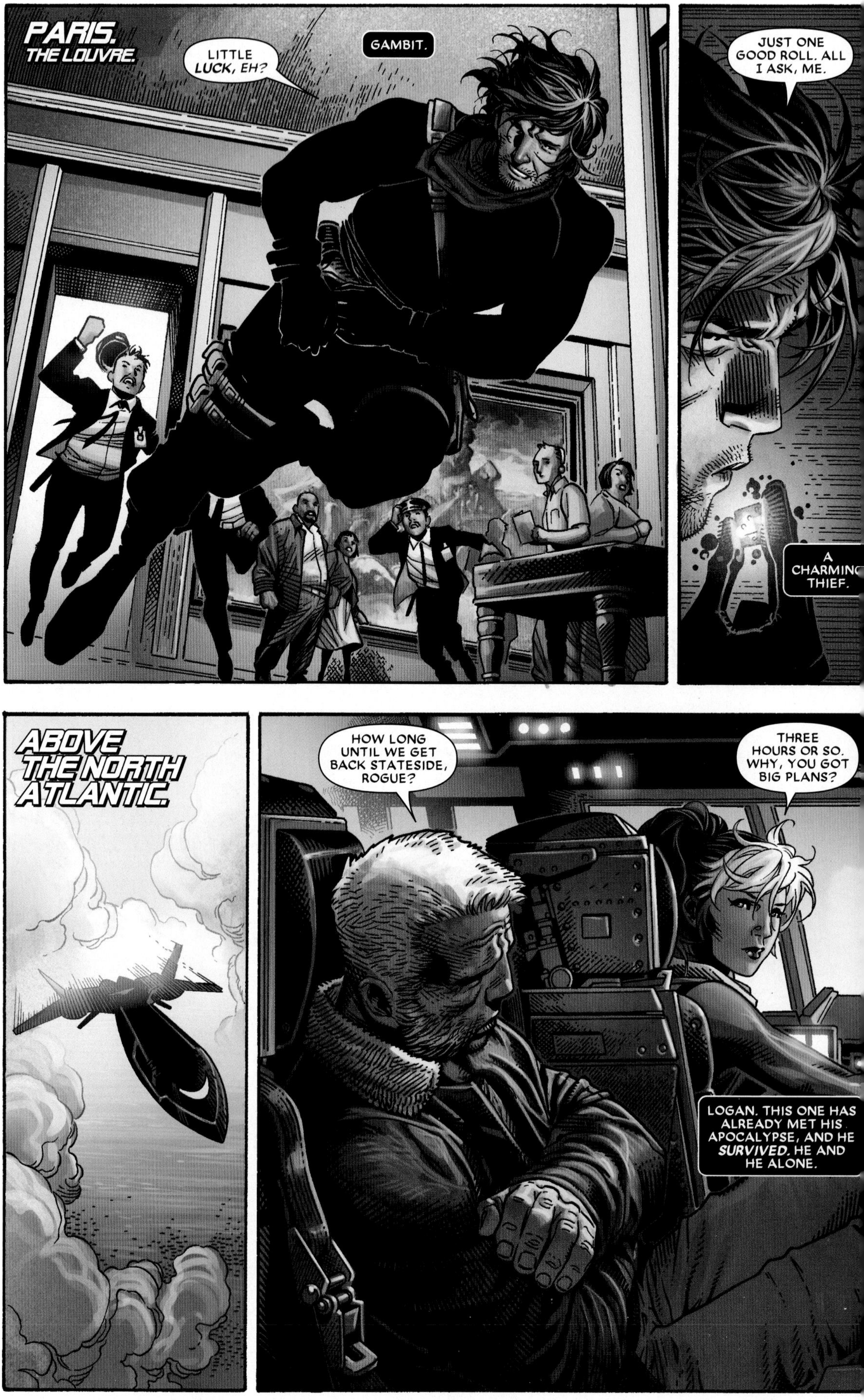
PARIS.
THE LOUVRE.
LITTLE LUCK, EH?
GAMBIT.
JUST ONE GOOD ROLL. ALL I ASK, ME.
A CHARMING THIEF.
ABOVE THE NORTH ATLANTIC.
HOW LONG UNTIL WE GET BACK STATESIDE, ROGUE?
THREE HOURS OR SO. WHY, YOU GOT BIG PLANS?
LOGAN. THIS ONE HAS ALREADY MET HIS APOCALYPSE, AND HE SURVIVED. HE AND HE ALONE.

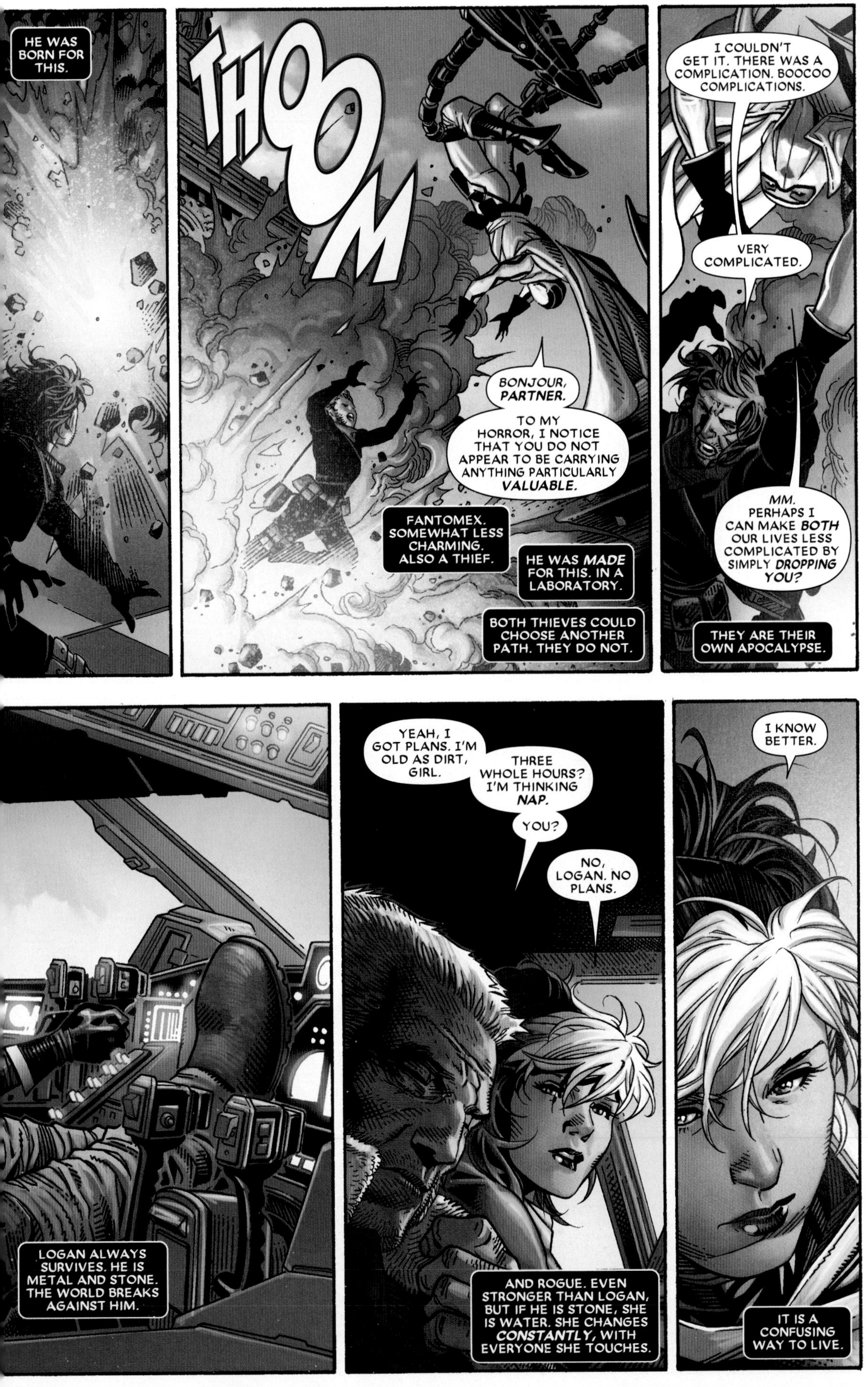
HE WAS BORN FOR THIS.
THOOOM
BONJOUR, PARTNER.
TO MY HORROR, I NOTICE THAT YOU DO NOT APPEAR TO BE CARRYING ANYTHING PARTICULARLY VALUABLE.
FANTOMEX. SOMEWHAT LESS CHARMING. ALSO A THIEF.
HE WAS MADE FOR THIS. IN A LABORATORY.
BOTH THIEVES COULD CHOOSE ANOTHER PATH. THEY DO NOT.
I COULDN'T GET IT. THERE WAS A COMPLICATION. BOOCOO COMPLICATIONS.
VERY COMPLICATED.
MM. PERHAPS I CAN MAKE BOTH OUR LIVES LESS COMPLICATED BY SIMPLY DROPPING YOU?
THEY ARE THEIR OWN APOCALYPSE.
LOGAN ALWAYS SURVIVES. HE IS METAL AND STONE. THE WORLD BREAKS AGAINST HIM.
YEAH, I GOT PLANS. I'M OLD AS DIRT, GIRL.
THREE WHOLE HOURS? I'M THINKING NAP.
YOU?
NO, LOGAN. NO PLANS.
AND ROGUE. EVEN STRONGER THAN LOGAN, BUT IF HE IS STONE, SHE IS WATER. SHE CHANGES CONSTANTLY, WITH EVERYONE SHE TOUCHES.
I KNOW BETTER.
IT IS A CONFUSING WAY TO LIVE.

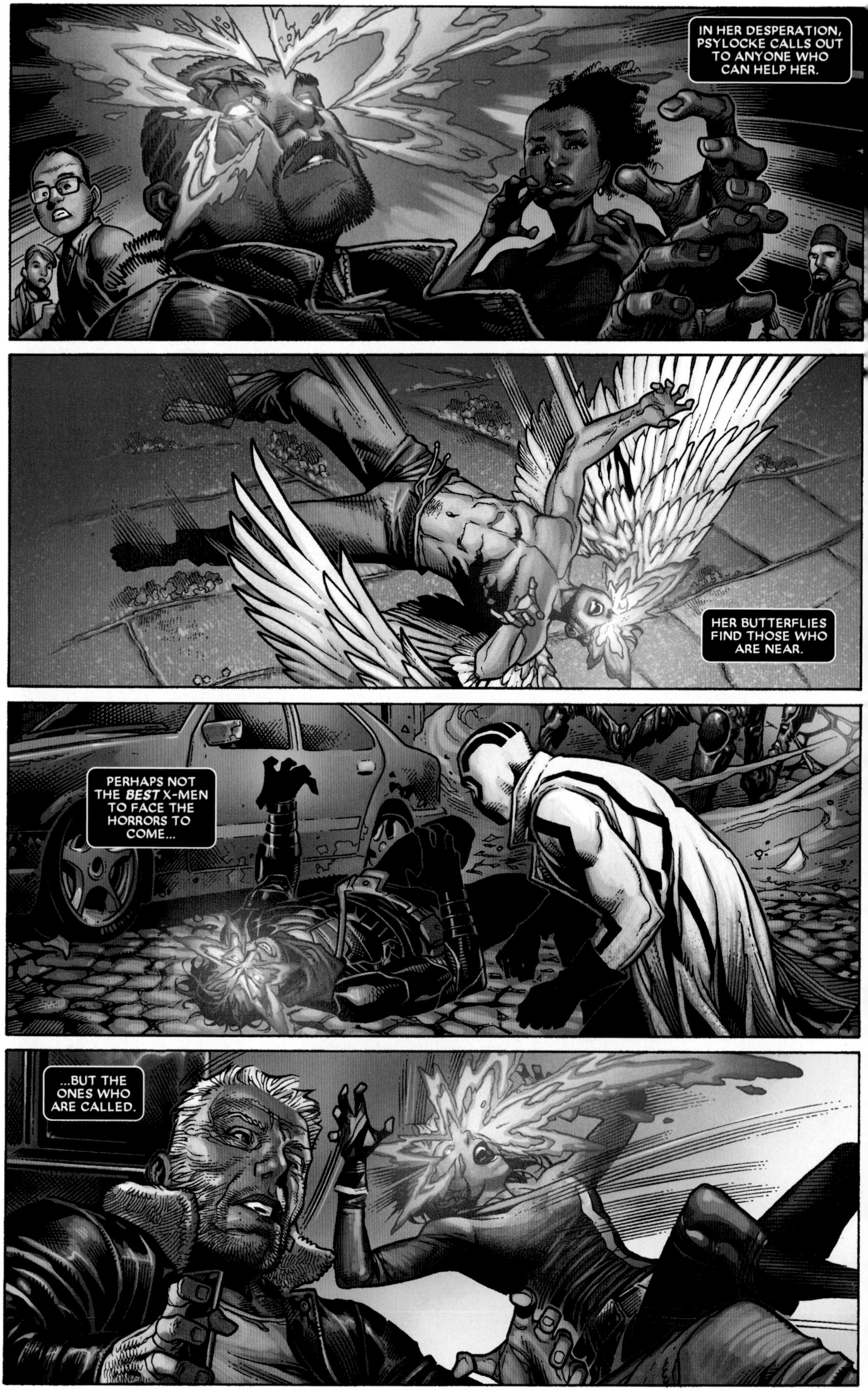
IN HER DESPERATION, PSYLOCKE CALLS OUT TO ANYONE WHO CAN HELP HER.
HER BUTTERFLIES FIND THOSE WHO ARE NEAR.
PERHAPS NOT THE *BEST* X-MEN TO FACE THE HORRORS TO COME...
...BUT THE ONES WHO ARE CALLED.

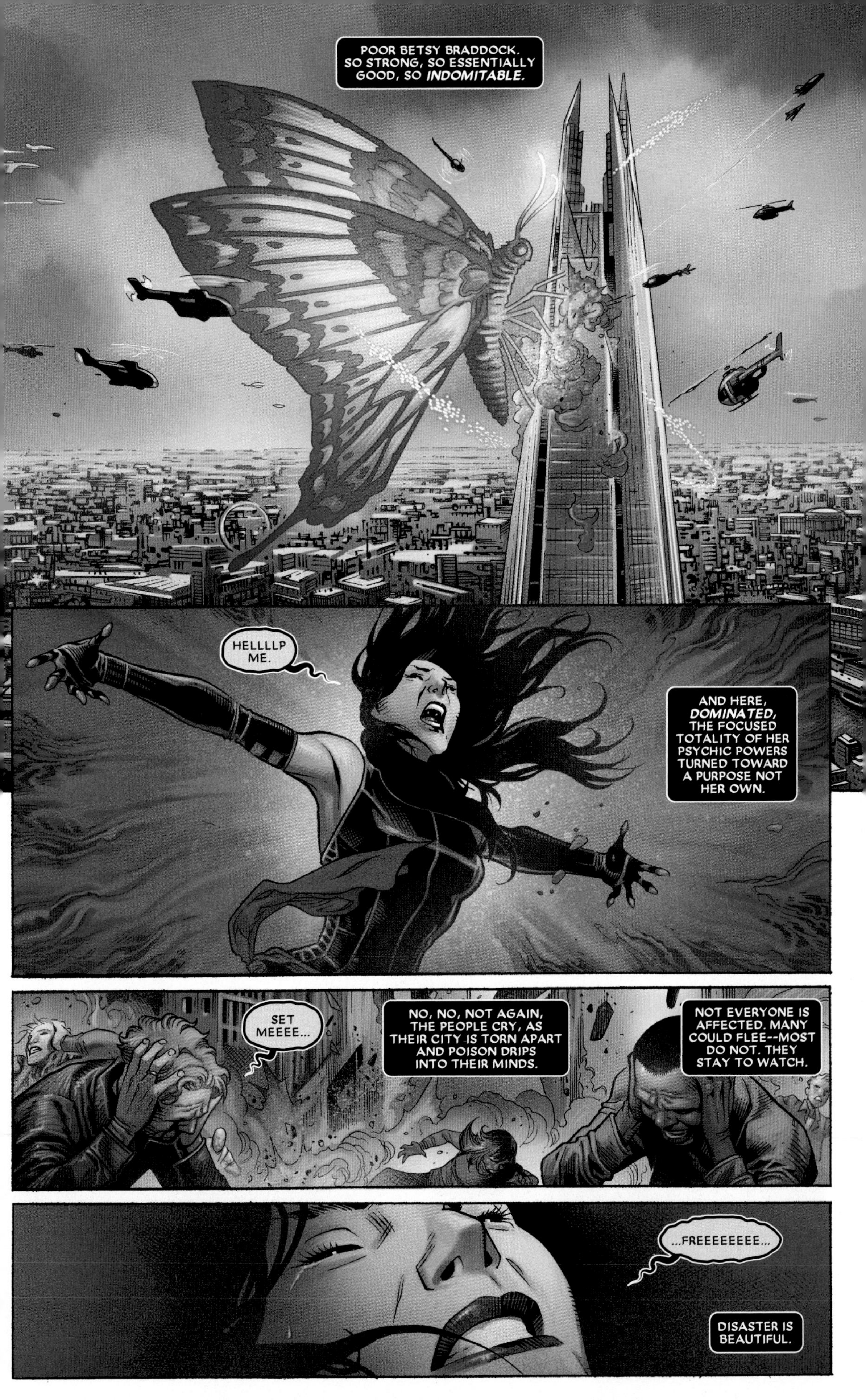
POOR BETSY BRADDOCK. SO STRONG, SO ESSENTIALLY GOOD, SO *INDOMITABLE.*
HELLLLP ME.
AND HERE, *DOMINATED,* THE FOCUSED TOTALITY OF HER PSYCHIC POWERS TURNED TOWARD A PURPOSE NOT HER OWN.
SET MEEEE...
NO, NO, NOT AGAIN, THE PEOPLE CRY, AS THEIR CITY IS TORN APART AND POISON DRIPS INTO THEIR MINDS.
NOT EVERYONE IS AFFECTED. MANY COULD FLEE--MOST DO NOT. THEY STAY TO WATCH.
...FREEEEEEEE...
DISASTER IS BEAUTIFUL.

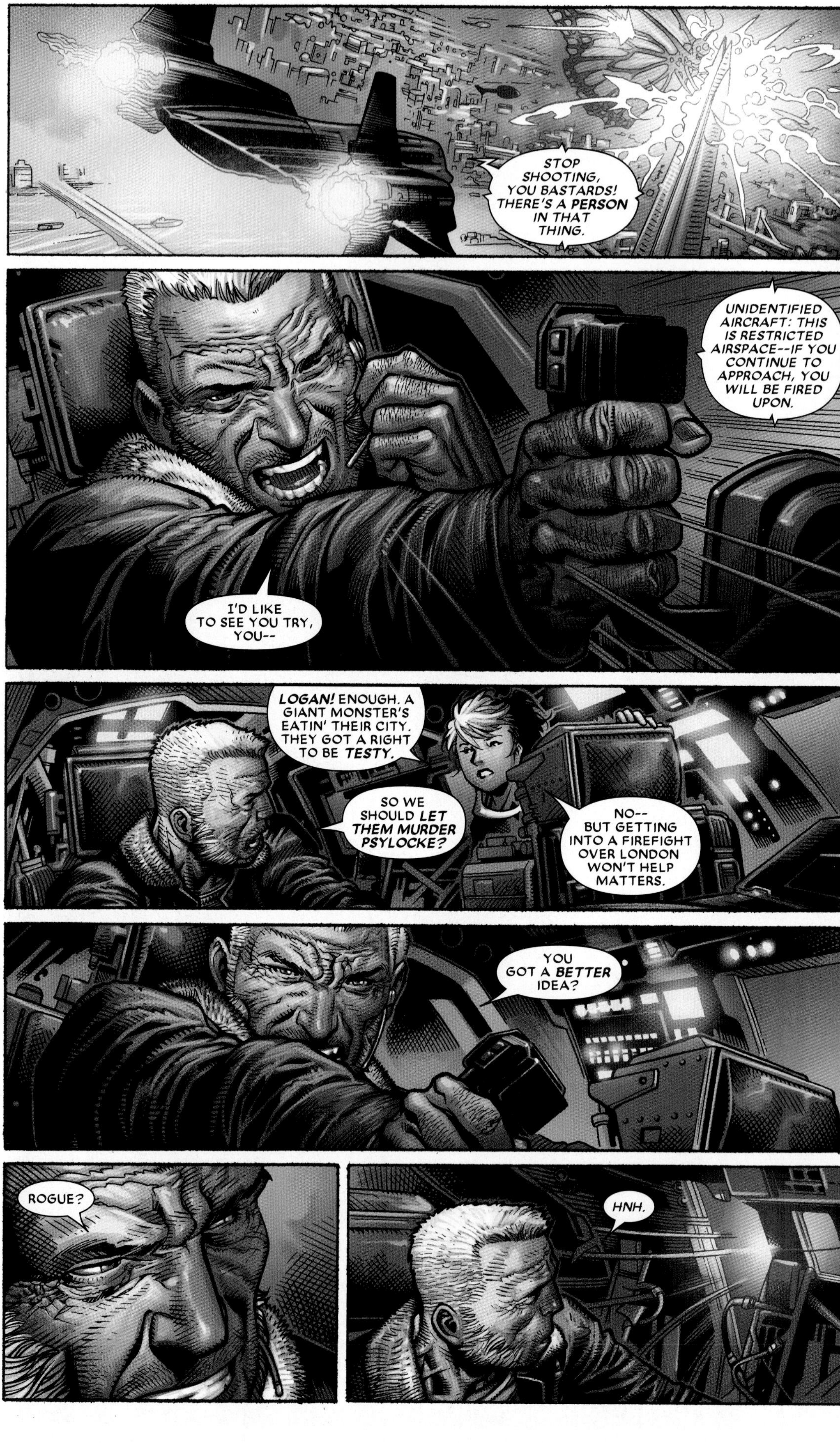
STOP SHOOTING, YOU BASTARDS! THERE'S A PERSON IN THAT THING.
UNIDENTIFIED AIRCRAFT: THIS IS RESTRICTED AIRSPACE--IF YOU CONTINUE TO APPROACH, YOU WILL BE FIRED UPON.
I'D LIKE TO SEE YOU TRY, YOU--
LOGAN! ENOUGH. A GIANT MONSTER'S EATIN' THEIR CITY. THEY GOT A RIGHT TO BE TESTY.
SO WE SHOULD LET THEM MURDER PSYLOCKE?
NO-- BUT GETTING INTO A FIREFIGHT OVER LONDON WON'T HELP MATTERS.
YOU GOT A BETTER IDEA?
ROGUE?
HNH.

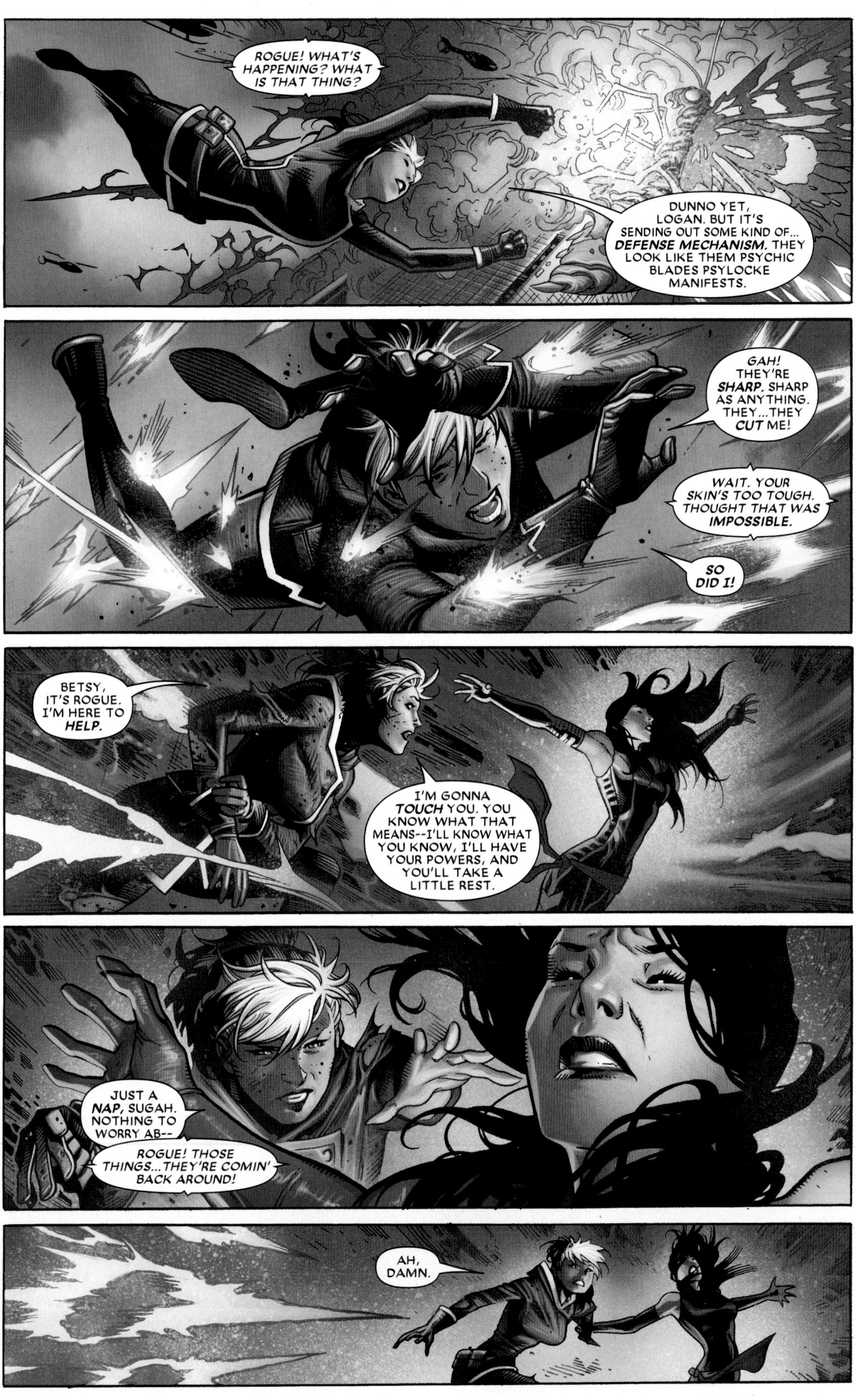
ROGUE! WHAT'S HAPPENING? WHAT IS THAT THING?
DUNNO YET, LOGAN. BUT IT'S SENDING OUT SOME KIND OF... DEFENSE MECHANISM. THEY LOOK LIKE THEM PSYCHIC BLADES PSYLOCKE MANIFESTS.
GAH! THEY'RE SHARP. SHARP AS ANYTHING. THEY...THEY CUT ME!
WAIT. YOUR SKIN'S TOO TOUGH. THOUGHT THAT WAS IMPOSSIBLE.
SO DID I!
BETSY, IT'S ROGUE. I'M HERE TO HELP.
I'M GONNA TOUCH YOU. YOU KNOW WHAT THAT MEANS--I'LL KNOW WHAT YOU KNOW, I'LL HAVE YOUR POWERS, AND YOU'LL TAKE A LITTLE REST.
JUST A NAP, SUGAH. NOTHING TO WORRY AB--
ROGUE! THOSE THINGS...THEY'RE COMIN' BACK AROUND!
AH, DAMN.

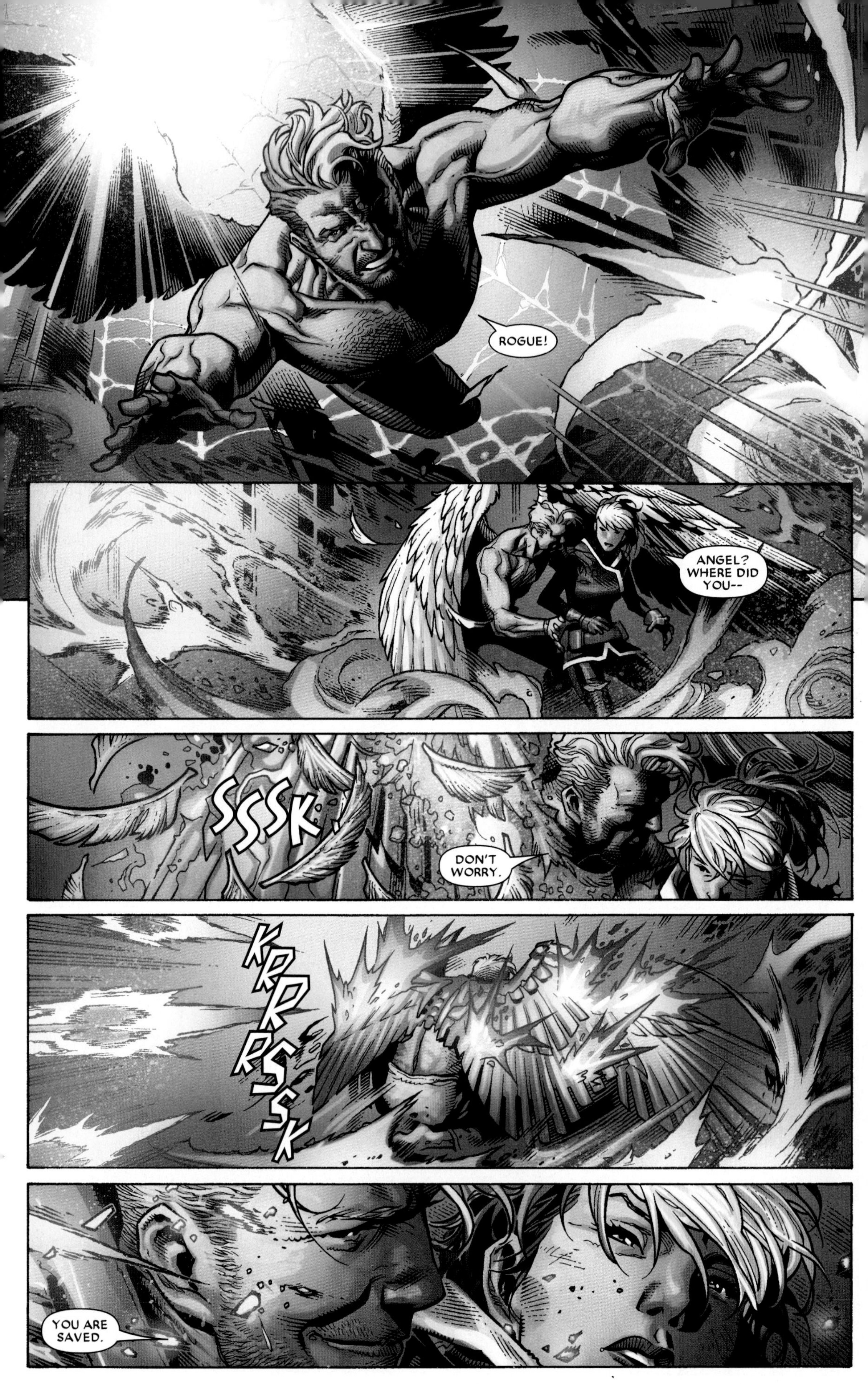
ROGUE!
ANGEL? WHERE DID YOU--
SSSK
DON'T WORRY.
KRRRRSSSK
YOU ARE SAVED.

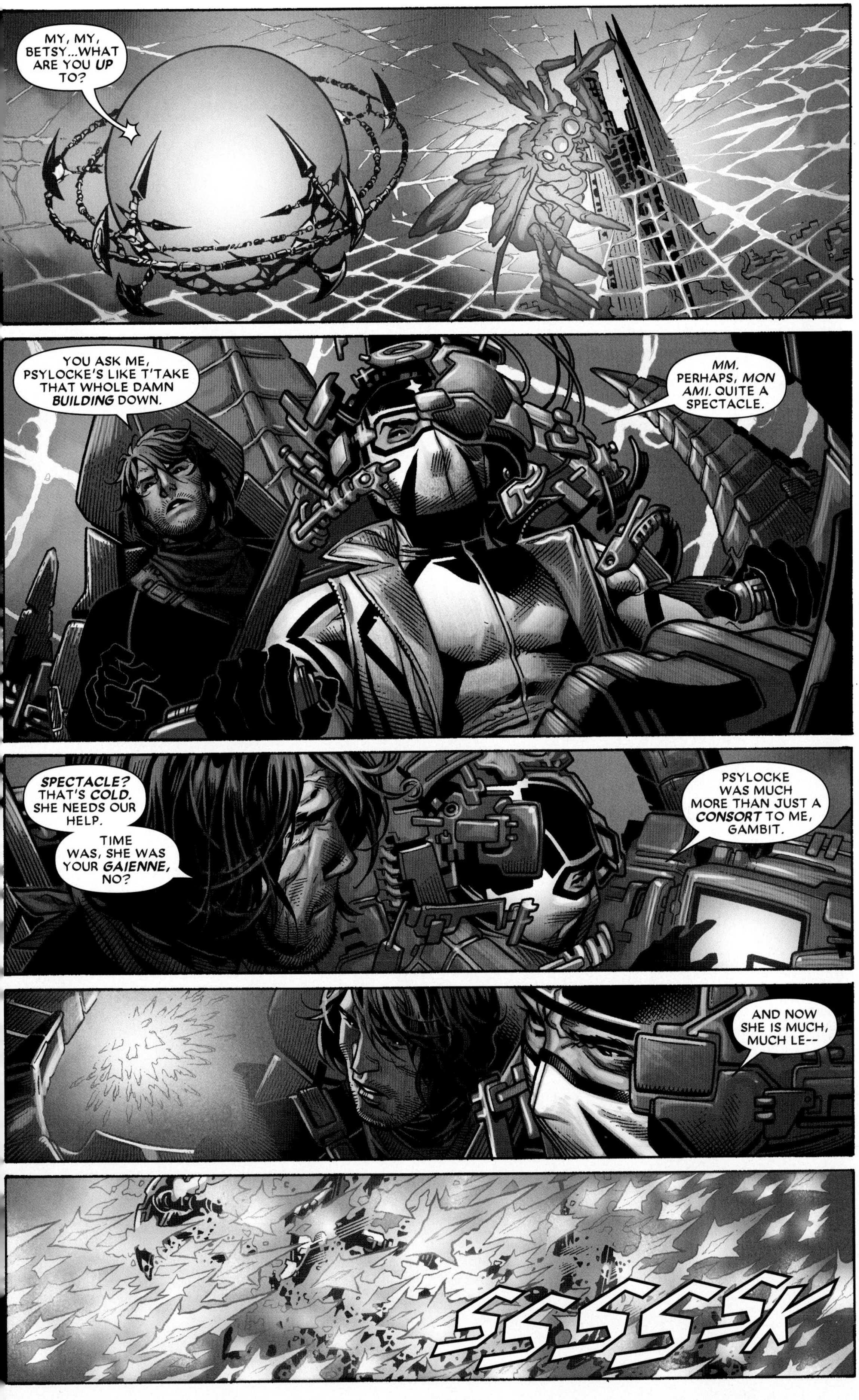

MY, MY, BETSY...WHAT ARE YOU *UP* TO?
YOU ASK ME, PSYLOCKE'S LIKE T'TAKE THAT WHOLE DAMN *BUILDING* DOWN.
MM. PERHAPS, *MON AMI.* QUITE A SPECTACLE.
SPECTACLE? THAT'S *COLD.* SHE NEEDS OUR HELP.
TIME WAS, SHE WAS YOUR *GAIENNE,* NO?
PSYLOCKE WAS MUCH MORE THAN JUST A *CONSORT* TO ME, GAMBIT.
AND NOW SHE IS MUCH, MUCH LE--
SSSSSK

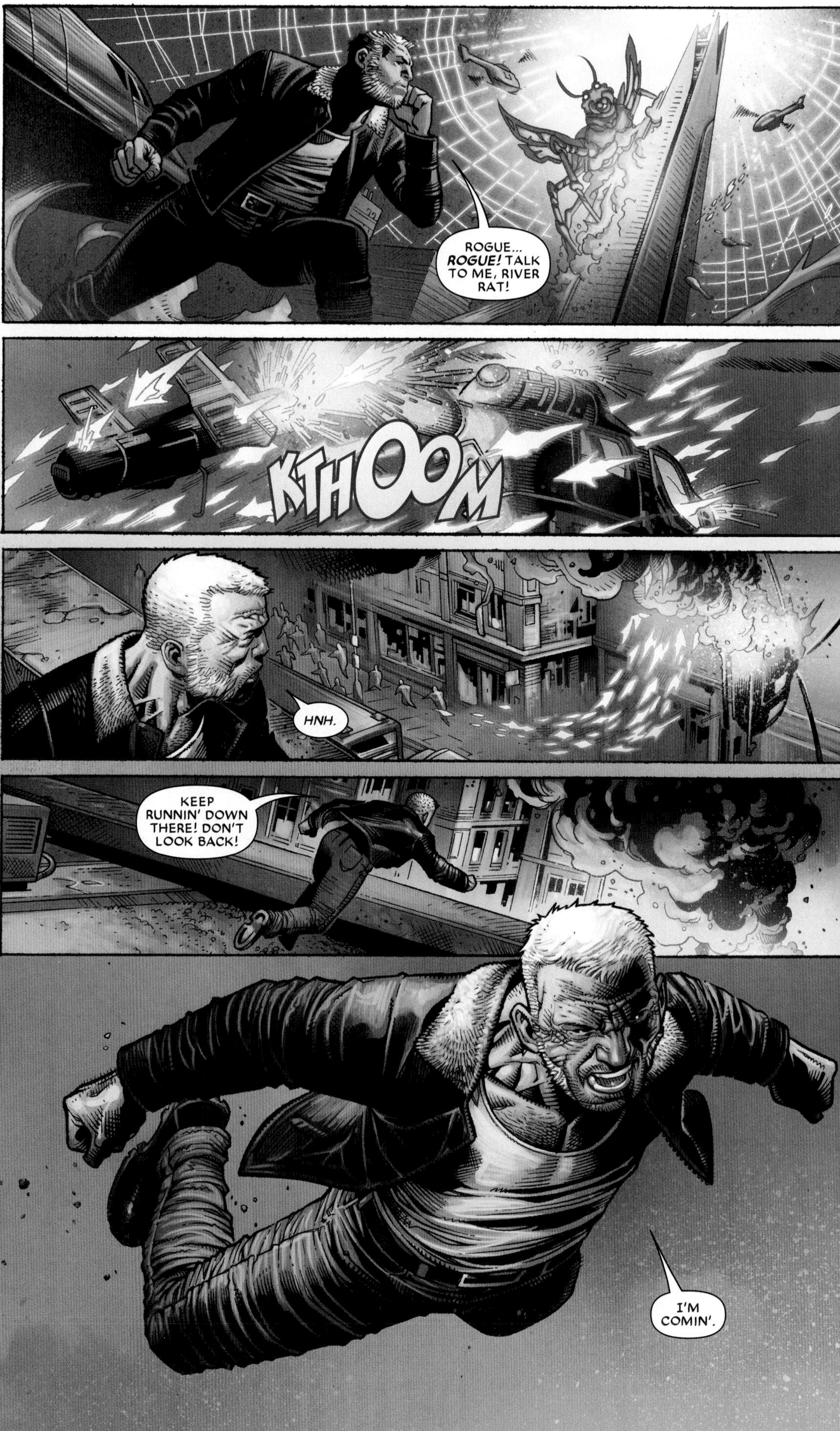
ROGUE... ROGUE! TALK TO ME, RIVER RAT!
KTHOOOM
HNH.
KEEP RUNNIN' DOWN THERE! DON'T LOOK BACK!
I'M COMIN'.

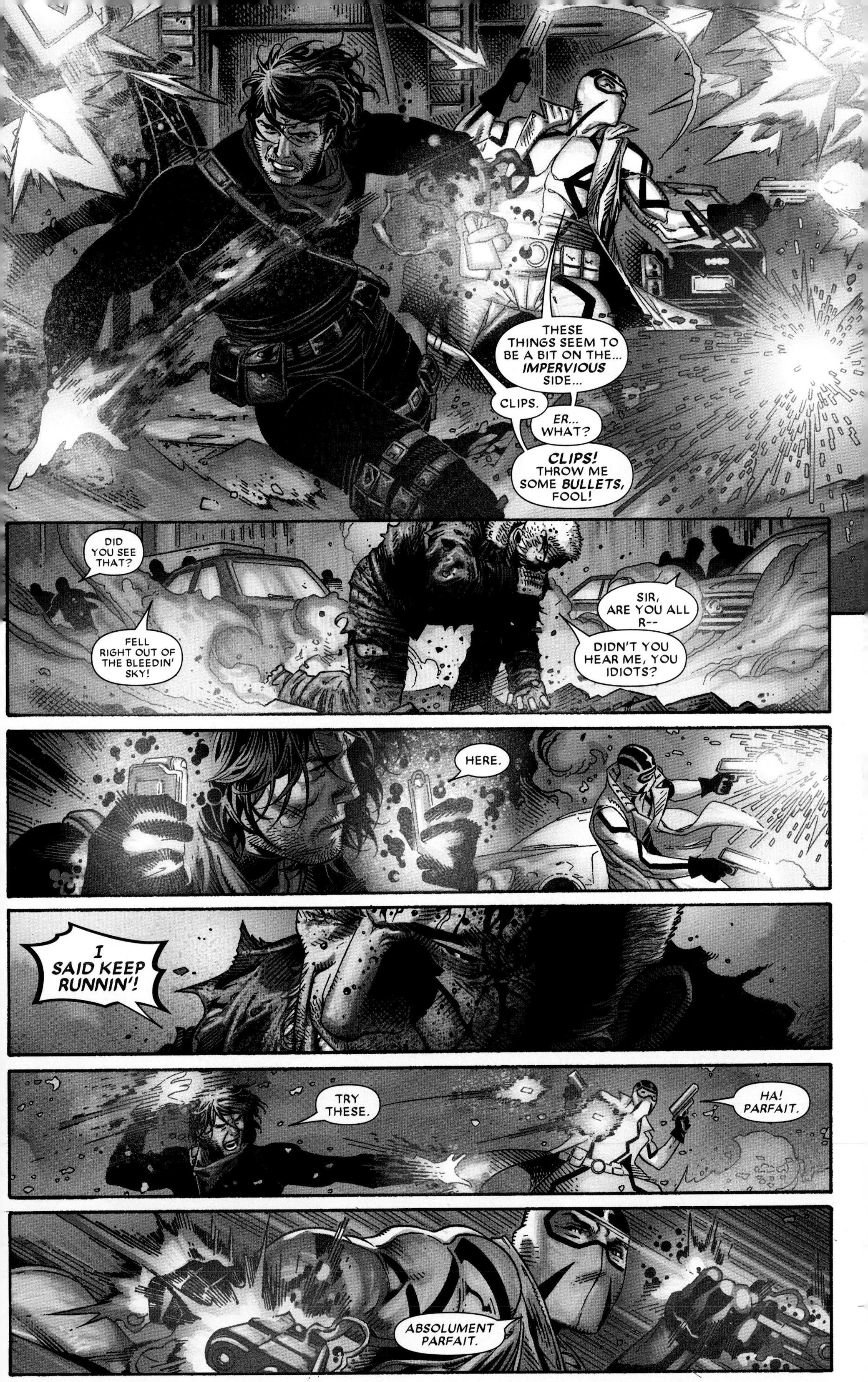
THESE THINGS SEEM TO BE A BIT ON THE... IMPERVIOUS SIDE...
CLIPS.
ER... WHAT?
CLIPS! THROW ME SOME BULLETS, FOOL!
DID YOU SEE THAT?
FELL RIGHT OUT OF THE BLEEDIN' SKY!
SIR, ARE YOU ALL R--
DIDN'T YOU HEAR ME, YOU IDIOTS?
HERE.
I SAID KEEP RUNNIN'!
TRY THESE.
HA! PARFAIT.
ABSOLUMENT PARFAIT.

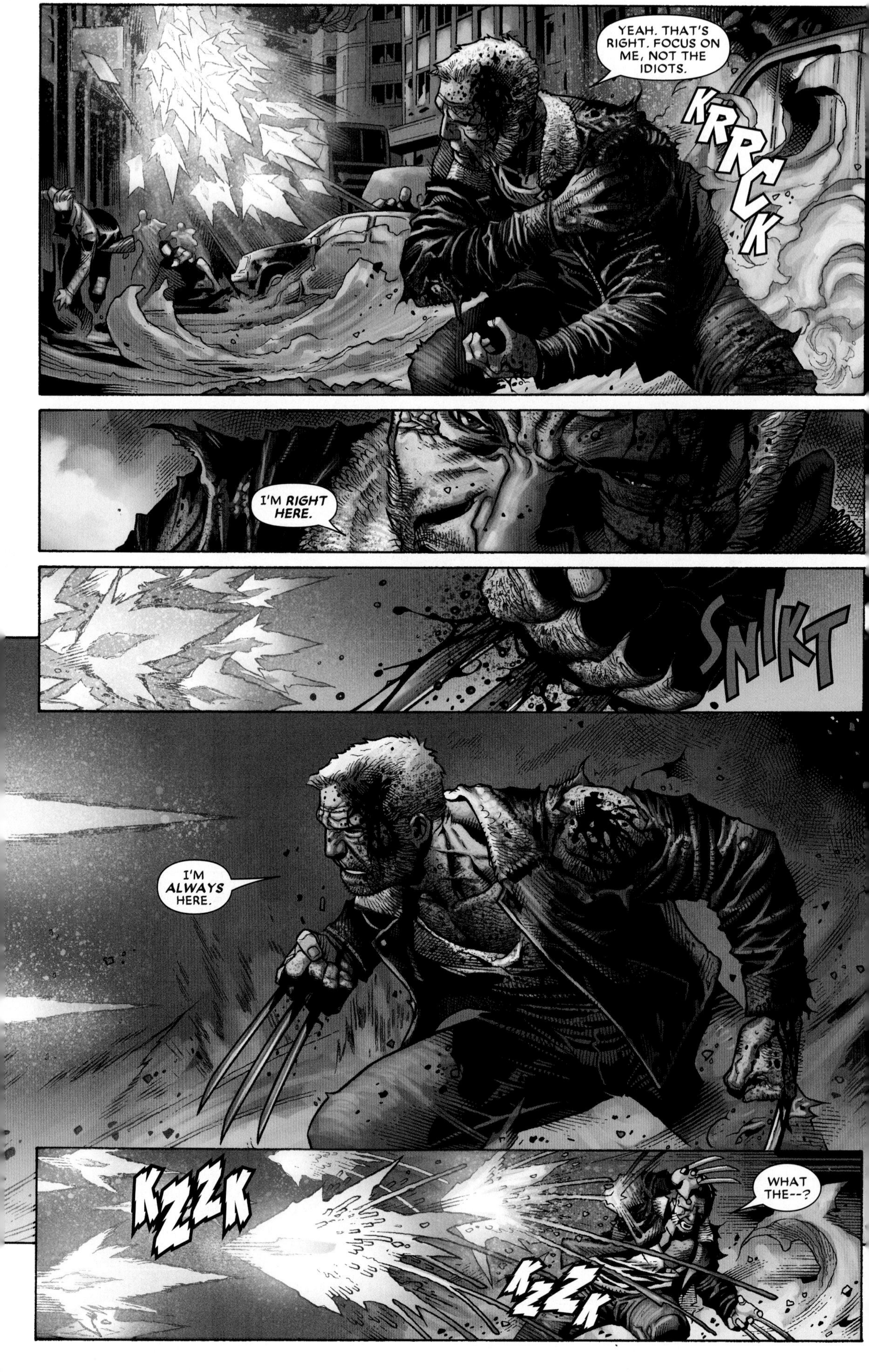

YEAH. THAT'S RIGHT. FOCUS ON ME, NOT THE IDIOTS.
KRRRCK
I'M RIGHT HERE.
SNIKT
I'M ALWAYS HERE.
KZZK
WHAT THE--?
KZZK

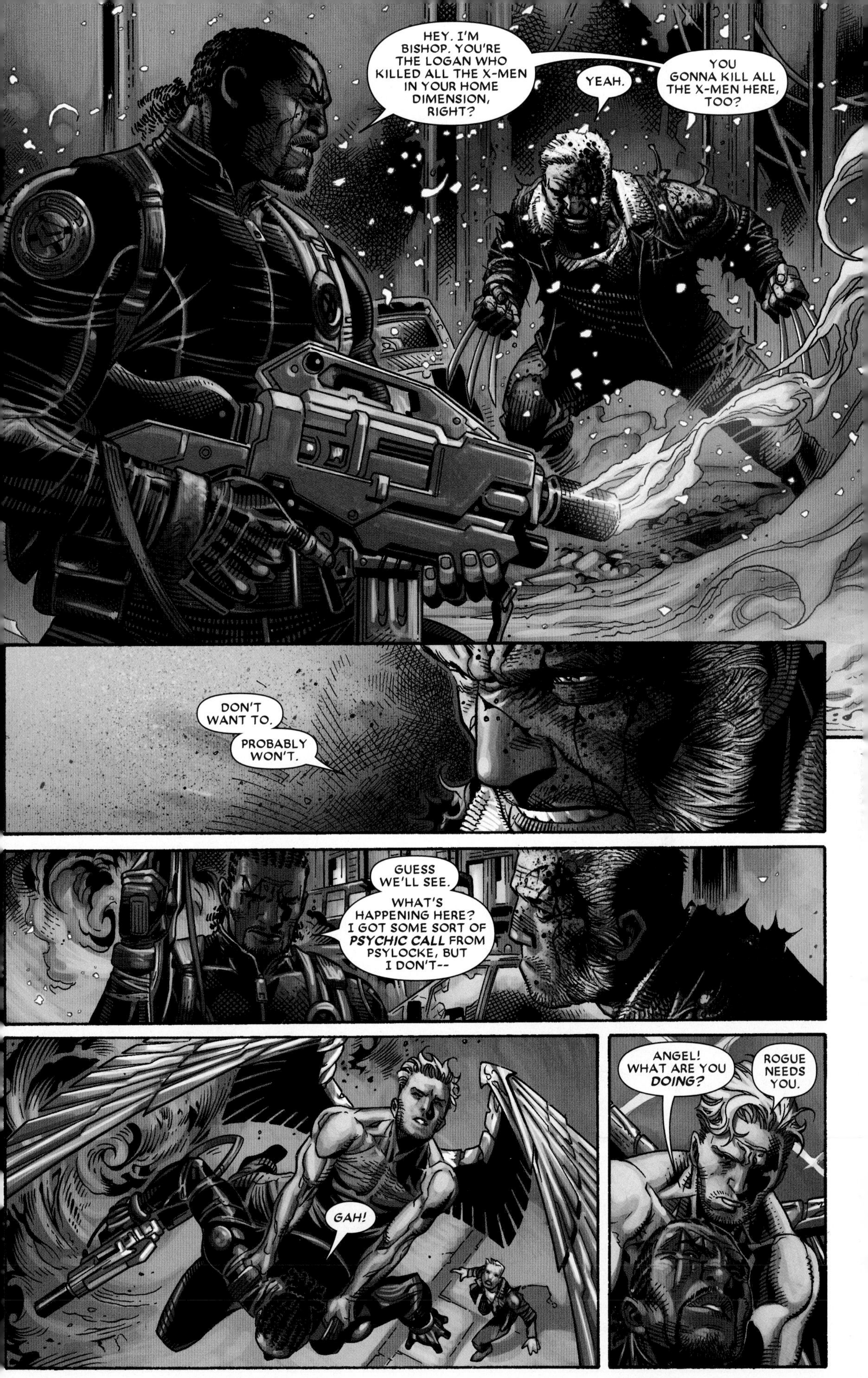
HEY. I'M BISHOP. YOU'RE THE LOGAN WHO KILLED ALL THE X-MEN IN YOUR HOME DIMENSION, RIGHT?
YEAH.
YOU GONNA KILL ALL THE X-MEN HERE, TOO?
DON'T WANT TO.
PROBABLY WON'T.
GUESS WE'LL SEE.
WHAT'S HAPPENING HERE? I GOT SOME SORT OF *PSYCHIC CALL* FROM PSYLOCKE, BUT I DON'T--
GAH!
ANGEL! WHAT ARE YOU *DOING?*
ROGUE NEEDS YOU.

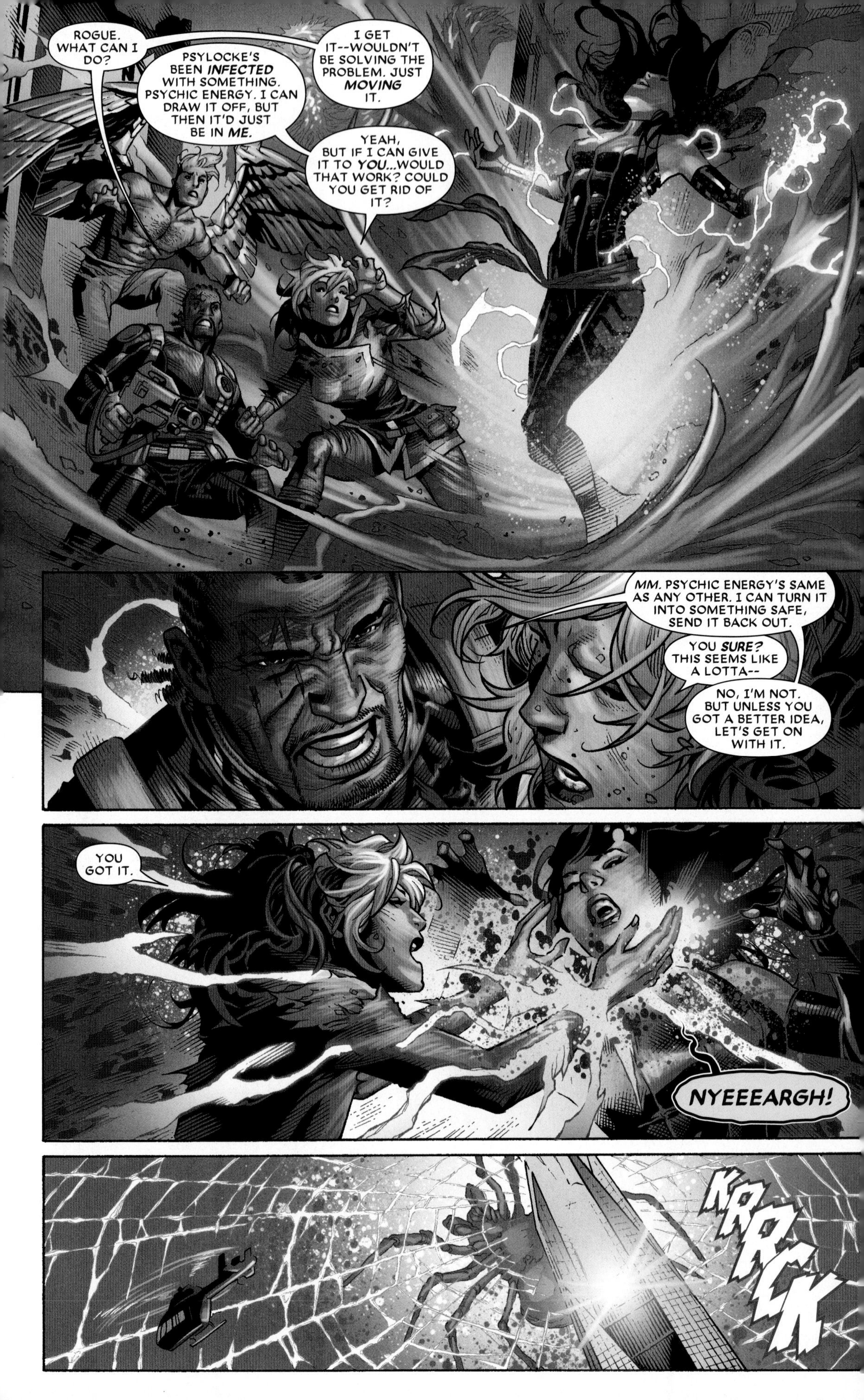
ROGUE. WHAT CAN I DO?
PSYLOCKE'S BEEN INFECTED WITH SOMETHING. PSYCHIC ENERGY. I CAN DRAW IT OFF, BUT THEN IT'D JUST BE IN ME.
I GET IT--WOULDN'T BE SOLVING THE PROBLEM. JUST MOVING IT.
YEAH, BUT IF I CAN GIVE IT TO YOU...WOULD THAT WORK? COULD YOU GET RID OF IT?
MM. PSYCHIC ENERGY'S SAME AS ANY OTHER. I CAN TURN IT INTO SOMETHING SAFE, SEND IT BACK OUT.
YOU SURE? THIS SEEMS LIKE A LOTTA--
NO, I'M NOT. BUT UNLESS YOU GOT A BETTER IDEA, LET'S GET ON WITH IT.
YOU GOT IT.
NYEEEARGH!
KRRCK

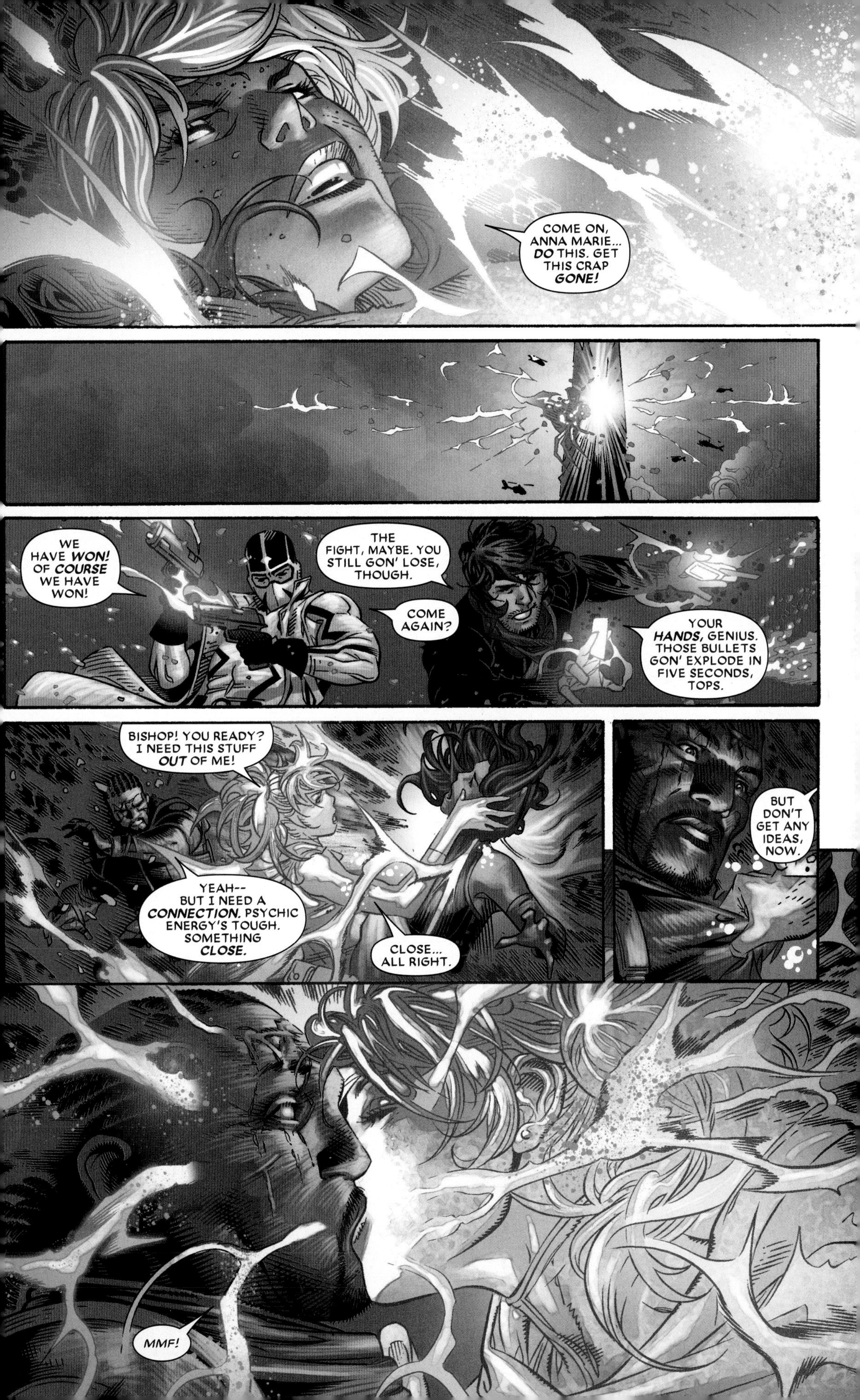
COME ON, ANNA MARIE... DO THIS. GET THIS CRAP GONE!
WE HAVE WON! OF COURSE WE HAVE WON!
THE FIGHT, MAYBE. YOU STILL GON' LOSE, THOUGH.
COME AGAIN?
YOUR HANDS, GENIUS. THOSE BULLETS GON' EXPLODE IN FIVE SECONDS, TOPS.
BISHOP! YOU READY? I NEED THIS STUFF OUT OF ME!
YEAH-- BUT I NEED A CONNECTION. PSYCHIC ENERGY'S TOUGH. SOMETHING CLOSE.
CLOSE... ALL RIGHT.
BUT DON'T GET ANY IDEAS, NOW.
MMF!

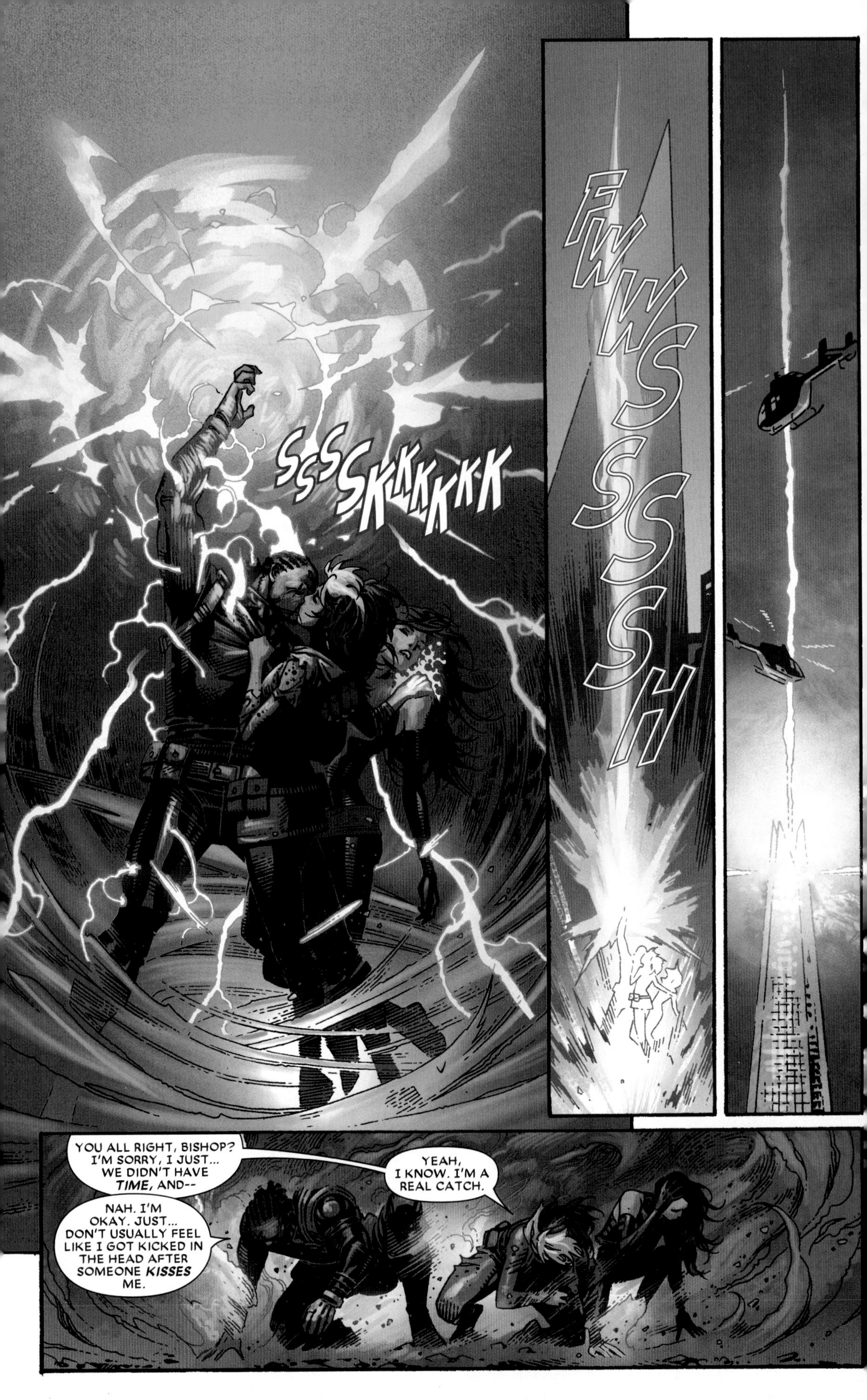
SSSSKKKKKKK
FWWSSSSH
YOU ALL RIGHT, BISHOP? I'M SORRY, I JUST... WE DIDN'T HAVE *TIME,* AND--
NAH. I'M OKAY. JUST... DON'T USUALLY FEEL LIKE I GOT KICKED IN THE HEAD AFTER SOMEONE *KISSES* ME.
YEAH, I KNOW. I'M A REAL CATCH.

WELL, THIS DAY HAS BEEN MOST *EMPHATICALLY* SAVED, NO?

REMIND ME WHAT YOU DID AGAIN?

WELL, PERHAPS NOT AS MUCH AS SOME.

BUT PROBABLY MORE THAN *MOST*.

KEEP IT UP, FANTOMEX.

I ALWAYS DO. ASK ANYONE.

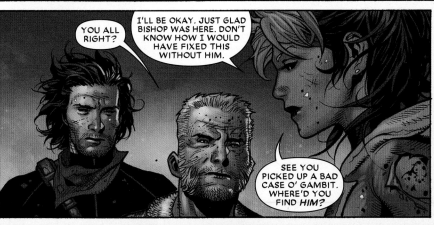

YOU ALL RIGHT?

I'LL BE OKAY. JUST GLAD BISHOP WAS HERE. DON'T KNOW HOW I WOULD HAVE FIXED THIS WITHOUT HIM.

SEE YOU PICKED UP A BAD CASE O' GAMBIT. WHERE'D YOU FIND *HIM*?

WELL, *THAT'S* A FINE HELLO TO THE *LOVE OF YOUR LIFE*.

STILL, REMY?

ALWAYS, *CHÈRE*.

FOUND GAMBIT ON THE STREET. FANTOMEX TOO. PSYLOCKE SENT OUT A CALL TO THEM, JUST LIKE US.

THEY AREN'T THE ONLY ONES, EITHER.

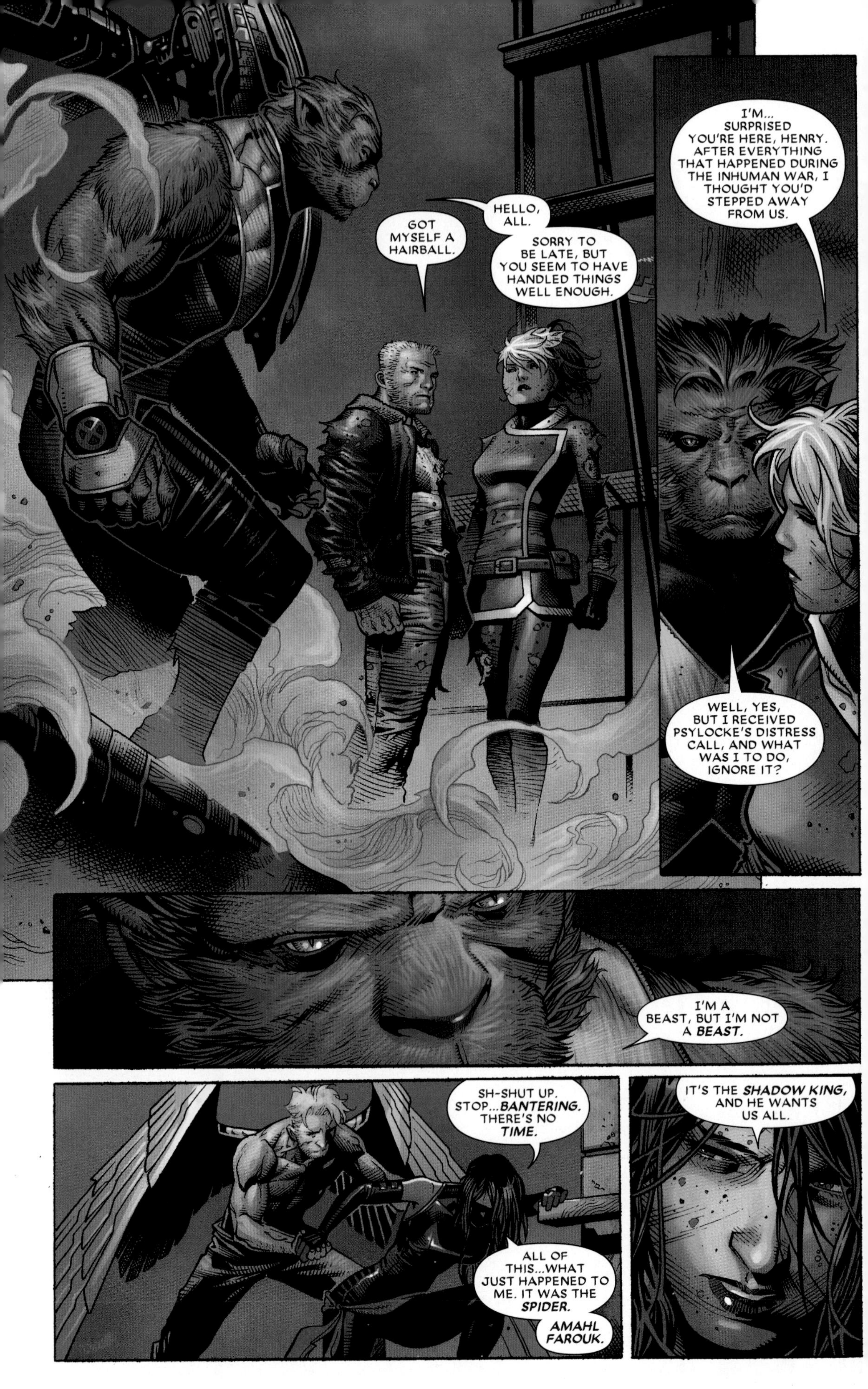
GOT MYSELF A HAIRBALL.
HELLO, ALL.
SORRY TO BE LATE, BUT YOU SEEM TO HAVE HANDLED THINGS WELL ENOUGH.
I'M... SURPRISED YOU'RE HERE, HENRY. AFTER EVERYTHING THAT HAPPENED DURING THE INHUMAN WAR, I THOUGHT YOU'D STEPPED AWAY FROM US.
WELL, YES, BUT I RECEIVED PSYLOCKE'S DISTRESS CALL, AND WHAT WAS I TO DO, IGNORE IT?
I'M A BEAST, BUT I'M NOT A *BEAST.*
SH-SHUT UP. STOP...*BANTERING.* THERE'S NO *TIME.*
ALL OF THIS...WHAT JUST HAPPENED TO ME. IT WAS THE *SPIDER.*
AMAHL FAROUK.
IT'S THE *SHADOW KING,* AND HE WANTS US ALL.

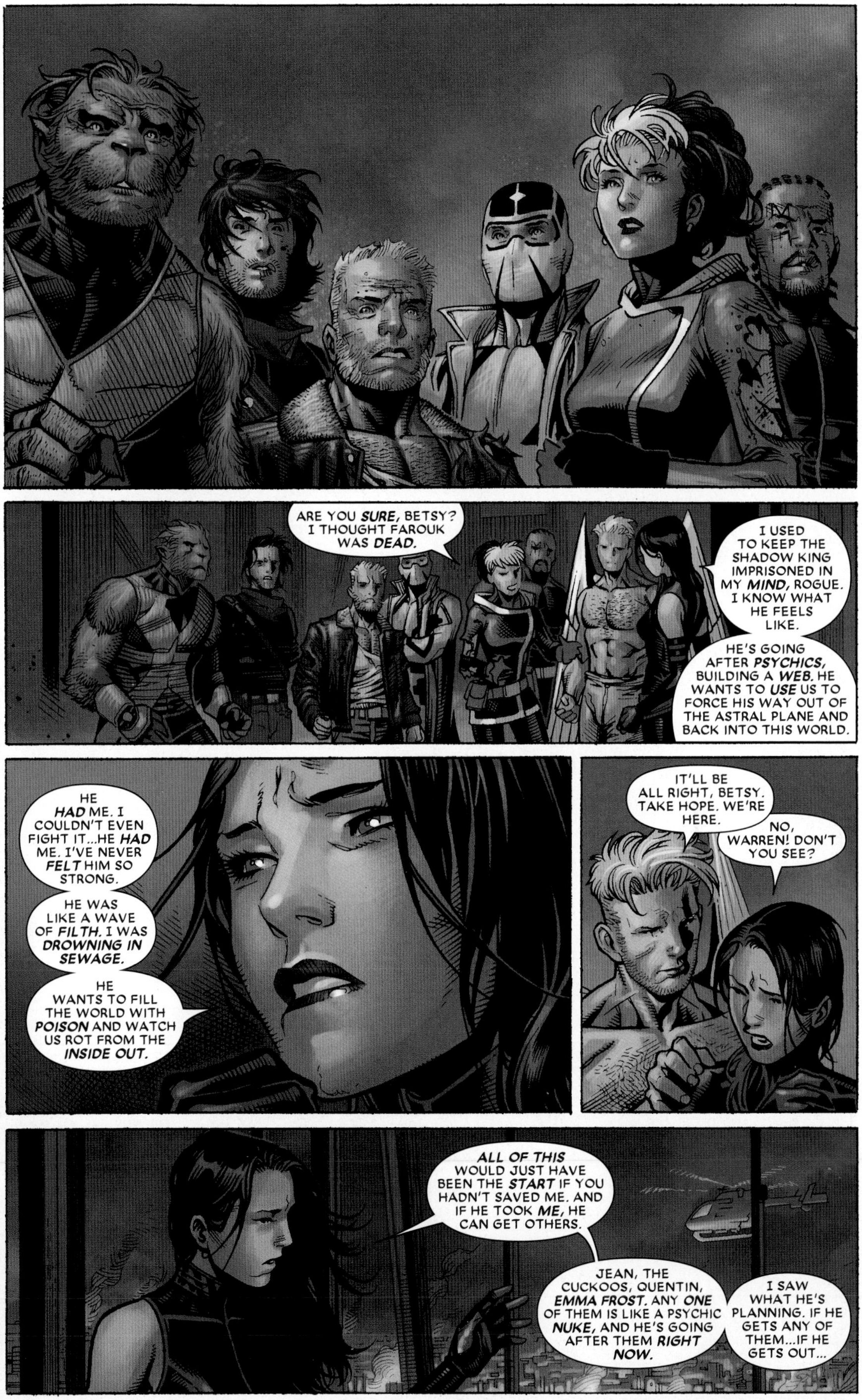
ARE YOU SURE, BETSY? I THOUGHT FAROUK WAS DEAD.
I USED TO KEEP THE SHADOW KING IMPRISONED IN MY MIND, ROGUE. I KNOW WHAT HE FEELS LIKE.
HE'S GOING AFTER PSYCHICS, BUILDING A WEB. HE WANTS TO USE US TO FORCE HIS WAY OUT OF THE ASTRAL PLANE AND BACK INTO THIS WORLD.
HE HAD ME. I COULDN'T EVEN FIGHT IT...HE HAD ME. I'VE NEVER FELT HIM SO STRONG.
HE WAS LIKE A WAVE OF FILTH. I WAS DROWNING IN SEWAGE.
HE WANTS TO FILL THE WORLD WITH POISON AND WATCH US ROT FROM THE INSIDE OUT.
IT'LL BE ALL RIGHT, BETSY. TAKE HOPE. WE'RE HERE.
NO, WARREN! DON'T YOU SEE?
ALL OF THIS WOULD JUST HAVE BEEN THE START IF YOU HADN'T SAVED ME. AND IF HE TOOK ME, HE CAN GET OTHERS.
JEAN, THE CUCKOOS, QUENTIN, EMMA FROST. ANY ONE OF THEM IS LIKE A PSYCHIC NUKE, AND HE'S GOING AFTER THEM RIGHT NOW.
I SAW WHAT HE'S PLANNING. IF HE GETS ANY OF THEM...IF HE GETS OUT...

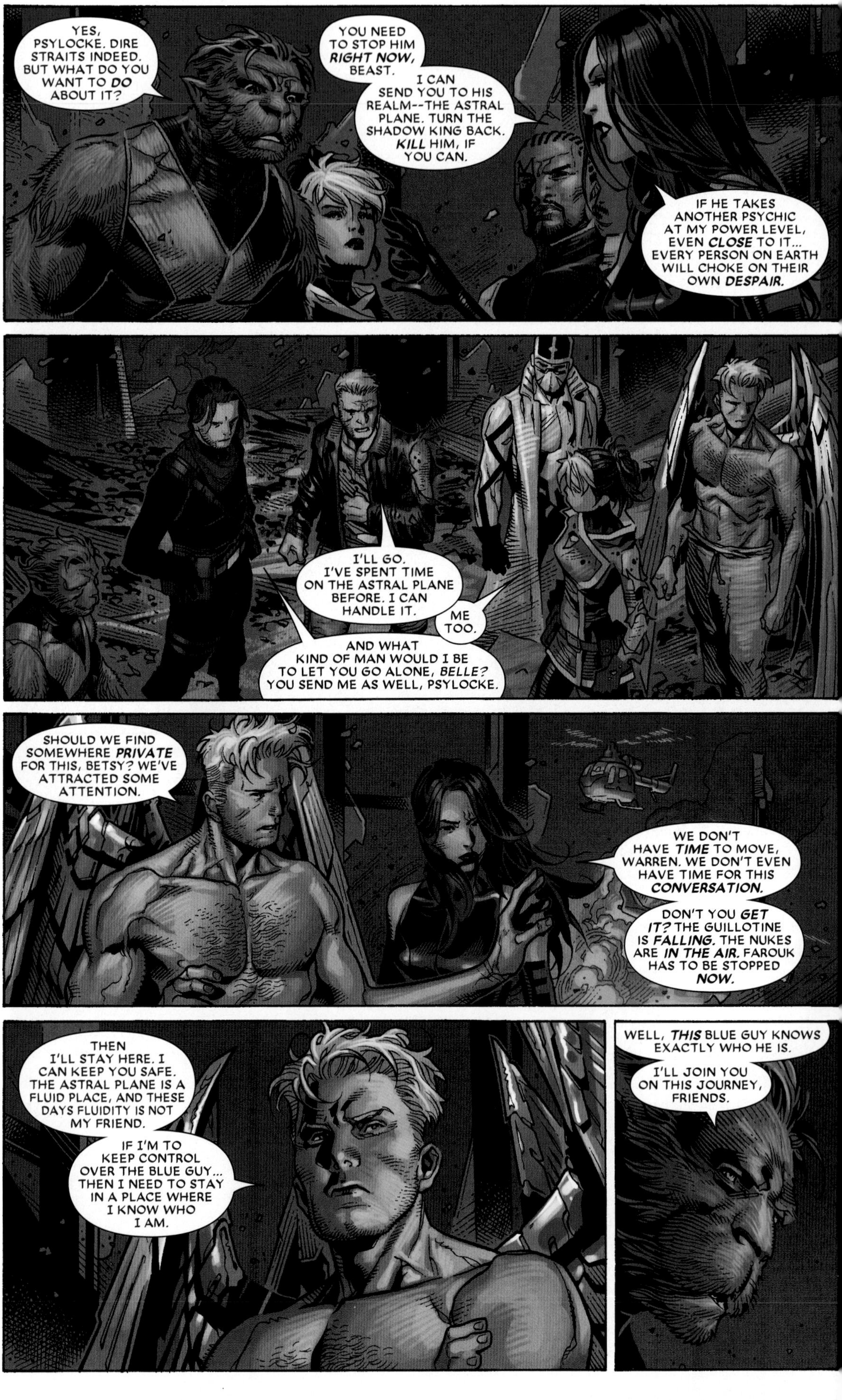

YES, PSYLOCKE. DIRE STRAITS INDEED. BUT WHAT DO YOU WANT TO DO ABOUT IT?
YOU NEED TO STOP HIM RIGHT NOW, BEAST.
I CAN SEND YOU TO HIS REALM--THE ASTRAL PLANE. TURN THE SHADOW KING BACK. KILL HIM, IF YOU CAN.
IF HE TAKES ANOTHER PSYCHIC AT MY POWER LEVEL, EVEN CLOSE TO IT... EVERY PERSON ON EARTH WILL CHOKE ON THEIR OWN DESPAIR.
I'LL GO. I'VE SPENT TIME ON THE ASTRAL PLANE BEFORE. I CAN HANDLE IT.
ME TOO.
AND WHAT KIND OF MAN WOULD I BE TO LET YOU GO ALONE, BELLE? YOU SEND ME AS WELL, PSYLOCKE.
SHOULD WE FIND SOMEWHERE PRIVATE FOR THIS, BETSY? WE'VE ATTRACTED SOME ATTENTION.
WE DON'T HAVE TIME TO MOVE, WARREN. WE DON'T EVEN HAVE TIME FOR THIS CONVERSATION.
DON'T YOU GET IT? THE GUILLOTINE IS FALLING. THE NUKES ARE IN THE AIR. FAROUK HAS TO BE STOPPED NOW.
THEN I'LL STAY HERE. I CAN KEEP YOU SAFE. THE ASTRAL PLANE IS A FLUID PLACE, AND THESE DAYS FLUIDITY IS NOT MY FRIEND.
IF I'M TO KEEP CONTROL OVER THE BLUE GUY... THEN I NEED TO STAY IN A PLACE WHERE I KNOW WHO I AM.
WELL, THIS BLUE GUY KNOWS EXACTLY WHO HE IS.
I'LL JOIN YOU ON THIS JOURNEY, FRIENDS.

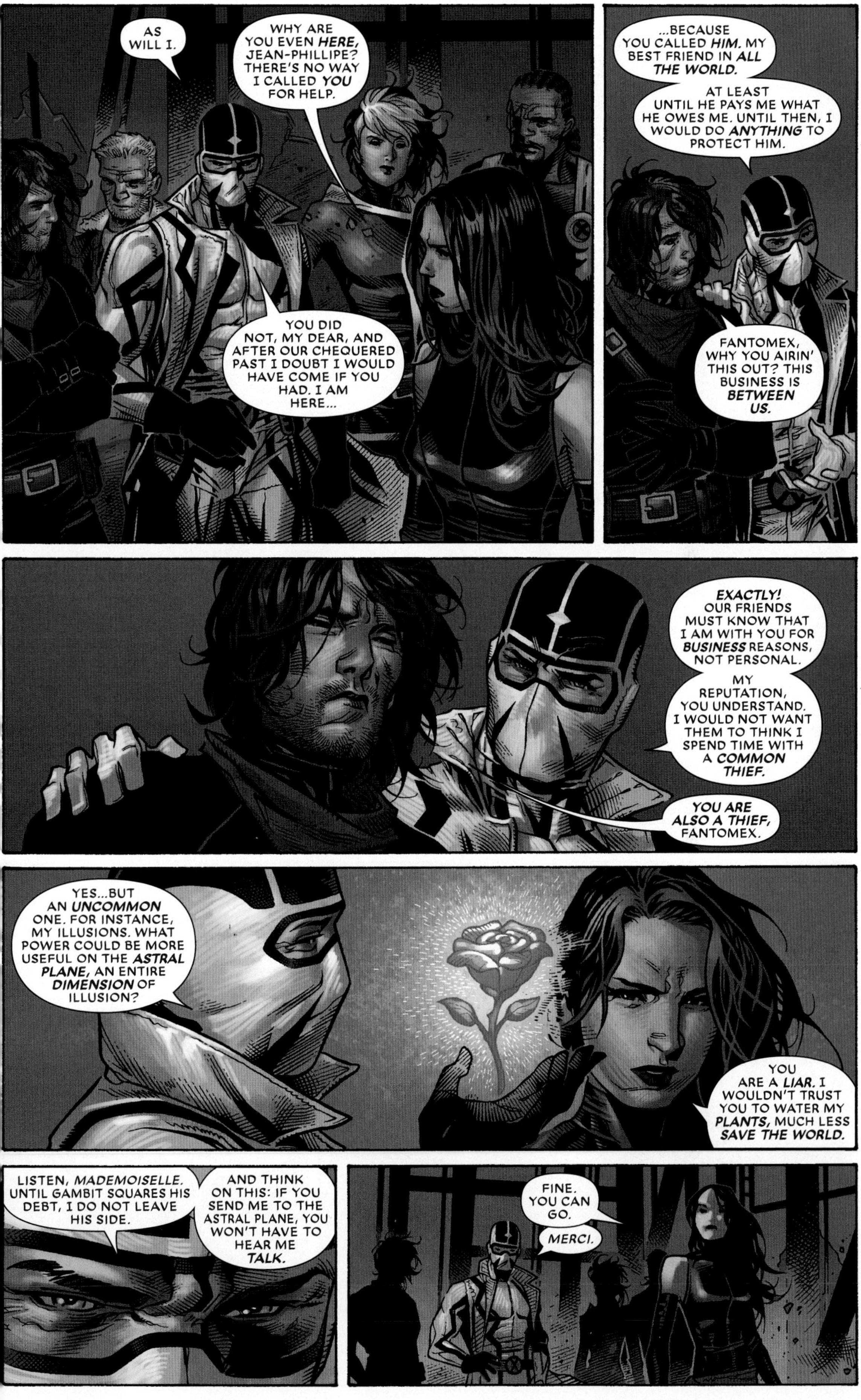
AS WILL I.
WHY ARE YOU EVEN HERE, JEAN-PHILLIPE? THERE'S NO WAY I CALLED YOU FOR HELP.
YOU DID NOT, MY DEAR, AND AFTER OUR CHEQUERED PAST I DOUBT I WOULD HAVE COME IF YOU HAD. I AM HERE...
...BECAUSE YOU CALLED HIM. MY BEST FRIEND IN ALL THE WORLD.
AT LEAST UNTIL HE PAYS ME WHAT HE OWES ME. UNTIL THEN, I WOULD DO ANYTHING TO PROTECT HIM.
FANTOMEX, WHY YOU AIRIN' THIS OUT? THIS BUSINESS IS BETWEEN US.
EXACTLY! OUR FRIENDS MUST KNOW THAT I AM WITH YOU FOR BUSINESS REASONS, NOT PERSONAL.
MY REPUTATION, YOU UNDERSTAND. I WOULD NOT WANT THEM TO THINK I SPEND TIME WITH A COMMON THIEF.
YOU ARE ALSO A THIEF, FANTOMEX.
YES...BUT AN UNCOMMON ONE. FOR INSTANCE, MY ILLUSIONS. WHAT POWER COULD BE MORE USEFUL ON THE ASTRAL PLANE, AN ENTIRE DIMENSION OF ILLUSION?
YOU ARE A LIAR. I WOULDN'T TRUST YOU TO WATER MY PLANTS, MUCH LESS SAVE THE WORLD.
LISTEN, MADEMOISELLE. UNTIL GAMBIT SQUARES HIS DEBT, I DO NOT LEAVE HIS SIDE.
AND THINK ON THIS: IF YOU SEND ME TO THE ASTRAL PLANE, YOU WON'T HAVE TO HEAR ME TALK.
FINE. YOU CAN GO.
MERCI.

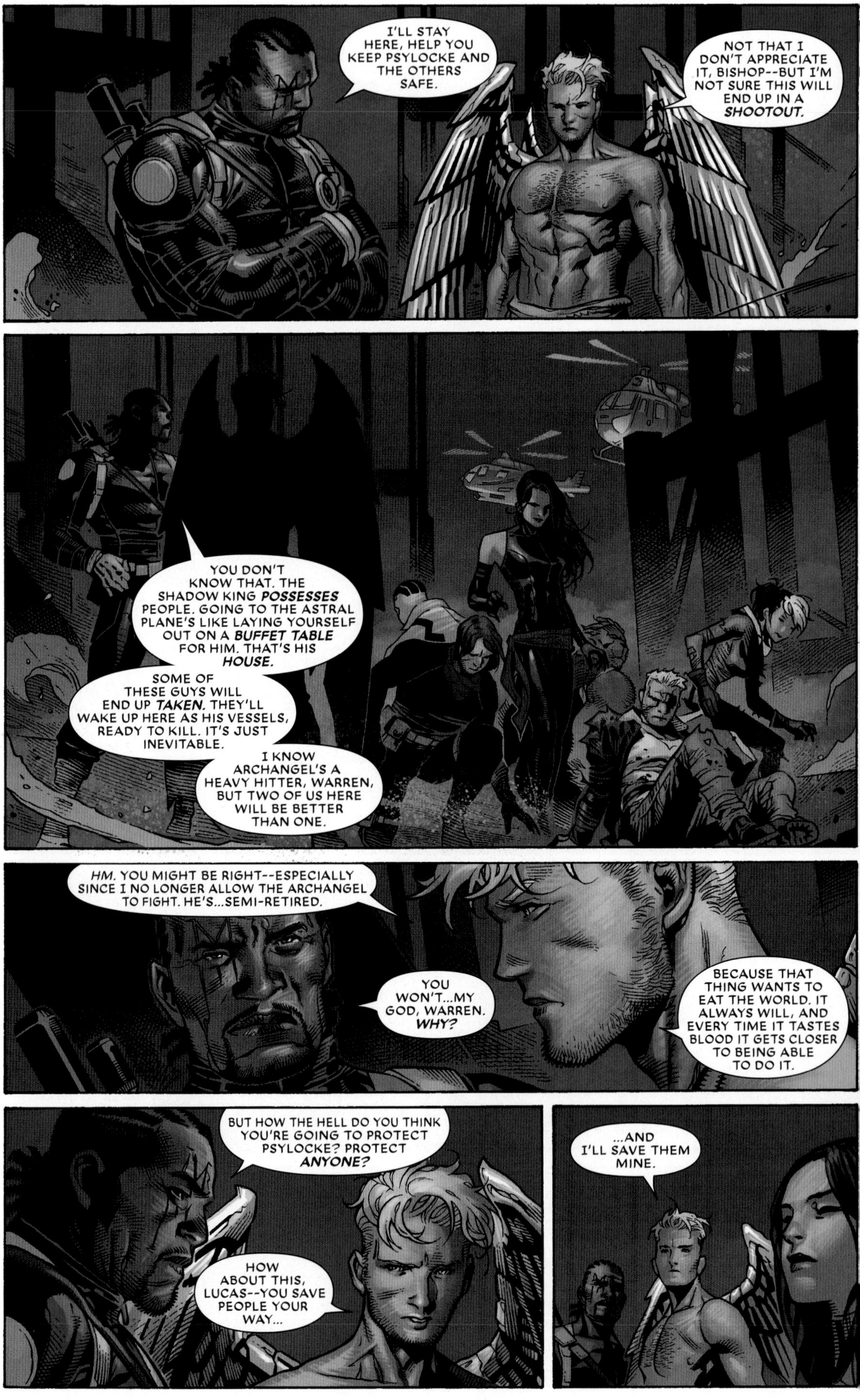

I'LL STAY HERE, HELP YOU KEEP PSYLOCKE AND THE OTHERS SAFE.
NOT THAT I DON'T APPRECIATE IT, BISHOP--BUT I'M NOT SURE THIS WILL END UP IN A *SHOOTOUT.*
YOU DON'T KNOW THAT. THE SHADOW KING *POSSESSES* PEOPLE. GOING TO THE ASTRAL PLANE'S LIKE LAYING YOURSELF OUT ON A *BUFFET TABLE* FOR HIM. THAT'S HIS *HOUSE.*
SOME OF THESE GUYS WILL END UP *TAKEN.* THEY'LL WAKE UP HERE AS HIS VESSELS, READY TO KILL. IT'S JUST INEVITABLE.
I KNOW ARCHANGEL'S A HEAVY HITTER, WARREN, BUT TWO OF US HERE WILL BE BETTER THAN ONE.
HM. YOU MIGHT BE RIGHT--ESPECIALLY SINCE I NO LONGER ALLOW THE ARCHANGEL TO FIGHT. HE'S...SEMI-RETIRED.
YOU WON'T...MY GOD, WARREN. *WHY?*
BECAUSE THAT THING WANTS TO EAT THE WORLD. IT ALWAYS WILL, AND EVERY TIME IT TASTES BLOOD IT GETS CLOSER TO BEING ABLE TO DO IT.
BUT HOW THE HELL DO YOU THINK YOU'RE GOING TO PROTECT PSYLOCKE? PROTECT *ANYONE?*
HOW ABOUT THIS, LUCAS--YOU SAVE PEOPLE YOUR WAY...
...AND I'LL SAVE THEM MINE.

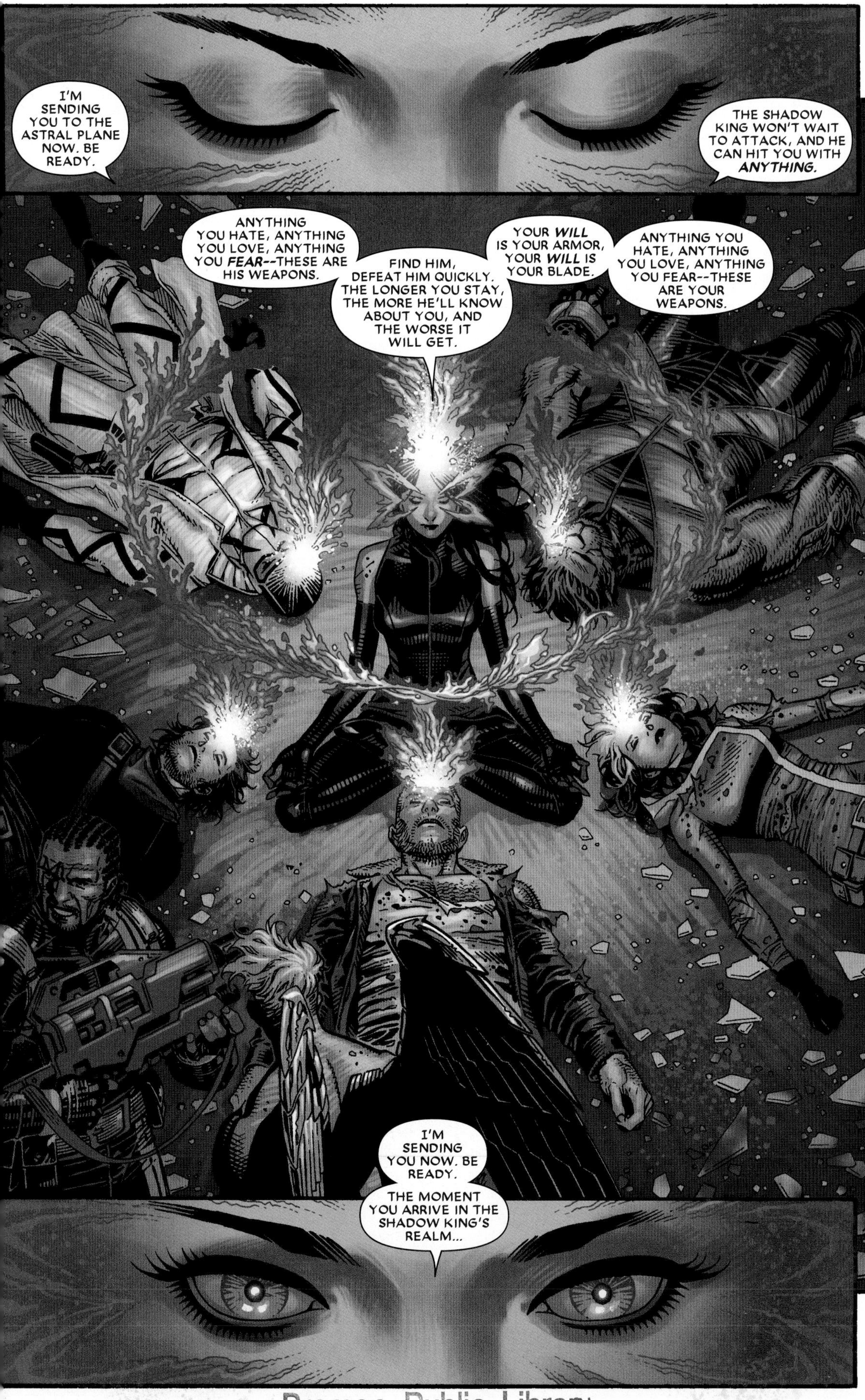
I'M SENDING YOU TO THE ASTRAL PLANE NOW. BE READY.
THE SHADOW KING WON'T WAIT TO ATTACK, AND HE CAN HIT YOU WITH *ANYTHING.*
ANYTHING YOU HATE, ANYTHING YOU LOVE, ANYTHING YOU *FEAR*--THESE ARE HIS WEAPONS.
FIND HIM, DEFEAT HIM QUICKLY. THE LONGER YOU STAY, THE MORE HE'LL KNOW ABOUT YOU, AND THE WORSE IT WILL GET.
YOUR *WILL* IS YOUR ARMOR, YOUR *WILL* IS YOUR BLADE.
ANYTHING YOU HATE, ANYTHING YOU LOVE, ANYTHING YOU FEAR--THESE ARE YOUR WEAPONS.
I'M SENDING YOU NOW. BE READY.
THE MOMENT YOU ARRIVE IN THE SHADOW KING'S REALM...

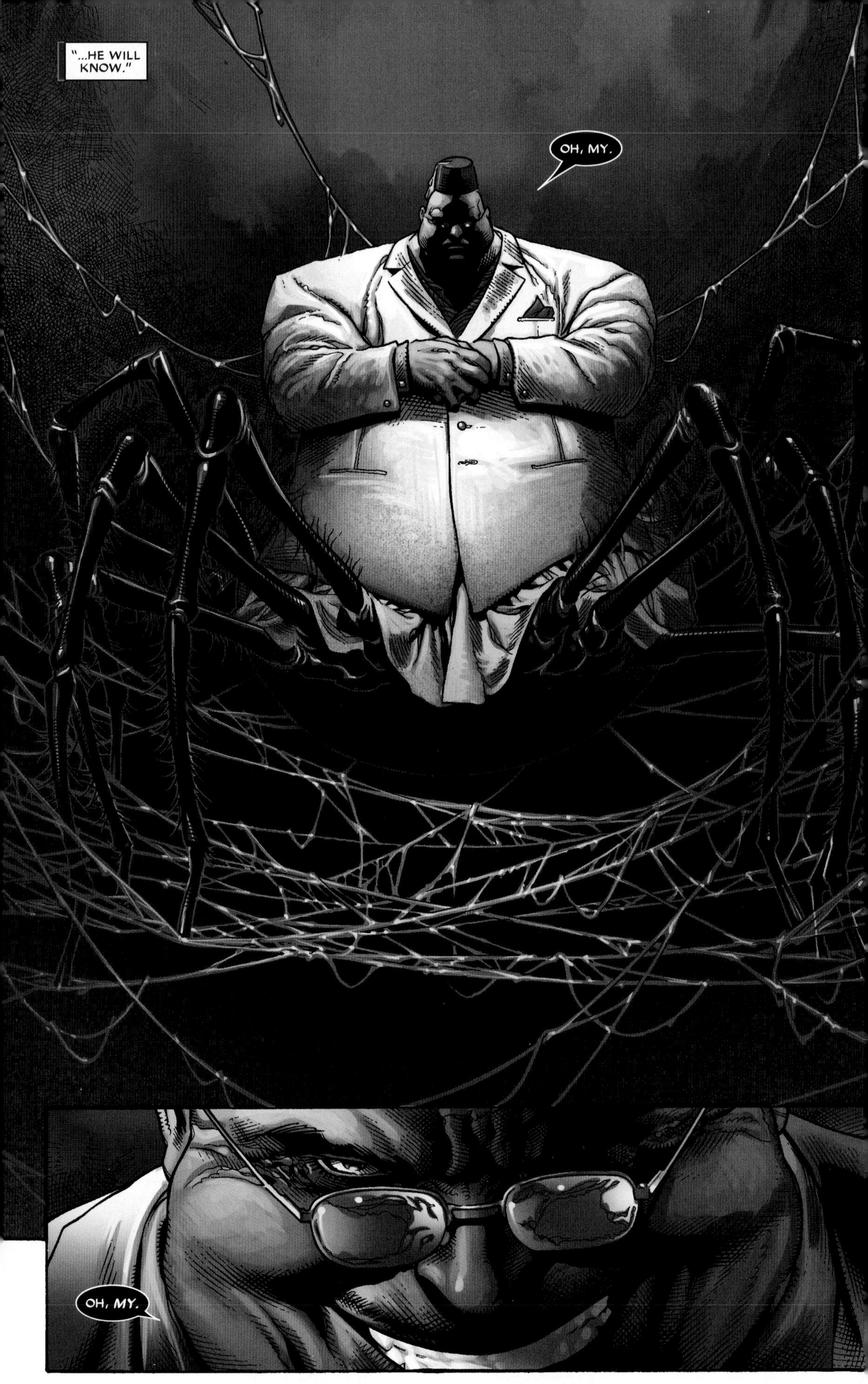
"...HE WILL KNOW."
OH, MY.
OH, MY.

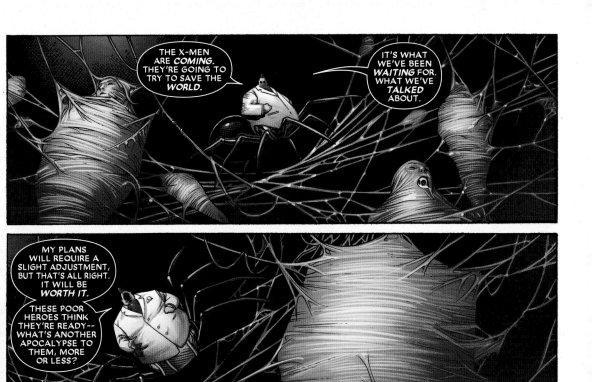

THE X-MEN ARE *COMING*. THEY'RE GOING TO TRY TO SAVE THE *WORLD*.

IT'S WHAT WE'VE BEEN *WAITING* FOR. WHAT WE'VE *TALKED* ABOUT.

MY PLANS WILL REQUIRE A SLIGHT ADJUSTMENT, BUT THAT'S ALL RIGHT. IT WILL BE *WORTH IT*.

THESE POOR HEROES THINK THEY'RE READY-- WHAT'S ANOTHER APOCALYPSE TO THEM, MORE OR LESS?

BUT THEY'VE FORGOTTEN THE SIMPLEST THING. WHAT ANY PSYCHIC COULD TELL THEM.

ON THE ASTRAL PLANE, THE APOCALYPSE ISN'T A WAR, OR MELTING ICE CAPS, OR A STRAY COMET. NOTHING LIKE THAT.

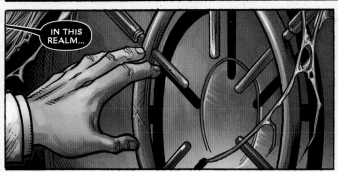

IN THIS REALM...

...THE APOCALYPSE IS *SECRETS*.

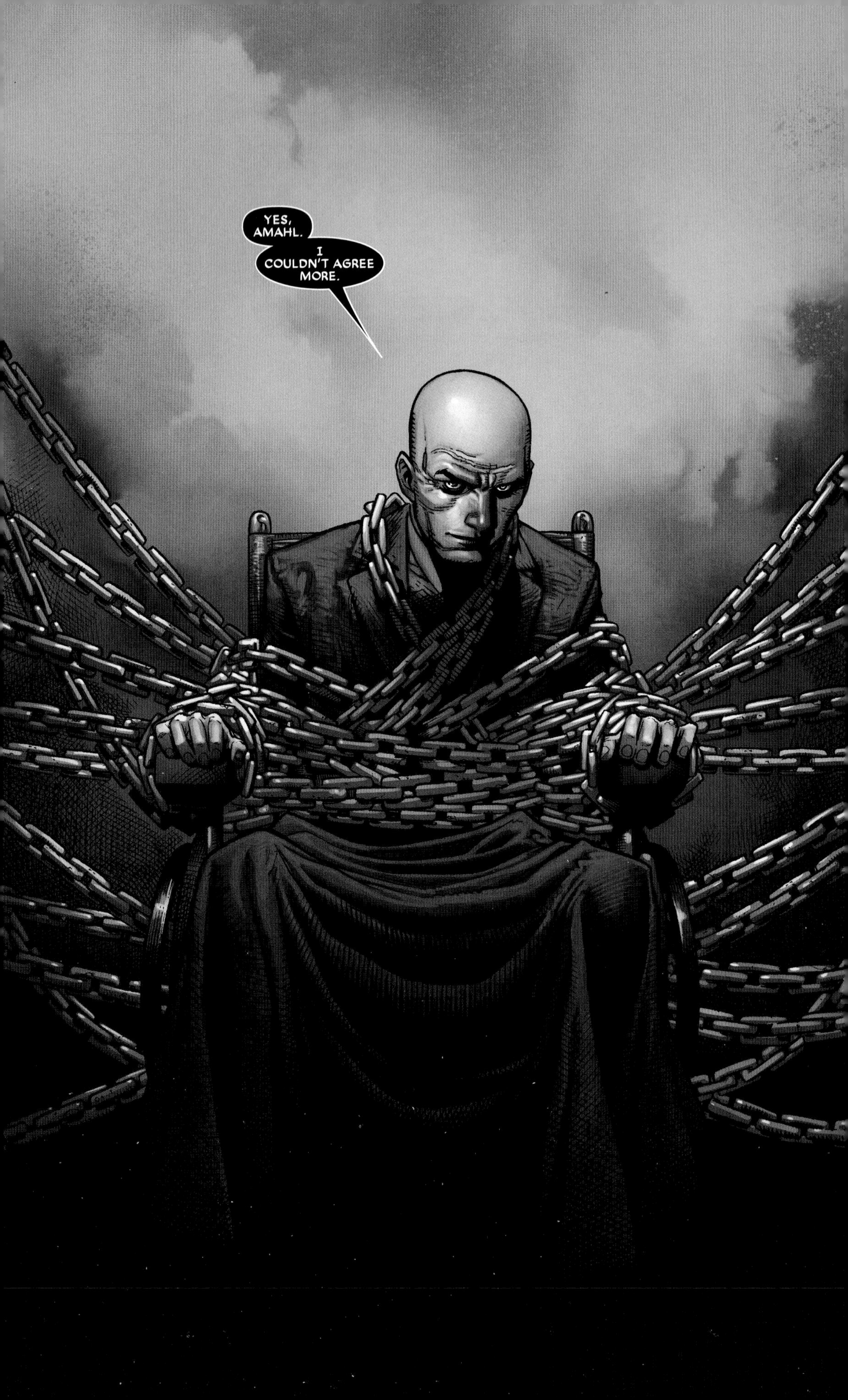
YES, AMAHL.
I COULDN'T AGREE MORE.

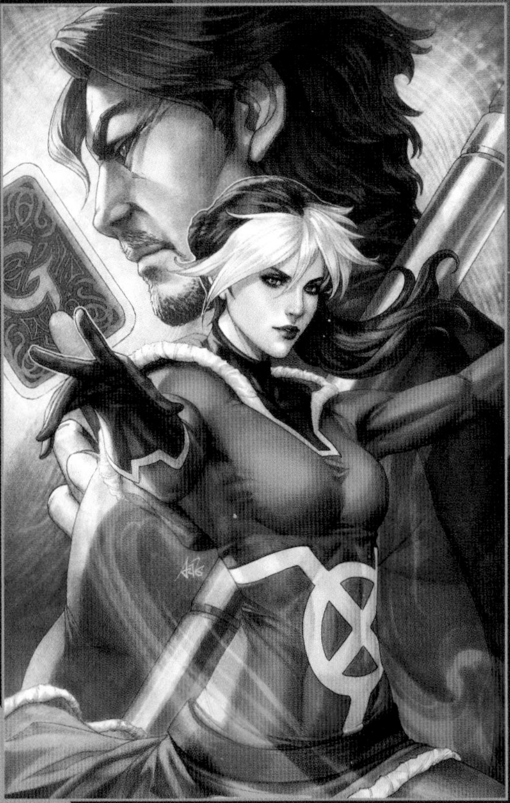

#1 VARIANT
BY **ARTGERM**

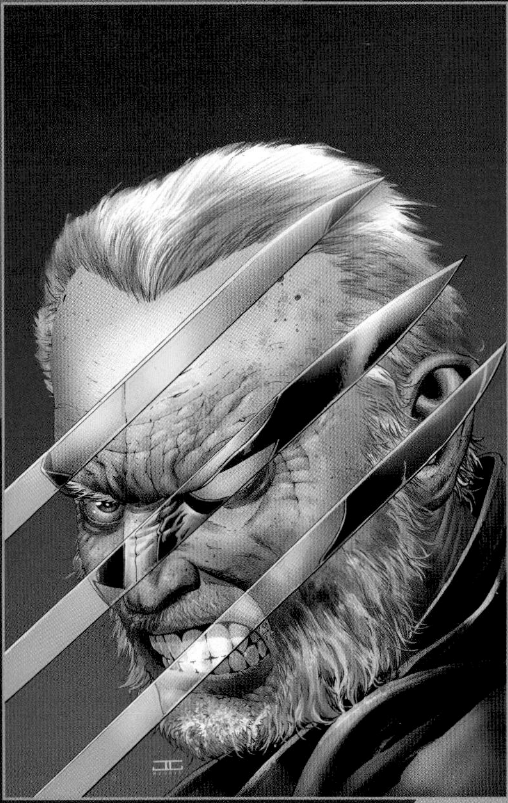

#1 VARIANT
BY **JOHN CASSADAY**
& **PAUL MOUNTS**

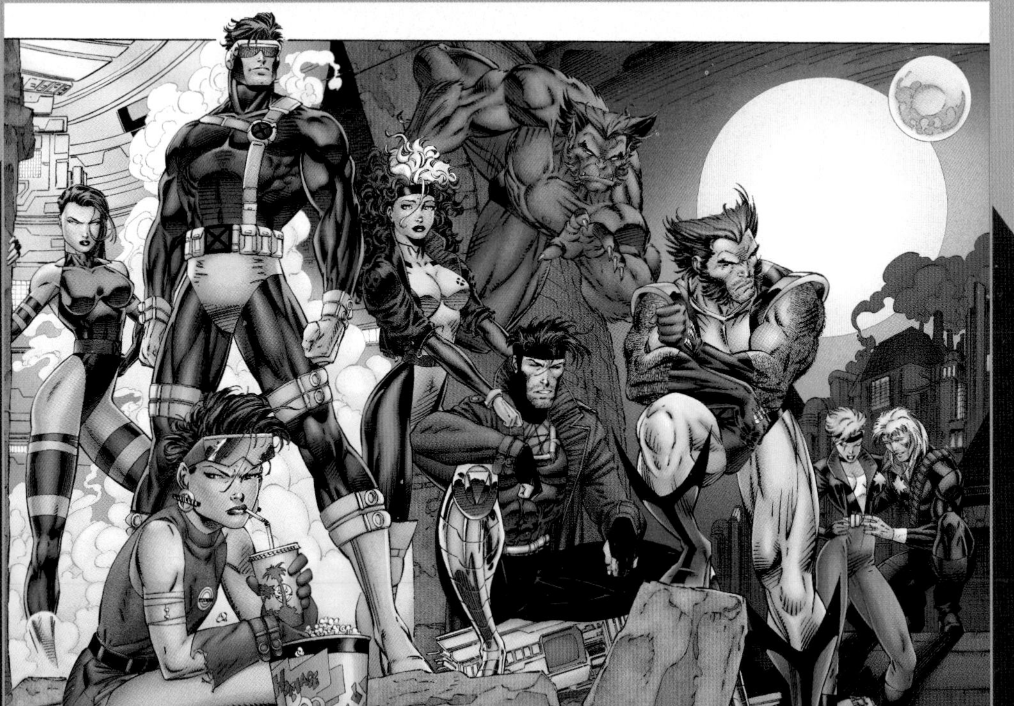

#1 REMASTERED VARIANT
BY **JIM LEE, SCOTT WILLIAMS** & **MORRY HOLLOWELL** WITH **JOE FRONTIRRE**

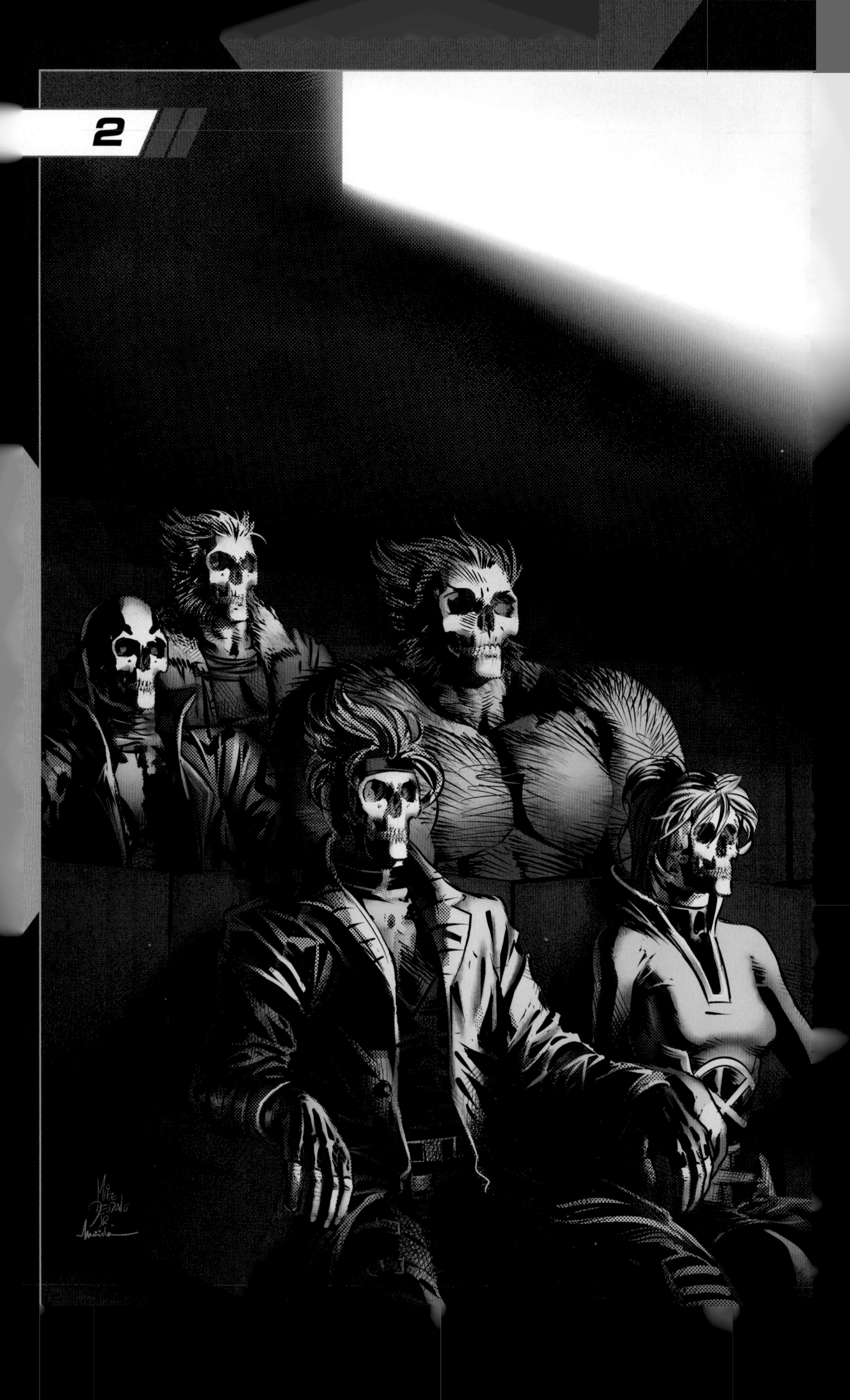
2

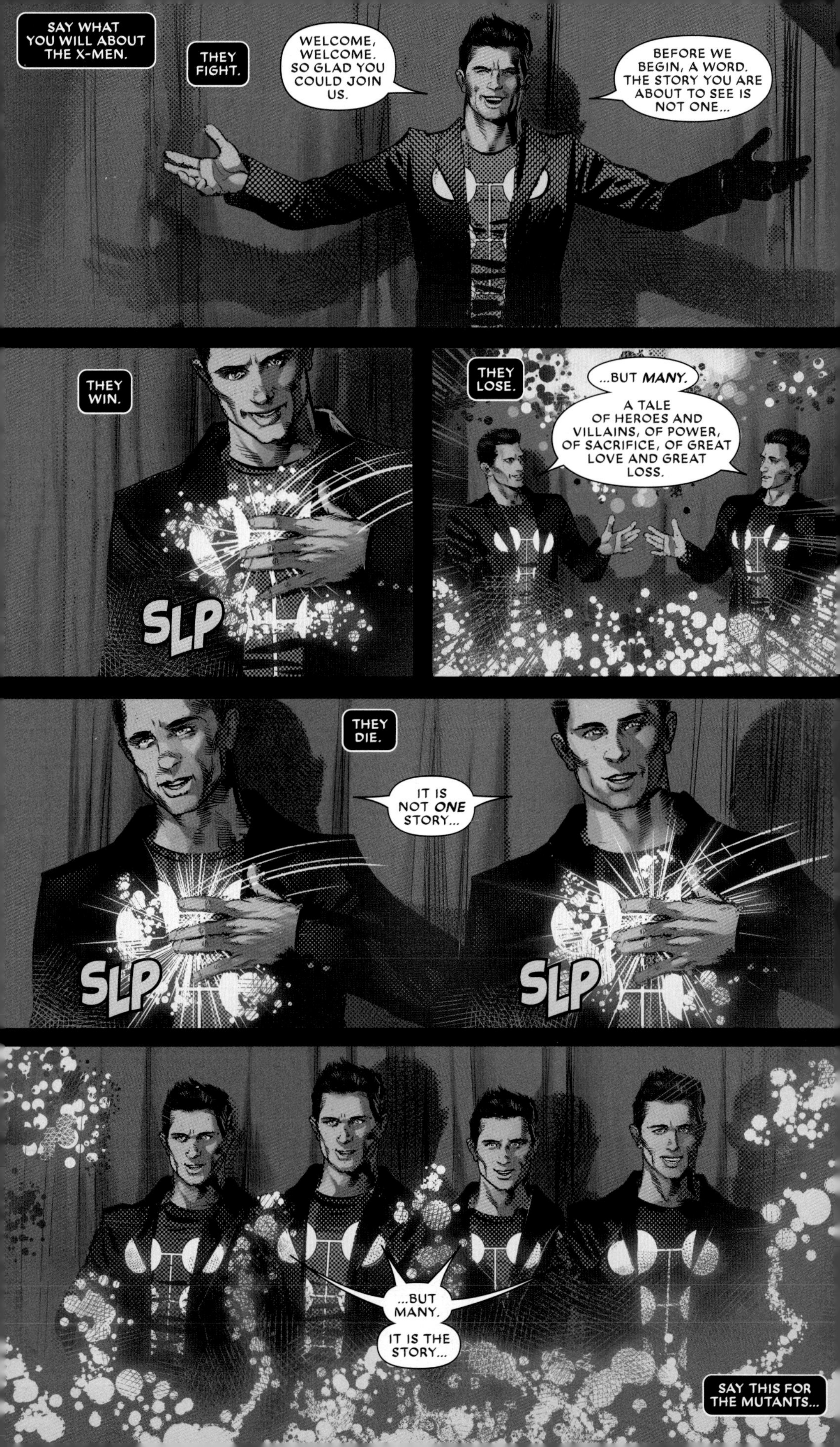
SAY WHAT YOU WILL ABOUT THE X-MEN.
THEY FIGHT.
WELCOME, WELCOME. SO GLAD YOU COULD JOIN US.
BEFORE WE BEGIN, A WORD. THE STORY YOU ARE ABOUT TO SEE IS NOT ONE...
THEY WIN.
SLP
THEY LOSE.
...BUT MANY.
A TALE OF HEROES AND VILLAINS, OF POWER, OF SACRIFICE, OF GREAT LOVE AND GREAT LOSS.
THEY DIE.
IT IS NOT ONE STORY...
SLP
SLP
...BUT MANY.
IT IS THE STORY...
SAY THIS FOR THE MUTANTS...

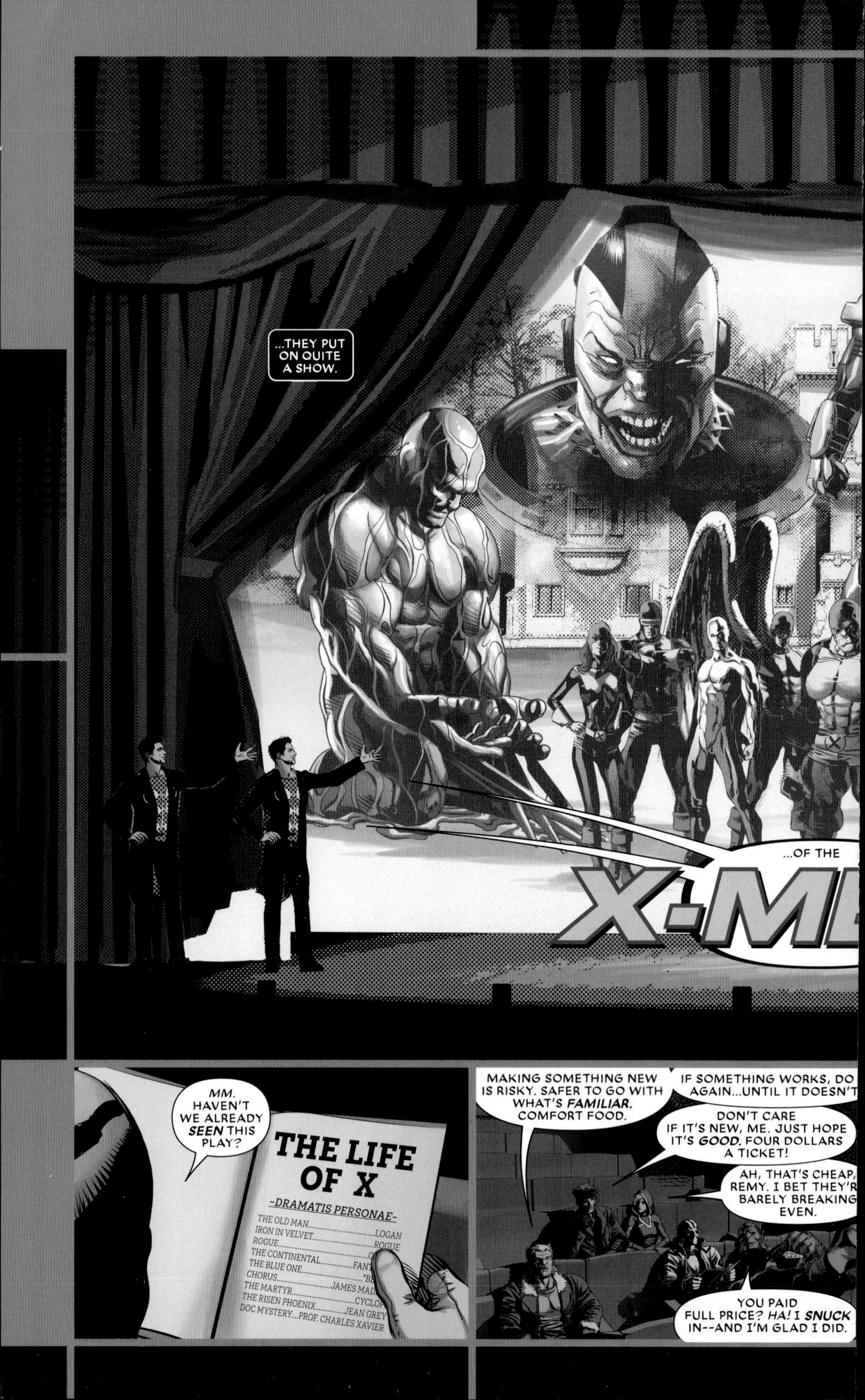
...THEY PUT ON QUITE A SHOW.
...OF THE
X-M
MM. HAVEN'T WE ALREADY SEEN THIS PLAY?
THE LIFE OF X
~DRAMATIS PERSONAE~
THE OLD MAN
IRON IN VELVET....LOGAN
ROGUE....ROGUE
THE CONTINENTAL....FANT
THE BLUE ONE
CHORUS
THE MARTYR....JAMES MAD
THE RISEN PHOENIX....CYCLOP
DOC MYSTERY....JEAN GREY
PROF. CHARLES XAVIER
MAKING SOMETHING NEW IS RISKY. SAFER TO GO WITH WHAT'S FAMILIAR. COMFORT FOOD.
IF SOMETHING WORKS, DO AGAIN...UNTIL IT DOESN'T
DON'T CARE IF IT'S NEW, ME. JUST HOPE IT'S GOOD. FOUR DOLLARS A TICKET!
AH, THAT'S CHEAP, REMY. I BET THEY'R BARELY BREAKING EVEN.
YOU PAID FULL PRICE? HA! I SNUCK IN--AND I'M GLAD I DID.

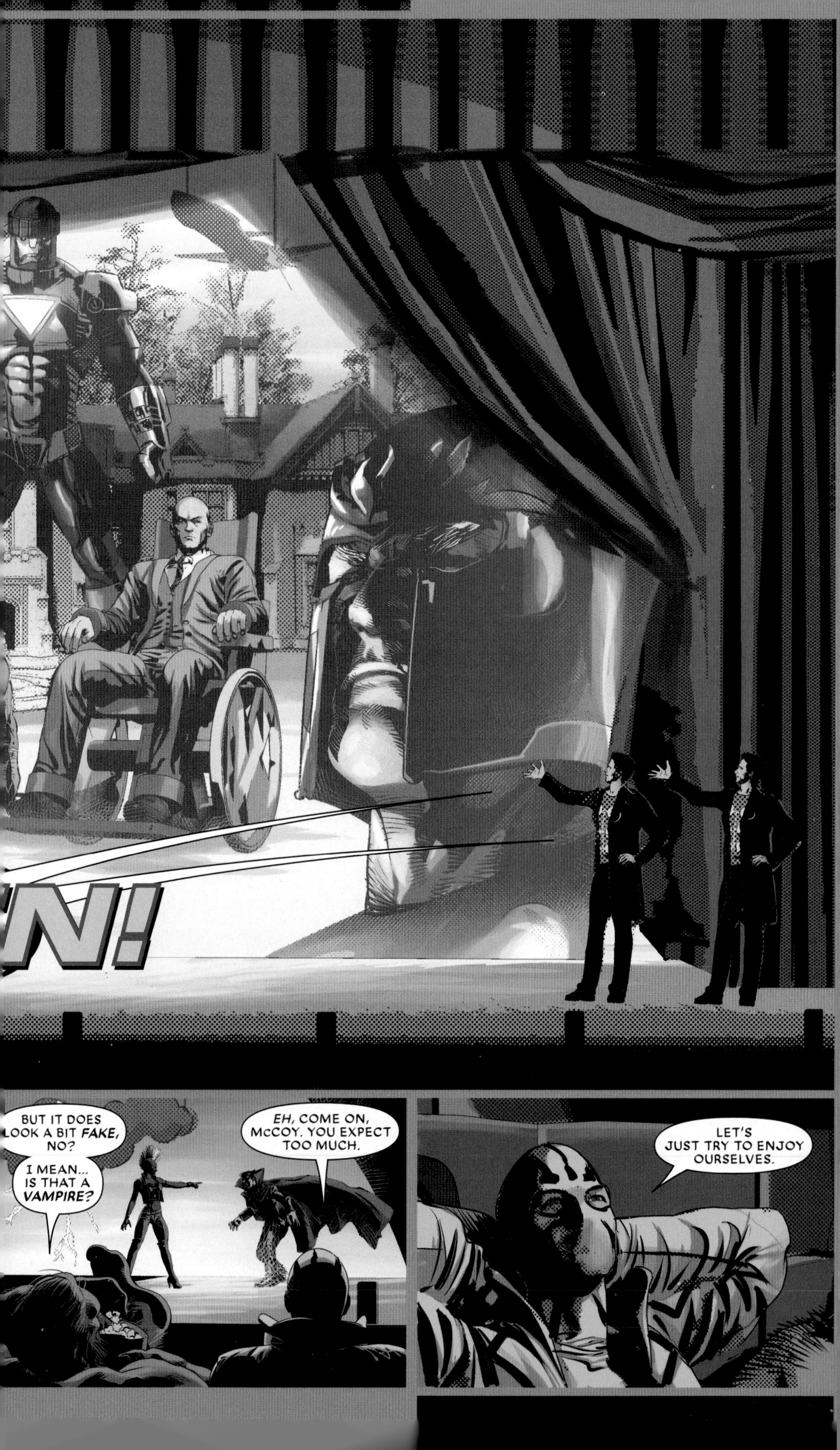
BUT IT DOES LOOK A BIT *FAKE,* NO?
I MEAN... IS THAT A *VAMPIRE?*
EH, COME ON, McCOY. YOU EXPECT TOO MUCH.
LET'S JUST TRY TO ENJOY OURSELVES.

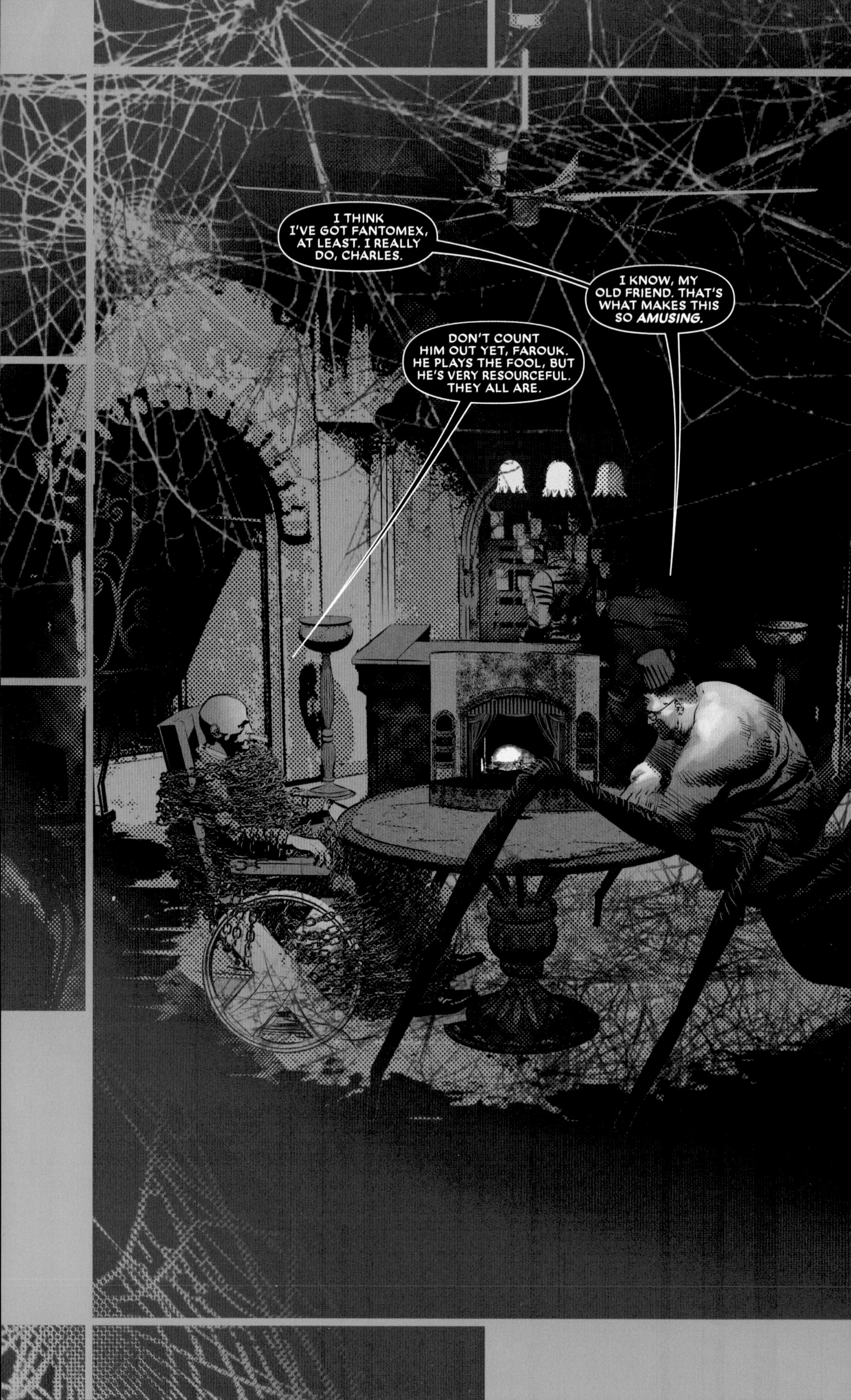
I THINK I'VE GOT FANTOMEX, AT LEAST. I REALLY DO, CHARLES.
I KNOW, MY OLD FRIEND. THAT'S WHAT MAKES THIS SO *AMUSING.*
DON'T COUNT HIM OUT YET, FAROUK. HE PLAYS THE FOOL, BUT HE'S VERY RESOURCEFUL. THEY ALL ARE.

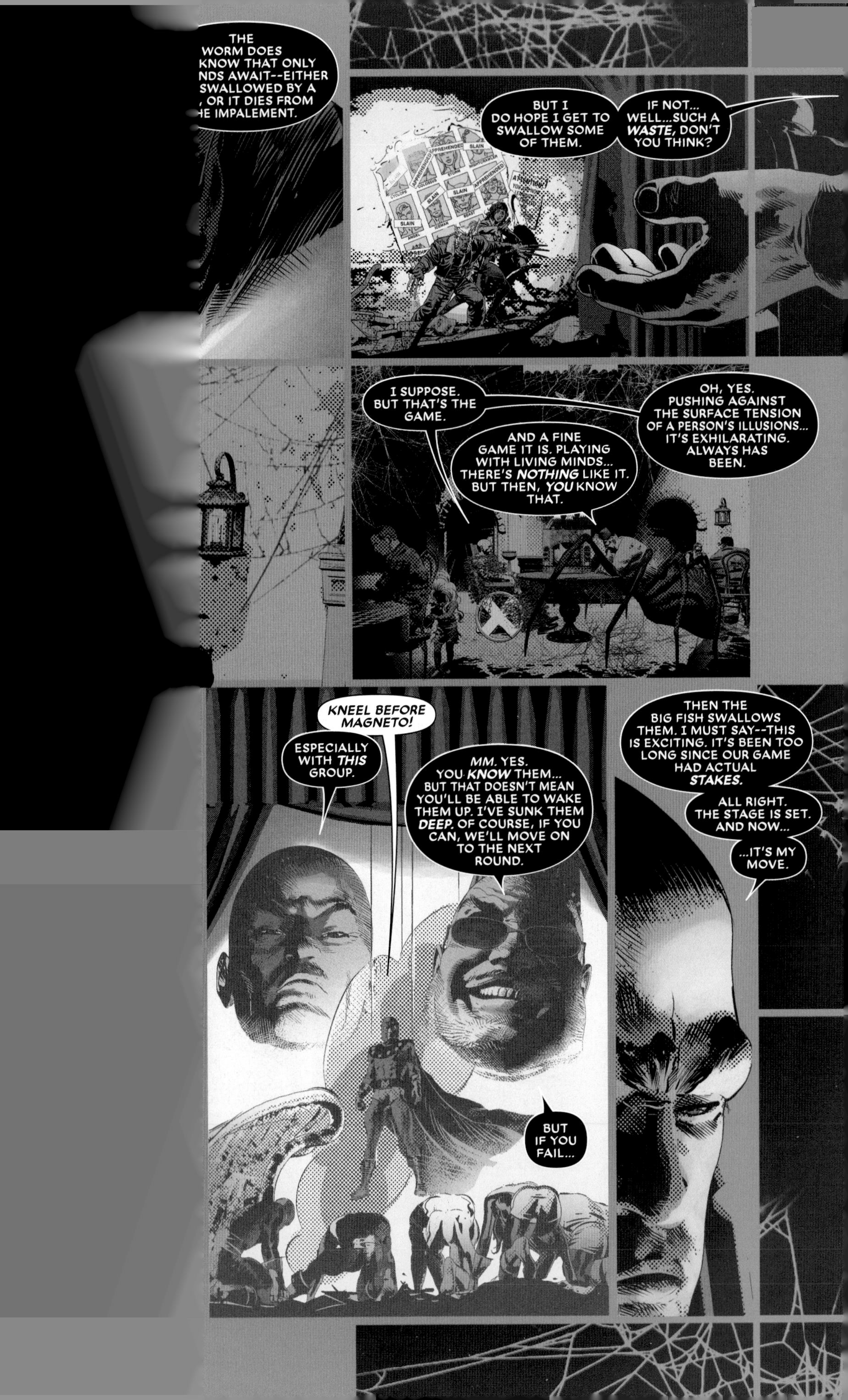
THE WORM DOES KNOW THAT ONLY NDS AWAIT--EITHER SWALLOWED BY A , OR IT DIES FROM HE IMPALEMENT.
BUT I DO HOPE I GET TO SWALLOW SOME OF THEM.
IF NOT... WELL...SUCH A WASTE, DON'T YOU THINK?
I SUPPOSE. BUT THAT'S THE GAME.
OH, YES. PUSHING AGAINST THE SURFACE TENSION OF A PERSON'S ILLUSIONS... IT'S EXHILARATING. ALWAYS HAS BEEN.
AND A FINE GAME IT IS. PLAYING WITH LIVING MINDS... THERE'S NOTHING LIKE IT. BUT THEN, YOU KNOW THAT.
KNEEL BEFORE MAGNETO!
ESPECIALLY WITH THIS GROUP.
MM. YES. YOU KNOW THEM... BUT THAT DOESN'T MEAN YOU'LL BE ABLE TO WAKE THEM UP. I'VE SUNK THEM DEEP. OF COURSE, IF YOU CAN, WE'LL MOVE ON TO THE NEXT ROUND.
BUT IF YOU FAIL...
THEN THE BIG FISH SWALLOWS THEM. I MUST SAY--THIS IS EXCITING. IT'S BEEN TOO LONG SINCE OUR GAME HAD ACTUAL STAKES.
ALL RIGHT. THE STAGE IS SET. AND NOW...
...IT'S MY MOVE.

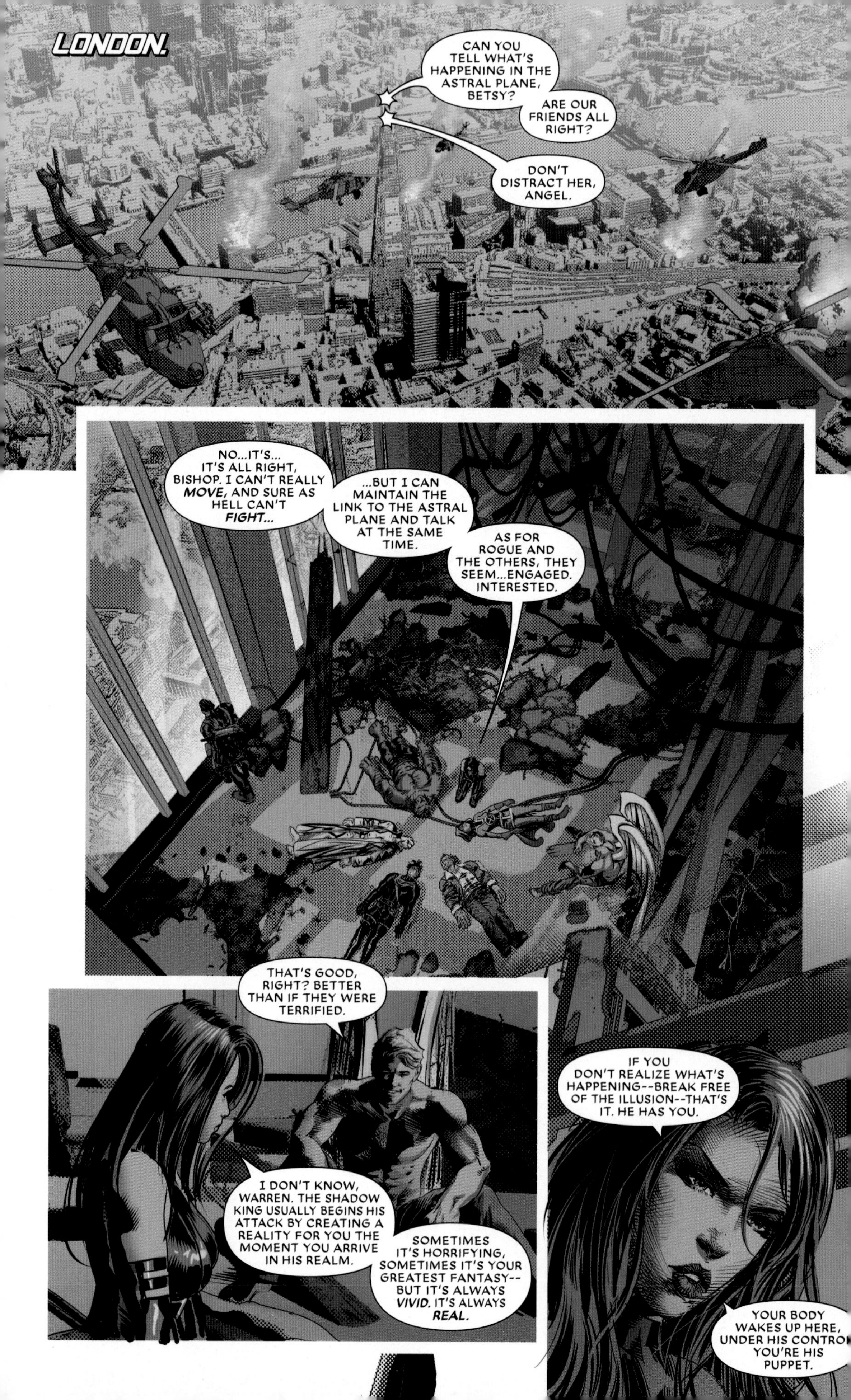
LONDON.
CAN YOU TELL WHAT'S HAPPENING IN THE ASTRAL PLANE, BETSY?
ARE OUR FRIENDS ALL RIGHT?
DON'T DISTRACT HER, ANGEL.
NO...IT'S... IT'S ALL RIGHT, BISHOP. I CAN'T REALLY MOVE, AND SURE AS HELL CAN'T FIGHT...
...BUT I CAN MAINTAIN THE LINK TO THE ASTRAL PLANE AND TALK AT THE SAME TIME.
AS FOR ROGUE AND THE OTHERS, THEY SEEM...ENGAGED. INTERESTED.
THAT'S GOOD, RIGHT? BETTER THAN IF THEY WERE TERRIFIED.
I DON'T KNOW, WARREN. THE SHADOW KING USUALLY BEGINS HIS ATTACK BY CREATING A REALITY FOR YOU THE MOMENT YOU ARRIVE IN HIS REALM.
SOMETIMES IT'S HORRIFYING, SOMETIMES IT'S YOUR GREATEST FANTASY--BUT IT'S ALWAYS VIVID. IT'S ALWAYS REAL.
IF YOU DON'T REALIZE WHAT'S HAPPENING--BREAK FREE OF THE ILLUSION--THAT'S IT. HE HAS YOU.
YOUR BODY WAKES UP HERE, UNDER HIS CONTRO YOU'RE HIS PUPPET.

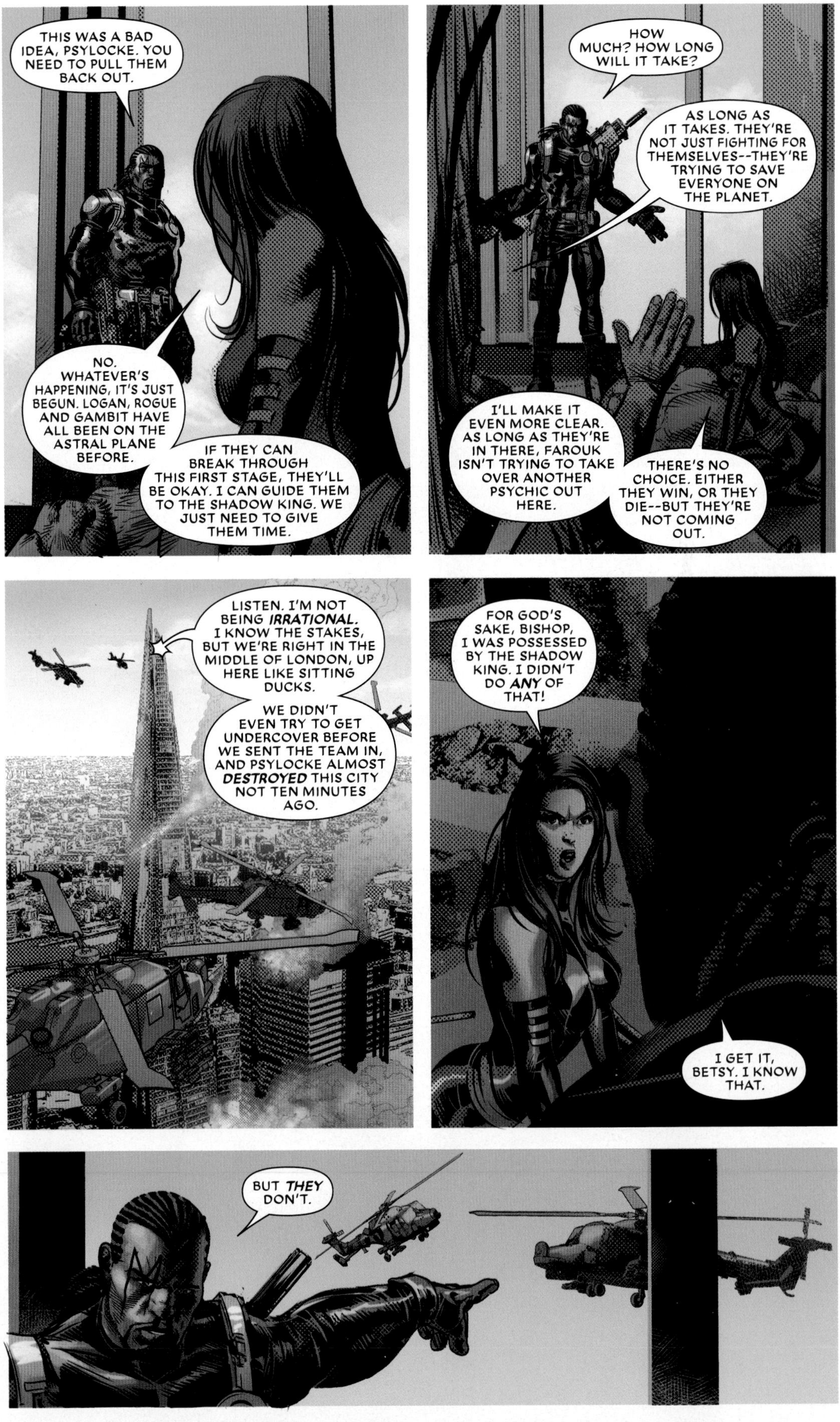

THIS WAS A BAD IDEA, PSYLOCKE. YOU NEED TO PULL THEM BACK OUT.
NO. WHATEVER'S HAPPENING, IT'S JUST BEGUN. LOGAN, ROGUE AND GAMBIT HAVE ALL BEEN ON THE ASTRAL PLANE BEFORE.
IF THEY CAN BREAK THROUGH THIS FIRST STAGE, THEY'LL BE OKAY. I CAN GUIDE THEM TO THE SHADOW KING. WE JUST NEED TO GIVE THEM TIME.
HOW MUCH? HOW LONG WILL IT TAKE?
AS LONG AS IT TAKES. THEY'RE NOT JUST FIGHTING FOR THEMSELVES--THEY'RE TRYING TO SAVE EVERYONE ON THE PLANET.
I'LL MAKE IT EVEN MORE CLEAR. AS LONG AS THEY'RE IN THERE, FAROUK ISN'T TRYING TO TAKE OVER ANOTHER PSYCHIC OUT HERE.
THERE'S NO CHOICE. EITHER THEY WIN, OR THEY DIE--BUT THEY'RE NOT COMING OUT.
LISTEN. I'M NOT BEING ***IRRATIONAL.*** I KNOW THE STAKES, BUT WE'RE RIGHT IN THE MIDDLE OF LONDON, UP HERE LIKE SITTING DUCKS.
WE DIDN'T EVEN TRY TO GET UNDERCOVER BEFORE WE SENT THE TEAM IN, AND PSYLOCKE ALMOST ***DESTROYED*** THIS CITY NOT TEN MINUTES AGO.
FOR GOD'S SAKE, BISHOP, I WAS POSSESSED BY THE SHADOW KING. I DIDN'T DO ***ANY*** OF THAT!
I GET IT, BETSY. I KNOW THAT.
BUT ***THEY*** DON'T.

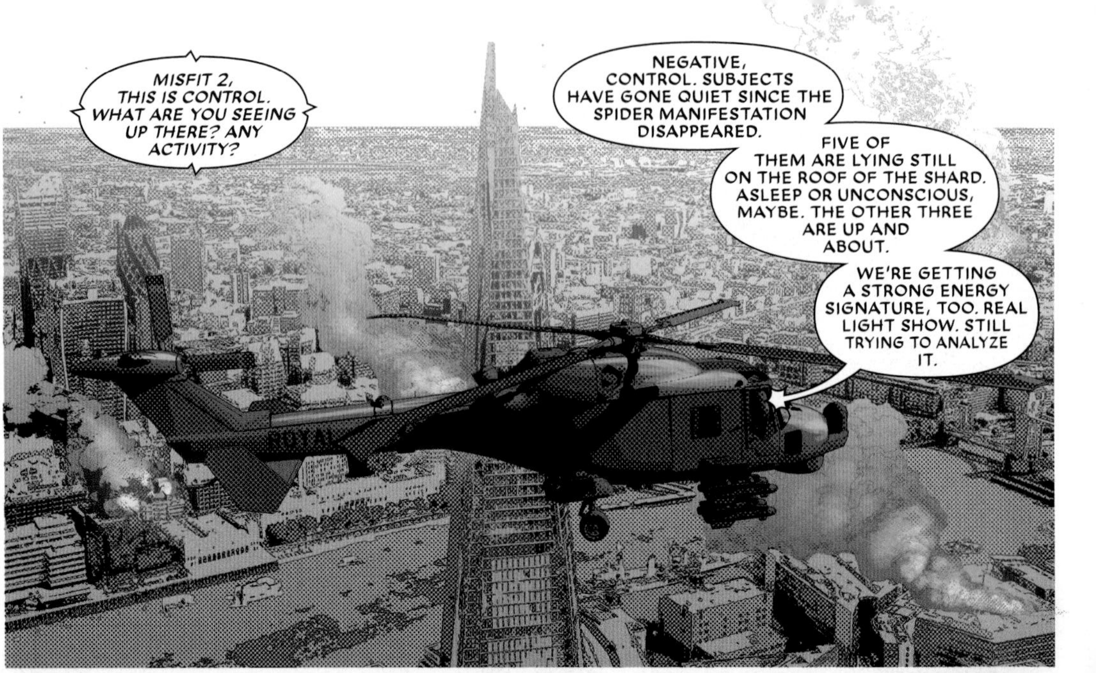
MISFIT 2, THIS IS CONTROL. WHAT ARE YOU SEEING UP THERE? ANY ACTIVITY?
NEGATIVE, CONTROL. SUBJECTS HAVE GONE QUIET SINCE THE SPIDER MANIFESTATION DISAPPEARED.
FIVE OF THEM ARE LYING STILL ON THE ROOF OF THE SHARD. ASLEEP OR UNCONSCIOUS, MAYBE. THE OTHER THREE ARE UP AND ABOUT.
WE'RE GETTING A STRONG ENERGY SIGNATURE, TOO. REAL LIGHT SHOW. STILL TRYING TO ANALYZE IT.
ROYAL

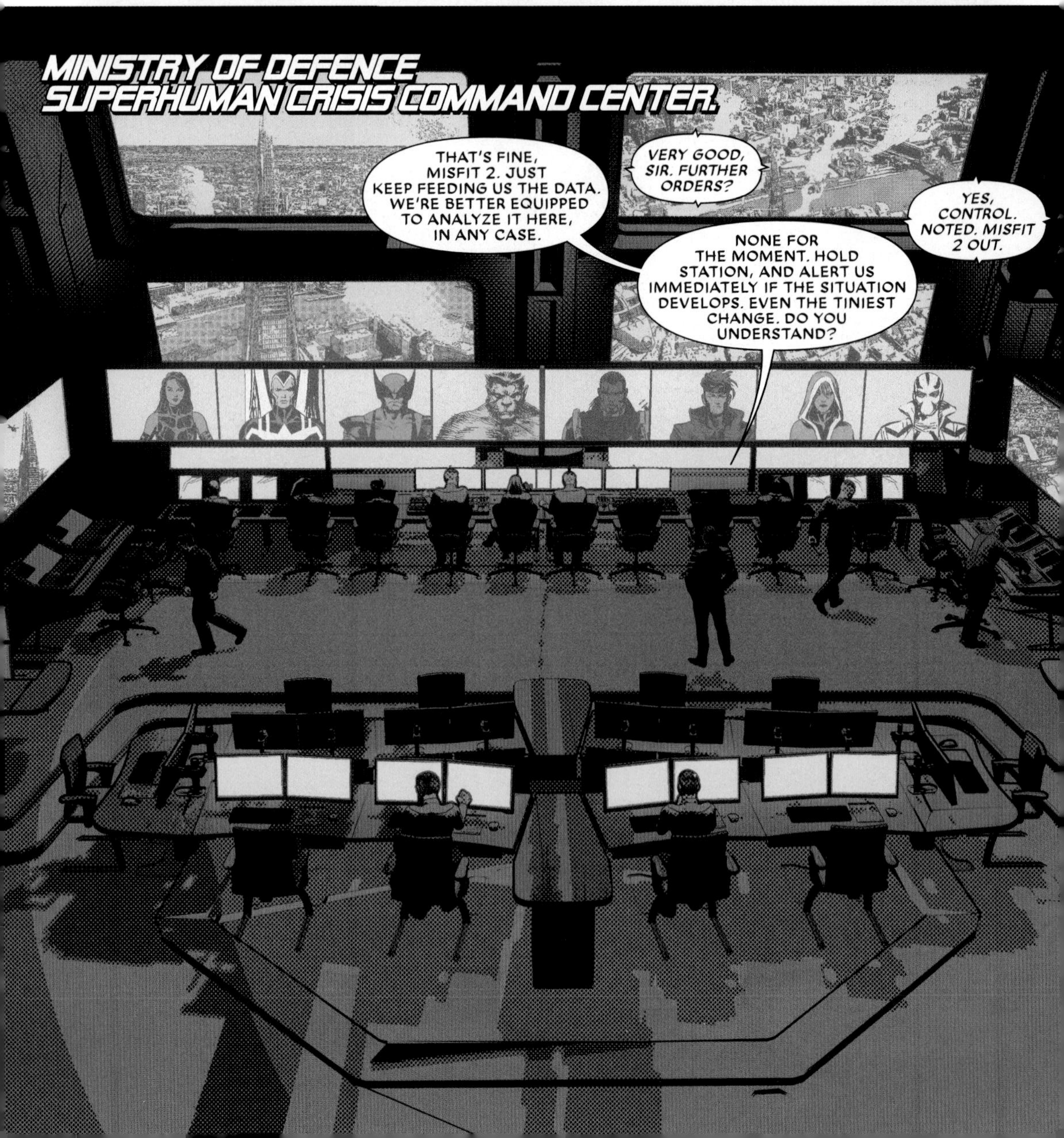
MINISTRY OF DEFENCE SUPERHUMAN CRISIS COMMAND CENTER.
THAT'S FINE, MISFIT 2. JUST KEEP FEEDING US THE DATA. WE'RE BETTER EQUIPPED TO ANALYZE IT HERE, IN ANY CASE.
VERY GOOD, SIR. FURTHER ORDERS?
NONE FOR THE MOMENT. HOLD STATION, AND ALERT US IMMEDIATELY IF THE SITUATION DEVELOPS. EVEN THE TINIEST CHANGE. DO YOU UNDERSTAND?
YES, CONTROL. NOTED. MISFIT 2 OUT.

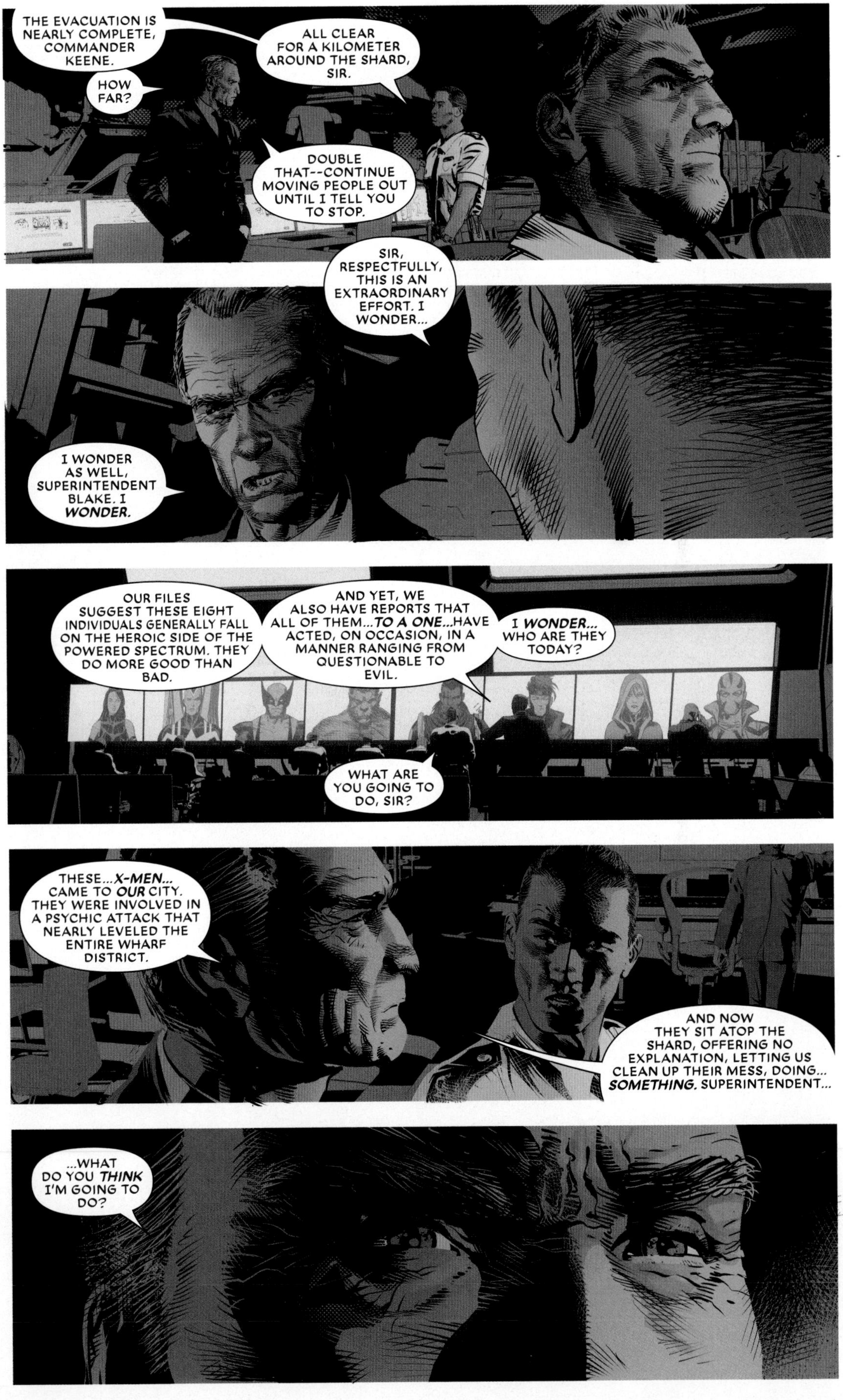
THE EVACUATION IS NEARLY COMPLETE, COMMANDER KEENE.
HOW FAR?
ALL CLEAR FOR A KILOMETER AROUND THE SHARD, SIR.
DOUBLE THAT--CONTINUE MOVING PEOPLE OUT UNTIL I TELL YOU TO STOP.
SIR, RESPECTFULLY, THIS IS AN EXTRAORDINARY EFFORT. I WONDER...
I WONDER AS WELL, SUPERINTENDENT BLAKE. I *WONDER.*
OUR FILES SUGGEST THESE EIGHT INDIVIDUALS GENERALLY FALL ON THE HEROIC SIDE OF THE POWERED SPECTRUM. THEY DO MORE GOOD THAN BAD.
AND YET, WE ALSO HAVE REPORTS THAT ALL OF THEM...*TO A ONE*...HAVE ACTED, ON OCCASION, IN A MANNER RANGING FROM QUESTIONABLE TO EVIL.
I *WONDER*... WHO ARE THEY TODAY?
WHAT ARE YOU GOING TO DO, SIR?
THESE...*X-MEN*... CAME TO *OUR* CITY. THEY WERE INVOLVED IN A PSYCHIC ATTACK THAT NEARLY LEVELED THE ENTIRE WHARF DISTRICT.
AND NOW THEY SIT ATOP THE SHARD, OFFERING NO EXPLANATION, LETTING US CLEAN UP THEIR MESS, DOING... *SOMETHING.* SUPERINTENDENT...
...WHAT DO YOU *THINK* I'M GOING TO DO?

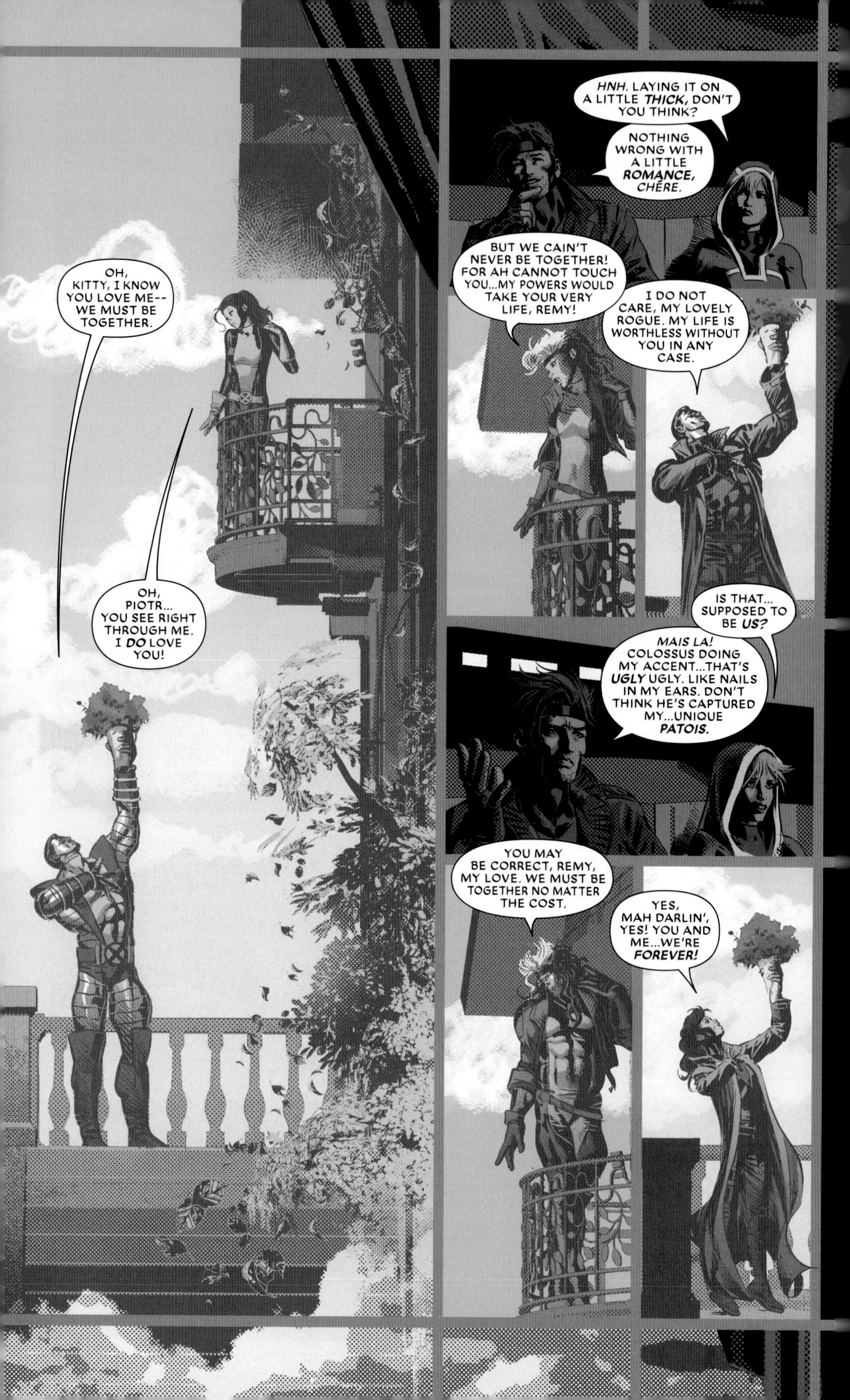
OH, KITTY, I KNOW YOU LOVE ME-- WE MUST BE TOGETHER.
OH, PIOTR... YOU SEE RIGHT THROUGH ME. I *DO* LOVE YOU!
HNH. LAYING IT ON A LITTLE *THICK,* DON'T YOU THINK?
NOTHING WRONG WITH A LITTLE *ROMANCE, CHÈRE.*
BUT WE CAIN'T NEVER BE TOGETHER! FOR AH CANNOT TOUCH YOU...MY POWERS WOULD TAKE YOUR VERY LIFE, REMY!
I DO NOT CARE, MY LOVELY ROGUE. MY LIFE IS WORTHLESS WITHOUT YOU IN ANY CASE.
IS THAT... SUPPOSED TO BE *US?*
MAIS LA! COLOSSUS DOING MY ACCENT...THAT'S *UGLY* UGLY. LIKE NAILS IN MY EARS. DON'T THINK HE'S CAPTURED MY...UNIQUE *PATOIS.*
YOU MAY BE CORRECT, REMY, MY LOVE. WE MUST BE TOGETHER NO MATTER THE COST.
YES, MAH DARLIN', YES! YOU AND ME...WE'RE *FOREVER!*

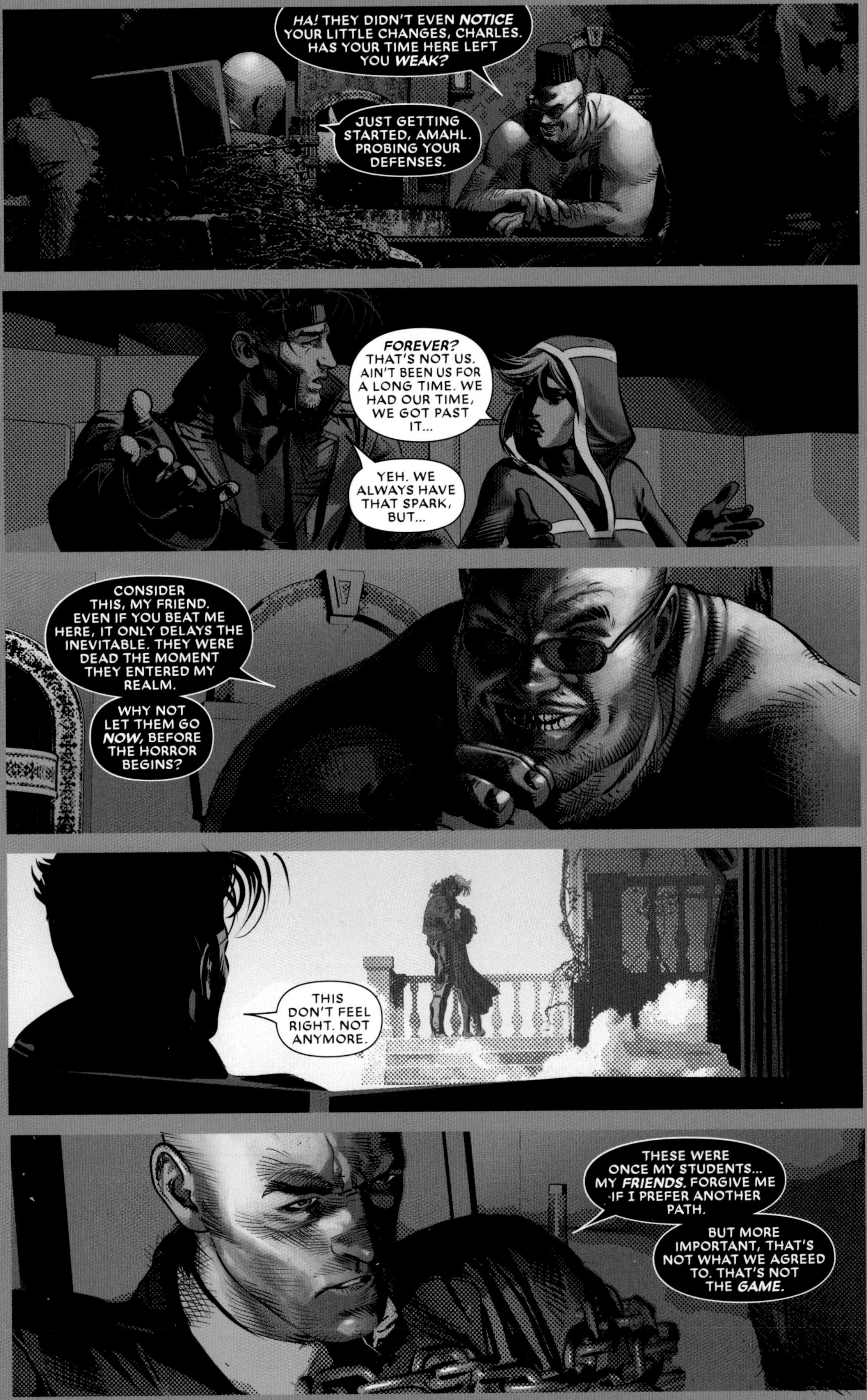
HA! THEY DIDN'T EVEN NOTICE YOUR LITTLE CHANGES, CHARLES. HAS YOUR TIME HERE LEFT YOU WEAK?
JUST GETTING STARTED, AMAHL. PROBING YOUR DEFENSES.
FOREVER? THAT'S NOT US. AIN'T BEEN US FOR A LONG TIME. WE HAD OUR TIME, WE GOT PAST IT...
YEH. WE ALWAYS HAVE THAT SPARK, BUT...
CONSIDER THIS, MY FRIEND. EVEN IF YOU BEAT ME HERE, IT ONLY DELAYS THE INEVITABLE. THEY WERE DEAD THE MOMENT THEY ENTERED MY REALM.
WHY NOT LET THEM GO NOW, BEFORE THE HORROR BEGINS?
THIS DON'T FEEL RIGHT. NOT ANYMORE.
THESE WERE ONCE MY STUDENTS... MY FRIENDS. FORGIVE ME IF I PREFER ANOTHER PATH.
BUT MORE IMPORTANT, THAT'S NOT WHAT WE AGREED TO. THAT'S NOT THE GAME.

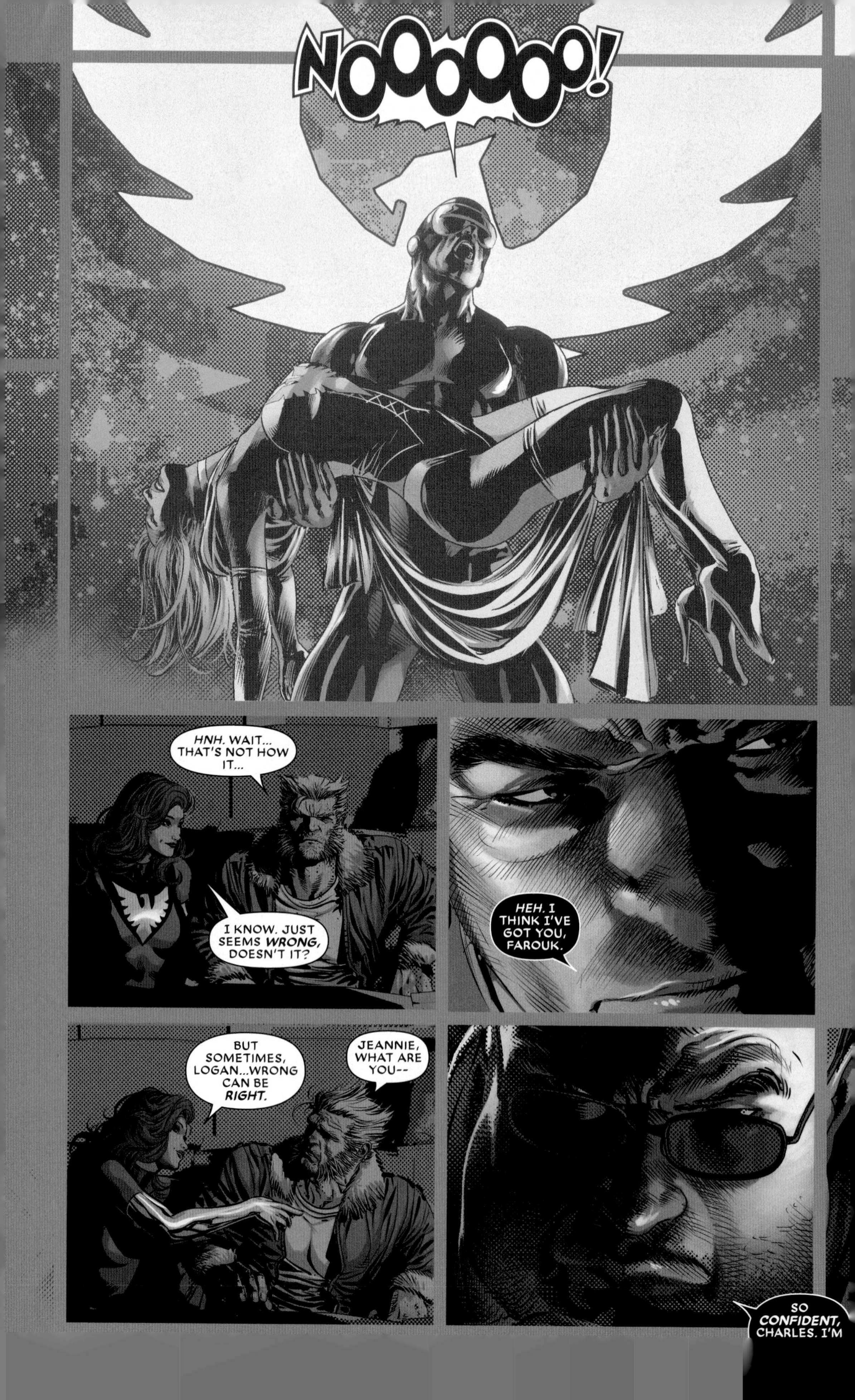
NOOOOOOO!
HNH. WAIT... THAT'S NOT HOW IT...
I KNOW. JUST SEEMS WRONG, DOESN'T IT?
HEH. I THINK I'VE GOT YOU, FAROUK.
BUT SOMETIMES, LOGAN...WRONG CAN BE RIGHT.
JEANNIE, WHAT ARE YOU--
SO CONFIDENT, CHARLES. I'M

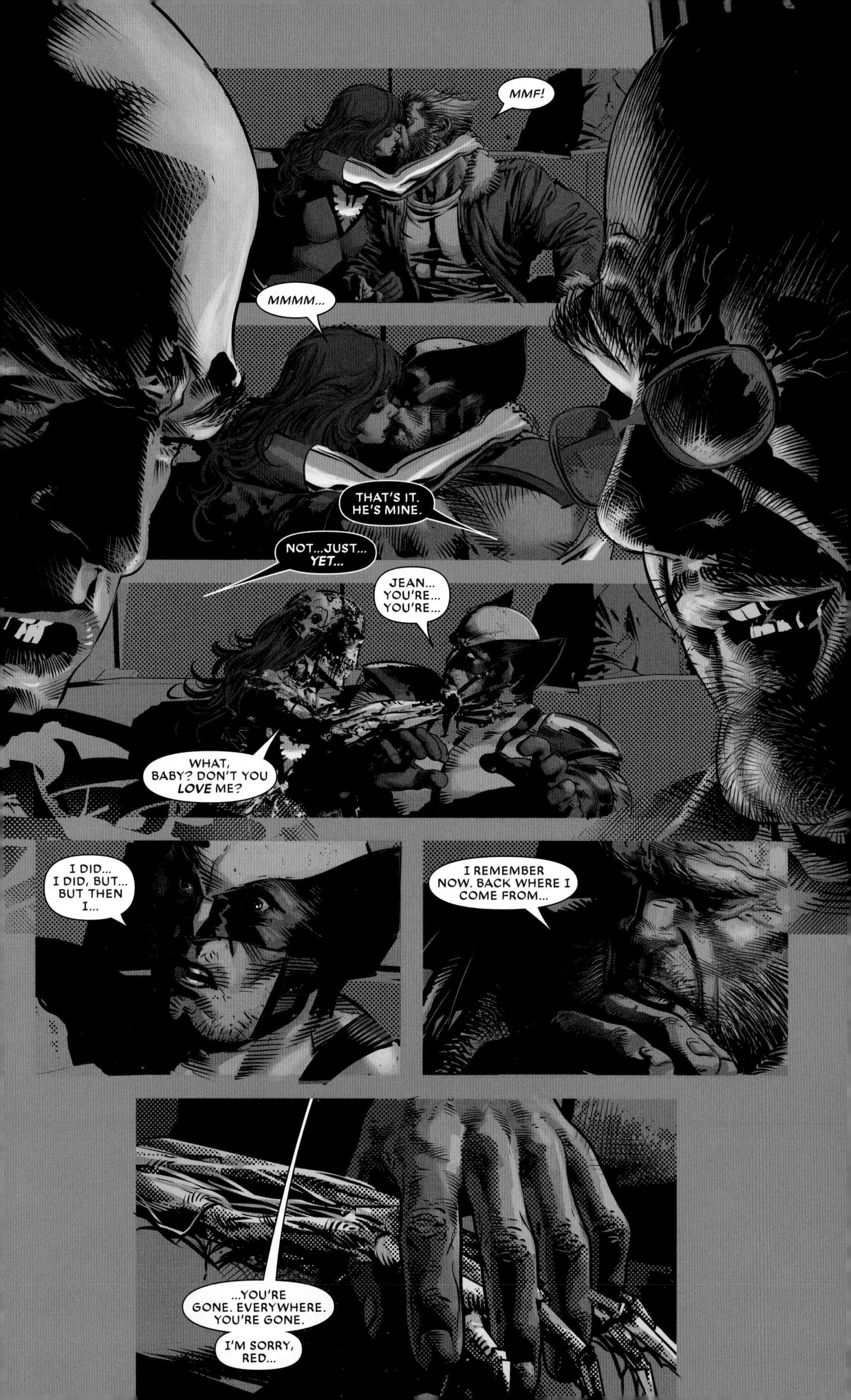
MMF!
MMMM...
THAT'S IT. HE'S MINE.
NOT...JUST... YET...
JEAN... YOU'RE... YOU'RE...
WHAT, BABY? DON'T YOU LOVE ME?
I DID... I DID, BUT... BUT THEN I...
I REMEMBER NOW. BACK WHERE I COME FROM...
...YOU'RE GONE. EVERYWHERE. YOU'RE GONE.
I'M SORRY, RED...

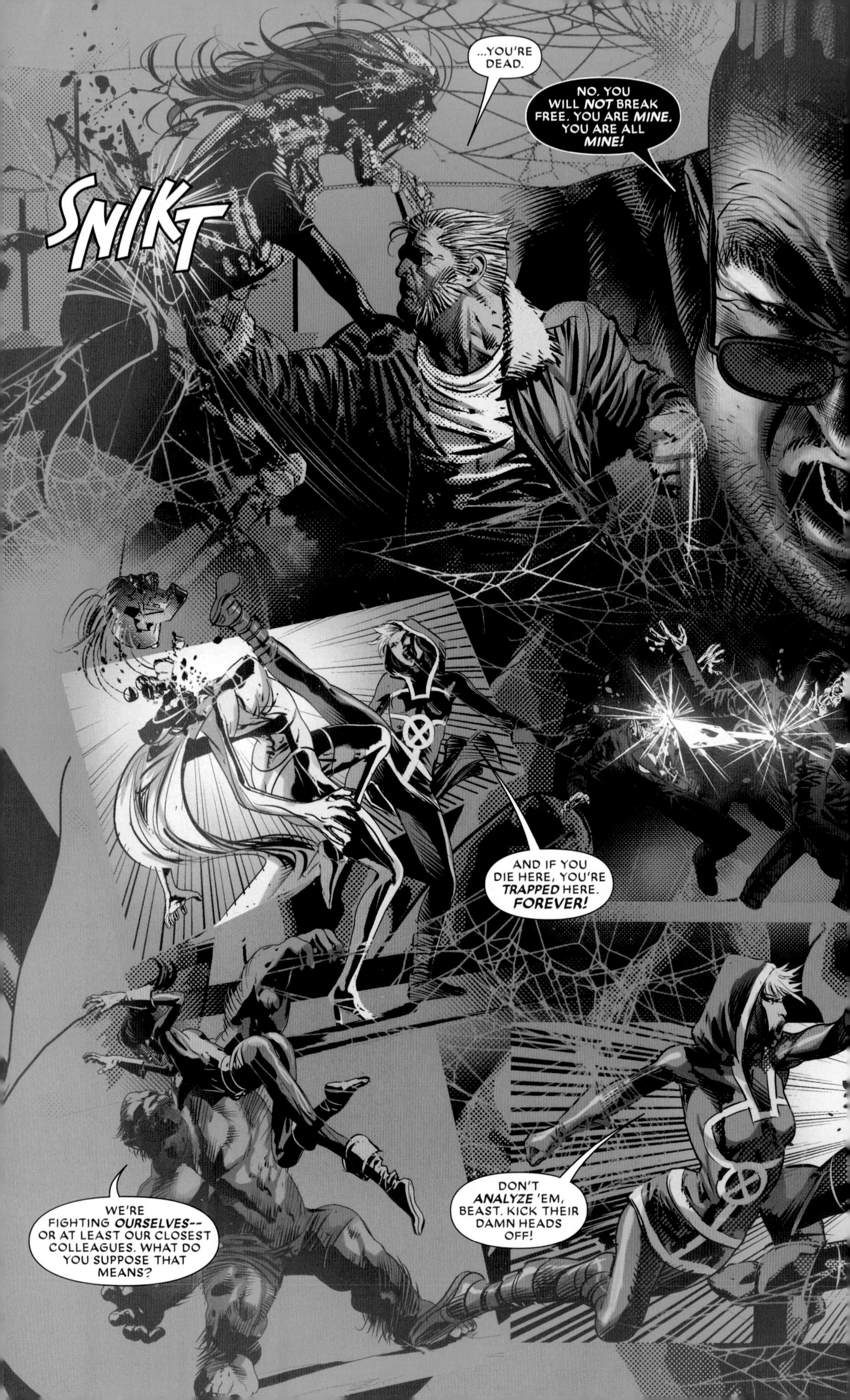
SNIKT
...YOU'RE DEAD.
NO. YOU WILL NOT BREAK FREE. YOU ARE MINE. YOU ARE ALL MINE!
AND IF YOU DIE HERE, YOU'RE TRAPPED HERE. FOREVER!
WE'RE FIGHTING OURSELVES-- OR AT LEAST OUR CLOSEST COLLEAGUES. WHAT DO YOU SUPPOSE THAT MEANS?
DON'T ANALYZE 'EM, BEAST. KICK THEIR DAMN HEADS OFF!

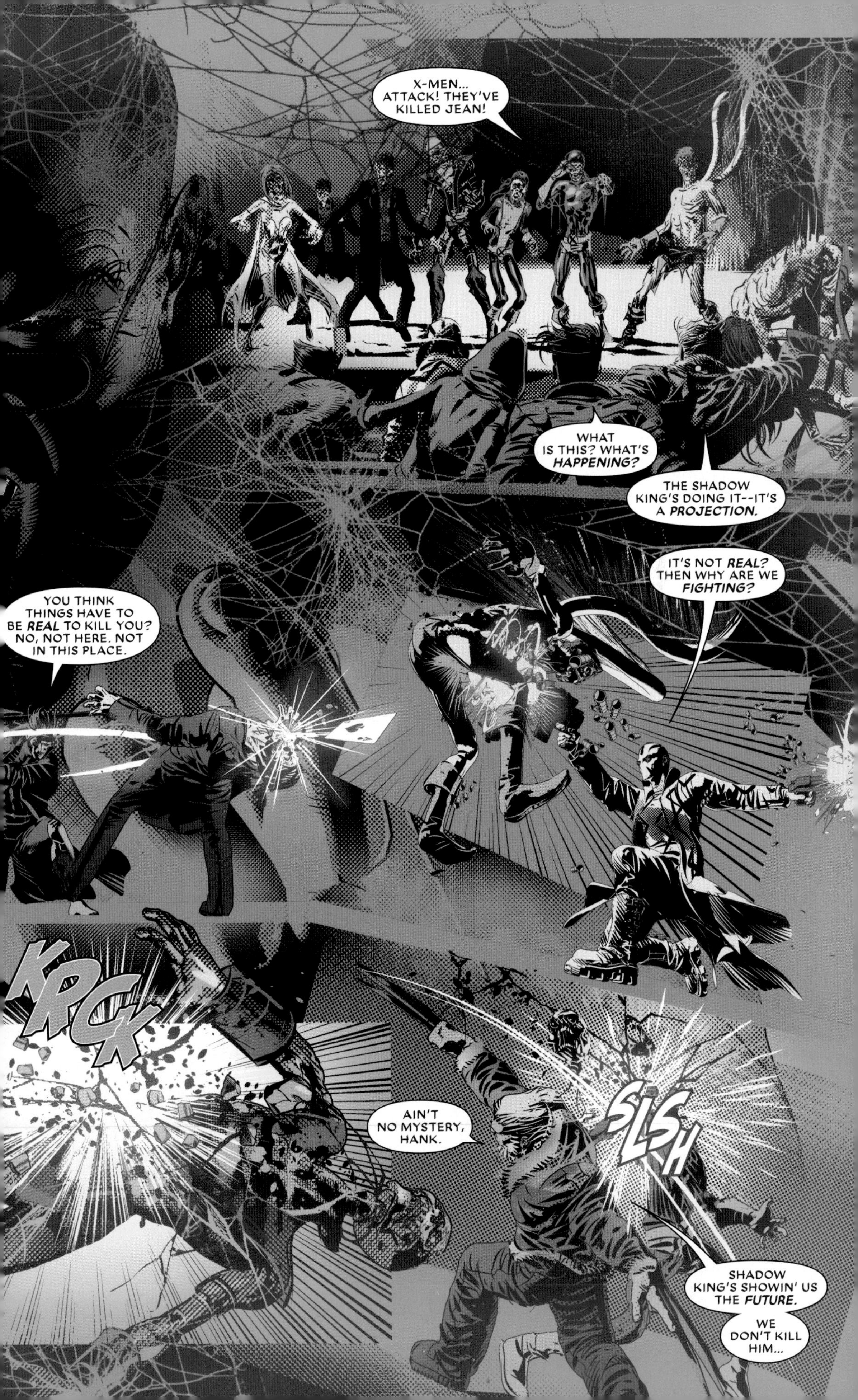
X-MEN... ATTACK! THEY'VE KILLED JEAN!
WHAT IS THIS? WHAT'S *HAPPENING?*
THE SHADOW KING'S DOING IT--IT'S A *PROJECTION.*
IT'S NOT *REAL?* THEN WHY ARE WE *FIGHTING?*
YOU THINK THINGS HAVE TO BE *REAL* TO KILL YOU? NO, NOT HERE. NOT IN THIS PLACE.
KRCK
AIN'T NO MYSTERY, HANK.
SLSH
SHADOW KING'S SHOWIN' US THE *FUTURE.*
WE DON'T KILL HIM...

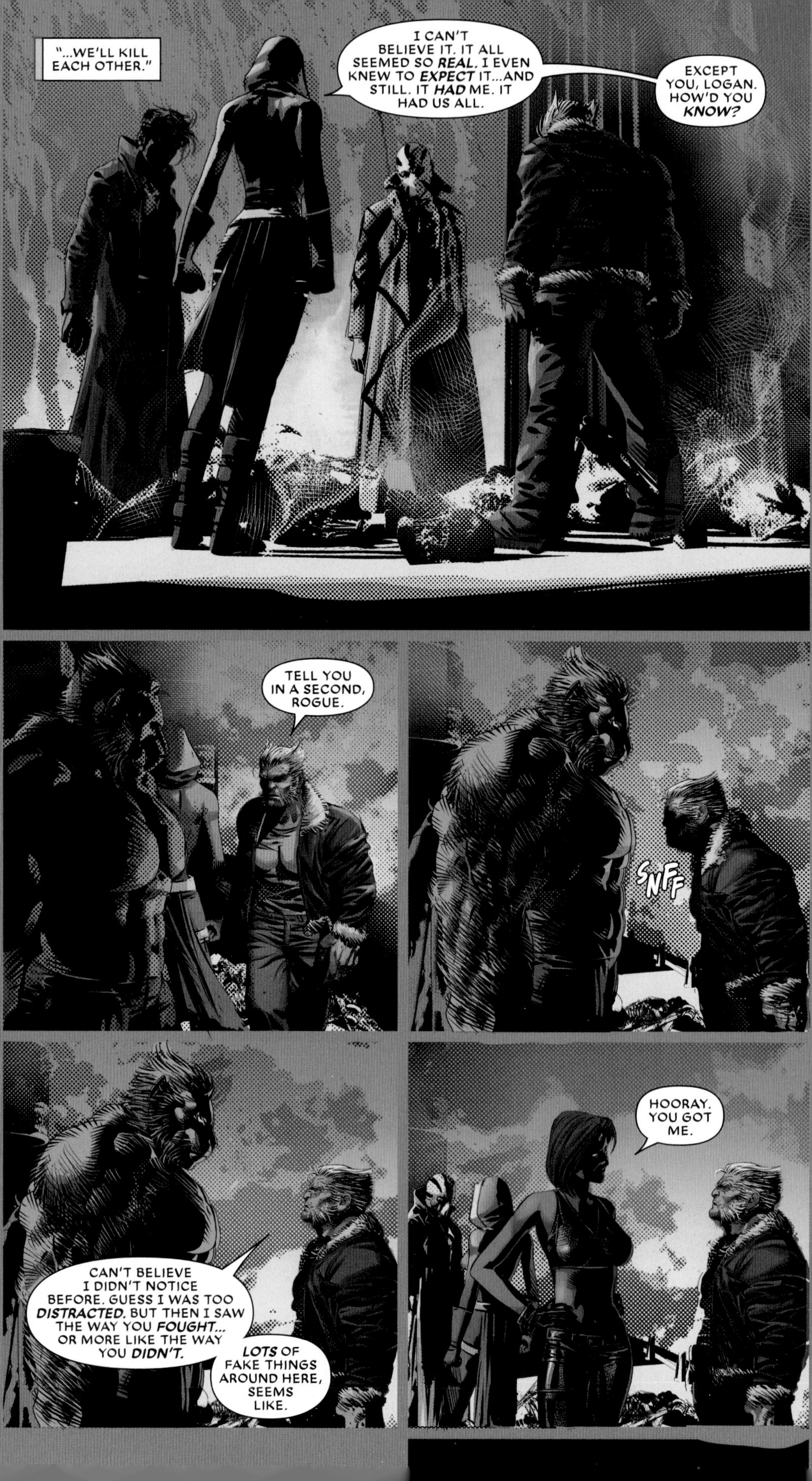

"...WE'LL KILL EACH OTHER."
I CAN'T BELIEVE IT. IT ALL SEEMED SO REAL. I EVEN KNEW TO EXPECT IT...AND STILL. IT HAD ME. IT HAD US ALL.
EXCEPT YOU, LOGAN. HOW'D YOU KNOW?
TELL YOU IN A SECOND, ROGUE.
SNFF
CAN'T BELIEVE I DIDN'T NOTICE BEFORE. GUESS I WAS TOO DISTRACTED. BUT THEN I SAW THE WAY YOU FOUGHT... OR MORE LIKE THE WAY YOU DIDN'T.
LOTS OF FAKE THINGS AROUND HERE, SEEMS LIKE.
HOORAY. YOU GOT ME.

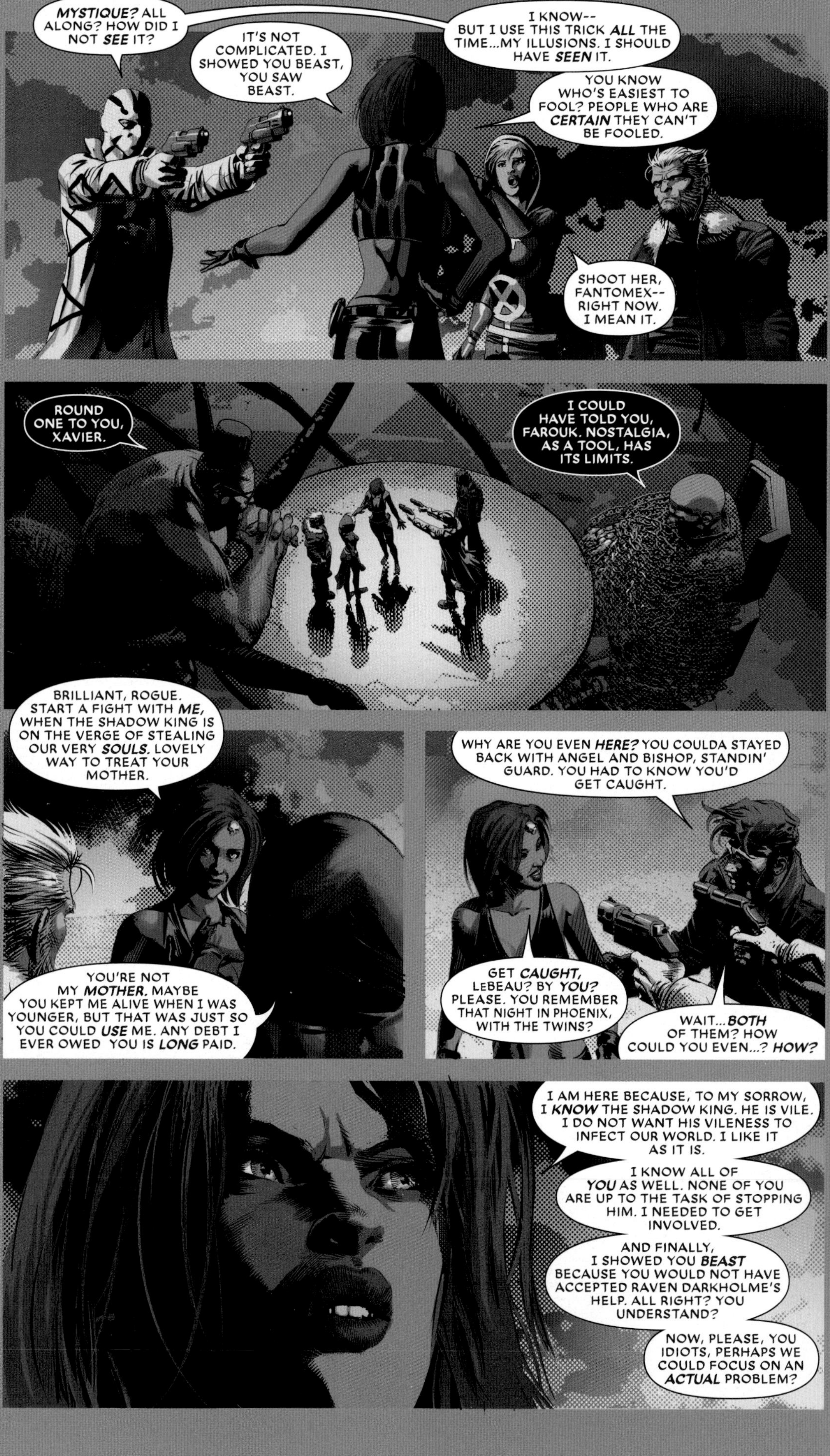
MYSTIQUE? ALL ALONG? HOW DID I NOT SEE IT?
IT'S NOT COMPLICATED. I SHOWED YOU BEAST, YOU SAW BEAST.
I KNOW-- BUT I USE THIS TRICK ALL THE TIME...MY ILLUSIONS. I SHOULD HAVE SEEN IT.
YOU KNOW WHO'S EASIEST TO FOOL? PEOPLE WHO ARE CERTAIN THEY CAN'T BE FOOLED.
SHOOT HER, FANTOMEX-- RIGHT NOW. I MEAN IT.
ROUND ONE TO YOU, XAVIER.
I COULD HAVE TOLD YOU, FAROUK. NOSTALGIA, AS A TOOL, HAS ITS LIMITS.
BRILLIANT, ROGUE. START A FIGHT WITH ME, WHEN THE SHADOW KING IS ON THE VERGE OF STEALING OUR VERY SOULS. LOVELY WAY TO TREAT YOUR MOTHER.
YOU'RE NOT MY MOTHER. MAYBE YOU KEPT ME ALIVE WHEN I WAS YOUNGER, BUT THAT WAS JUST SO YOU COULD USE ME. ANY DEBT I EVER OWED YOU IS LONG PAID.
WHY ARE YOU EVEN HERE? YOU COULDA STAYED BACK WITH ANGEL AND BISHOP, STANDIN' GUARD. YOU HAD TO KNOW YOU'D GET CAUGHT.
GET CAUGHT, LeBEAU? BY YOU? PLEASE. YOU REMEMBER THAT NIGHT IN PHOENIX, WITH THE TWINS?
WAIT...BOTH OF THEM? HOW COULD YOU EVEN...? HOW?
I AM HERE BECAUSE, TO MY SORROW, I KNOW THE SHADOW KING. HE IS VILE. I DO NOT WANT HIS VILENESS TO INFECT OUR WORLD. I LIKE IT AS IT IS.
I KNOW ALL OF YOU AS WELL. NONE OF YOU ARE UP TO THE TASK OF STOPPING HIM. I NEEDED TO GET INVOLVED.
AND FINALLY, I SHOWED YOU BEAST BECAUSE YOU WOULD NOT HAVE ACCEPTED RAVEN DARKHOLME'S HELP. ALL RIGHT? YOU UNDERSTAND?
NOW, PLEASE, YOU IDIOTS, PERHAPS WE COULD FOCUS ON AN ACTUAL PROBLEM?

OH, WHAT THE HELL IS *THIS?*

AH, OUI. LE PROCHAIN CAUCHEMAR. FANTASTIQUE.

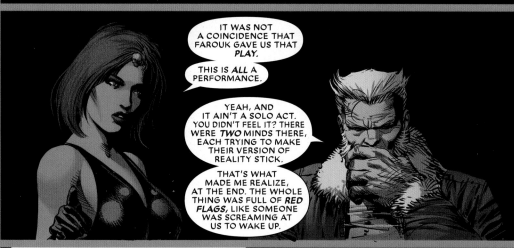

IT WAS NOT A COINCIDENCE THAT FAROUK GAVE US THAT *PLAY.*

THIS IS *ALL* A PERFORMANCE.

YEAH, AND IT AIN'T A SOLO ACT. YOU DIDN'T FEEL IT? THERE WERE *TWO* MINDS THERE, EACH TRYING TO MAKE THEIR VERSION OF REALITY STICK.

THAT'S WHAT MADE ME REALIZE, AT THE END. THE WHOLE THING WAS FULL OF *RED FLAGS,* LIKE SOMEONE WAS SCREAMING AT US TO WAKE UP.

YES. IN RETROSPECT...ALL RATHER *CLUMSY.* AT THE END, WITH THE BATTLE...LIKE A DISTRACTION. A DESPERATE EFFORT TO PULL US BACK INTO THE SCENARIO.

AND WERE NOT MOST OF THE ACTORS *DEAD?* EVEN *BEFORE* THE ZOMBIES ARRIVED?

LOTS OF DEAD THINGS END UP IN THE ASTRAL PLANE. FOR ALL WE KNOW, THAT *WAS* SCOTT AND JEAN AND JAMIE.

DON'T LIKE THAT. DON'T LIKE THAT AT *ALL.*

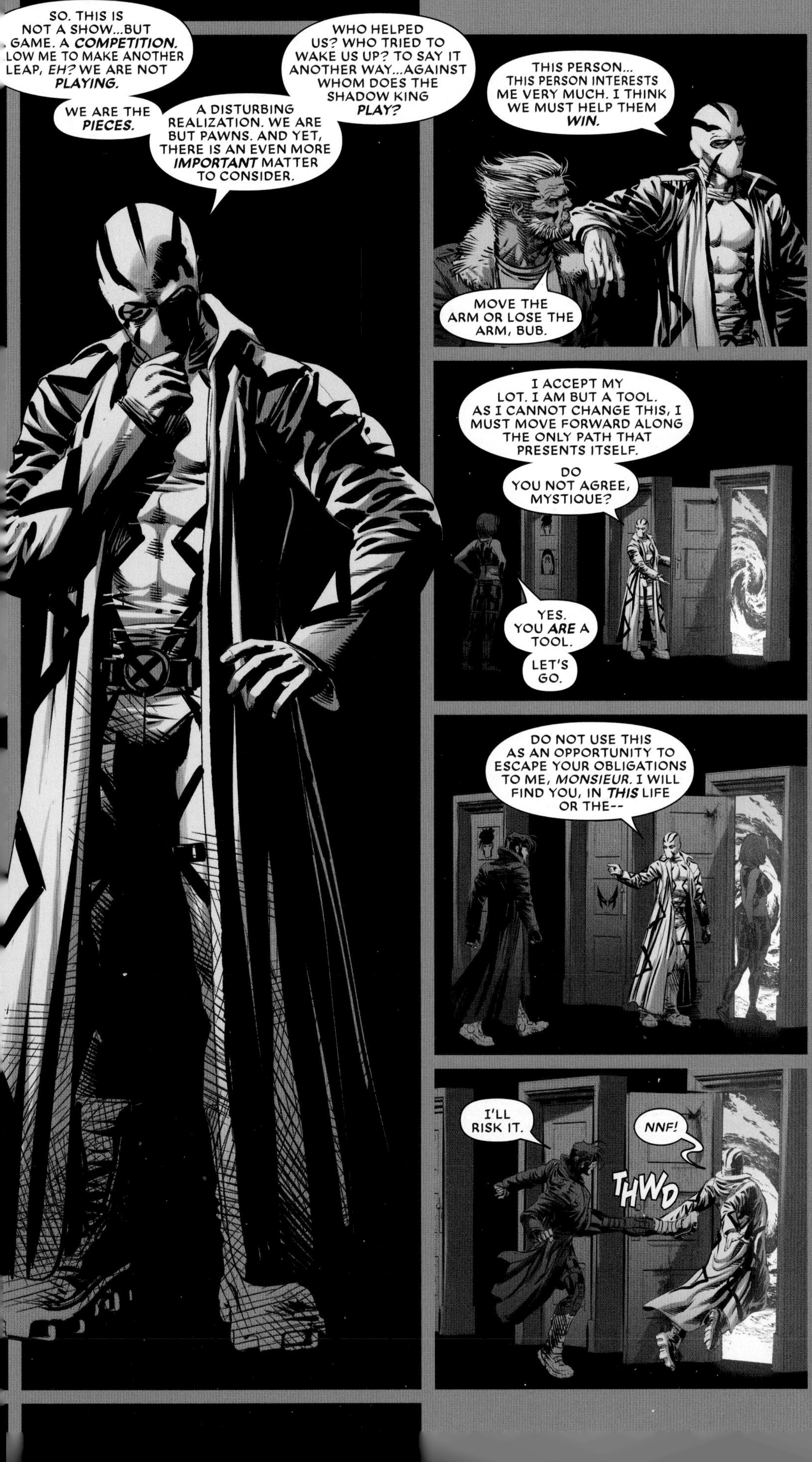
SO. THIS IS NOT A SHOW...BUT GAME. A COMPETITION. LOW ME TO MAKE ANOTHER LEAP, EH? WE ARE NOT PLAYING.
WE ARE THE PIECES.
A DISTURBING REALIZATION. WE ARE BUT PAWNS. AND YET, THERE IS AN EVEN MORE IMPORTANT MATTER TO CONSIDER.
WHO HELPED US? WHO TRIED TO WAKE US UP? TO SAY IT ANOTHER WAY...AGAINST WHOM DOES THE SHADOW KING PLAY?
THIS PERSON... THIS PERSON INTERESTS ME VERY MUCH. I THINK WE MUST HELP THEM WIN.
MOVE THE ARM OR LOSE THE ARM, BUB.
I ACCEPT MY LOT. I AM BUT A TOOL. AS I CANNOT CHANGE THIS, I MUST MOVE FORWARD ALONG THE ONLY PATH THAT PRESENTS ITSELF.
DO YOU NOT AGREE, MYSTIQUE?
YES. YOU ARE A TOOL.
LET'S GO.
DO NOT USE THIS AS AN OPPORTUNITY TO ESCAPE YOUR OBLIGATIONS TO ME, MONSIEUR. I WILL FIND YOU, IN THIS LIFE OR THE--
I'LL RISK IT.
NNF!
THWD

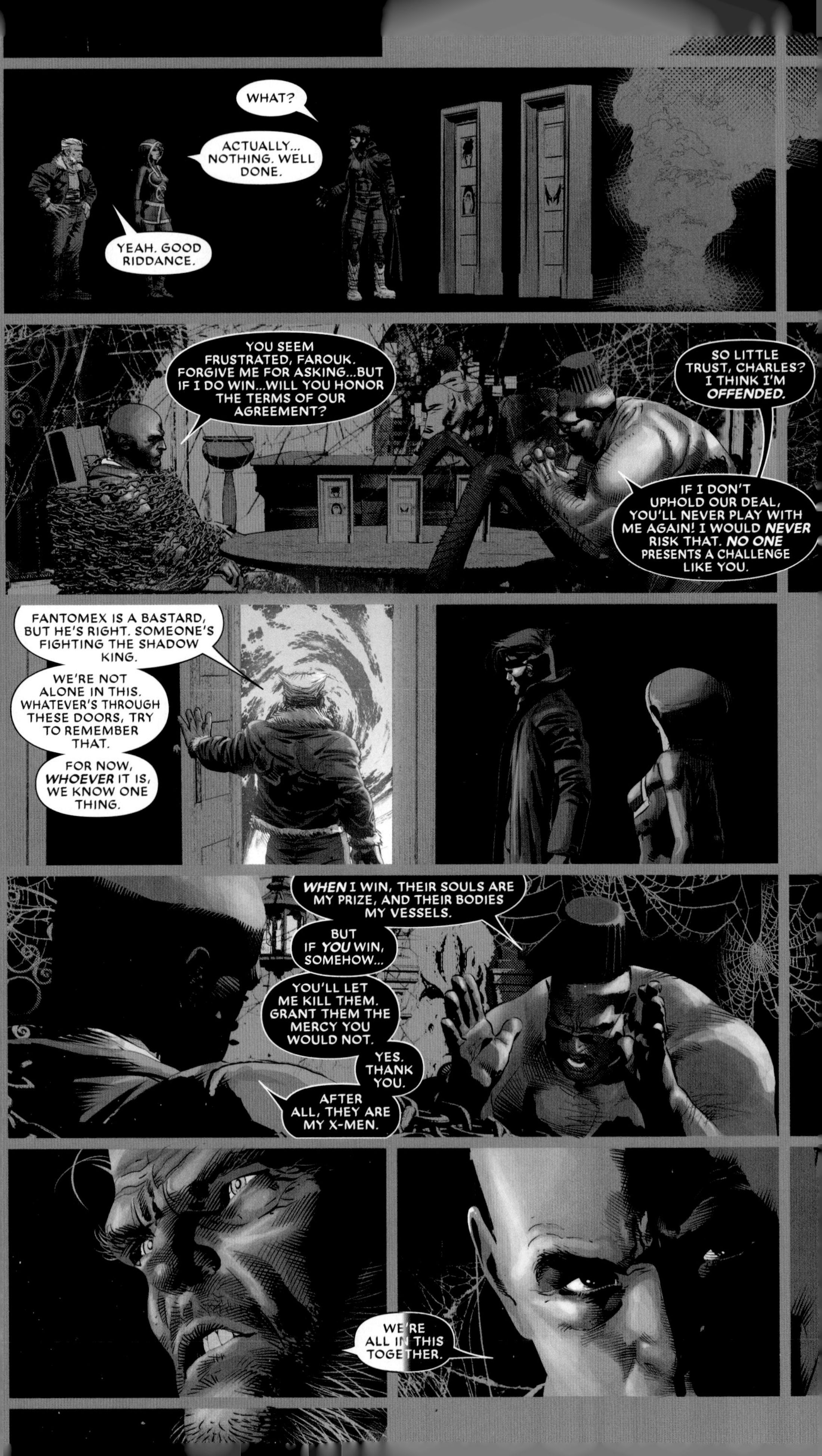
WHAT?
ACTUALLY... NOTHING. WELL DONE.
YEAH. GOOD RIDDANCE.
YOU SEEM FRUSTRATED, FAROUK. FORGIVE ME FOR ASKING...BUT IF I DO WIN...WILL YOU HONOR THE TERMS OF OUR AGREEMENT?
SO LITTLE TRUST, CHARLES? I THINK I'M *OFFENDED.*
IF I DON'T UPHOLD OUR DEAL, YOU'LL NEVER PLAY WITH ME AGAIN! I WOULD *NEVER* RISK THAT. *NO ONE* PRESENTS A CHALLENGE LIKE YOU.
FANTOMEX IS A BASTARD, BUT HE'S RIGHT. SOMEONE'S FIGHTING THE SHADOW KING.
WE'RE NOT ALONE IN THIS. WHATEVER'S THROUGH THESE DOORS, TRY TO REMEMBER THAT.
FOR NOW, *WHOEVER* IT IS, WE KNOW ONE THING.
WHEN I WIN, THEIR SOULS ARE MY PRIZE, AND THEIR BODIES MY VESSELS.
BUT IF *YOU* WIN, SOMEHOW...
YOU'LL LET ME KILL THEM. GRANT THEM THE MERCY YOU WOULD NOT.
YES. THANK YOU.
AFTER ALL, THEY ARE MY X-MEN.
WE'RE ALL IN THIS TOGETHER.

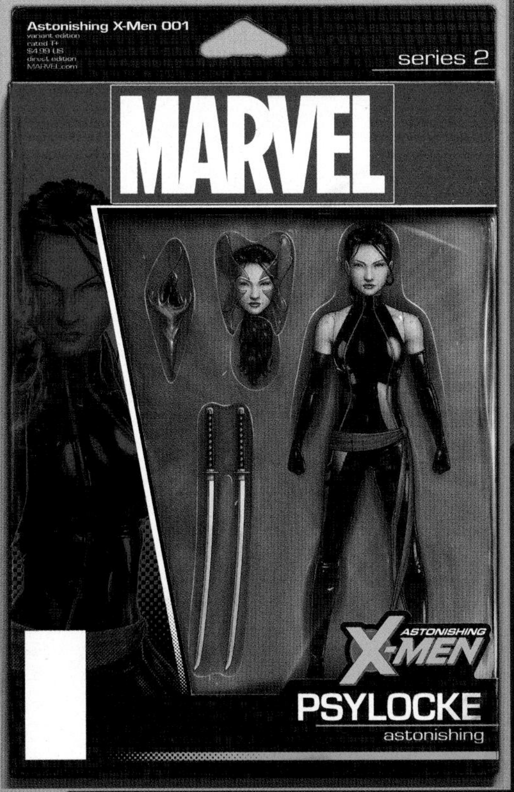
Astonishing X-Men 001
series 2
MARVEL
ASTONISHING
X-MEN
PSYLOCKE
astonishing

#1 ACTION FIGURE VARIANT
BY ***JOHN TYLER CHRISTOPHER***

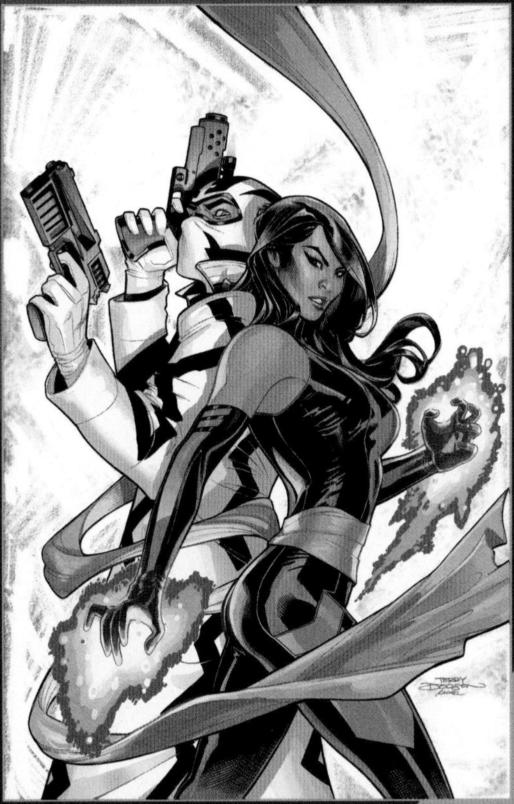

#1 VARIANT
BY ***TERRY DODSON***
& ***RACHEL DODSON***

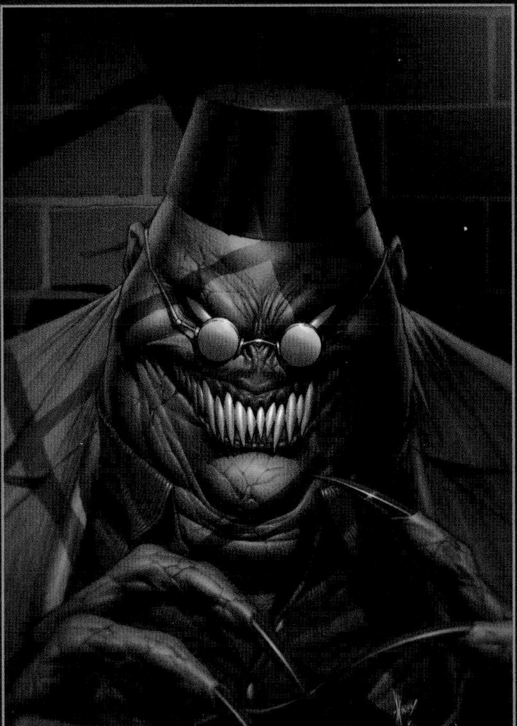

#1 VILLAIN VARIANT
BY ***DALE KEOWN***

3

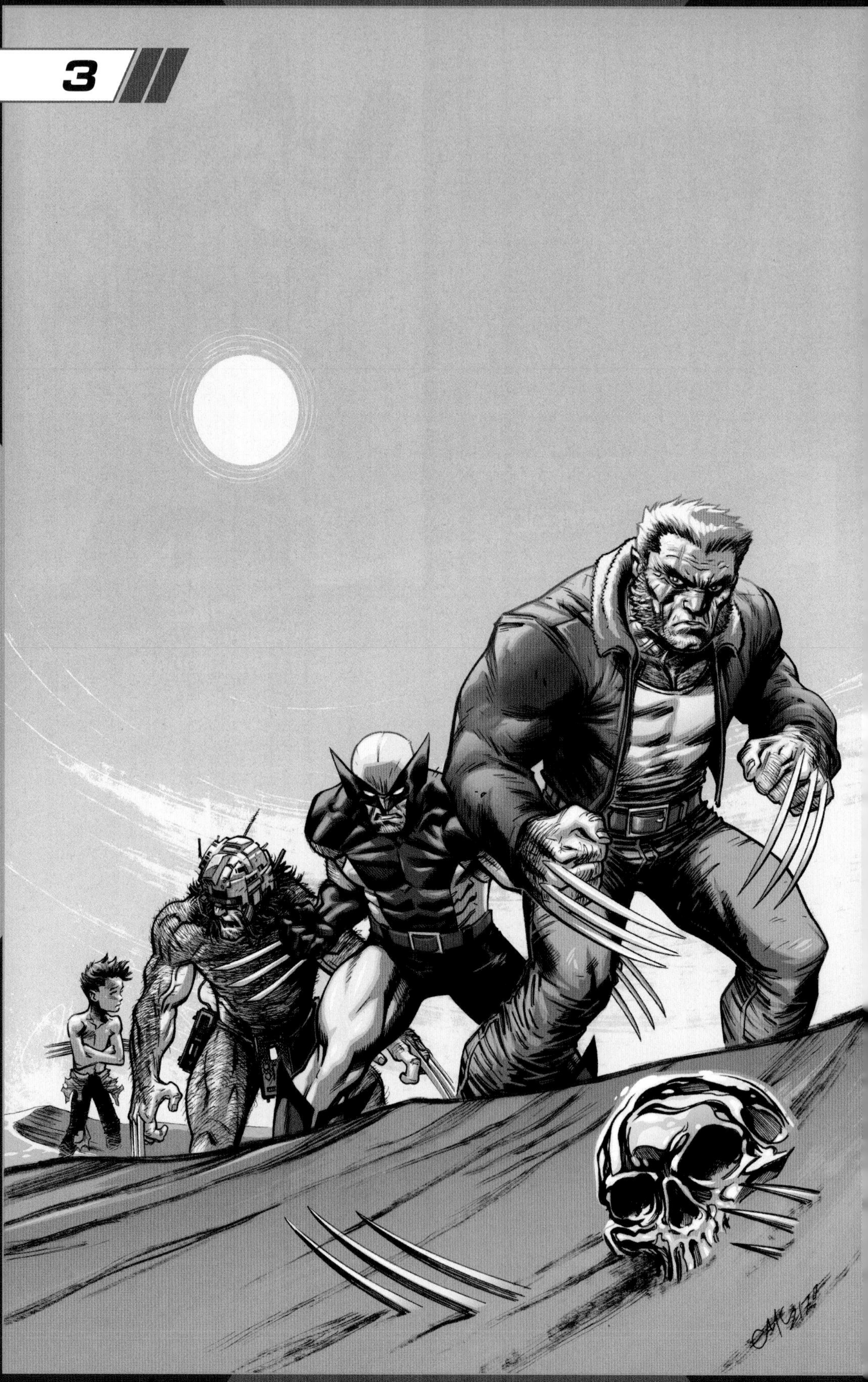

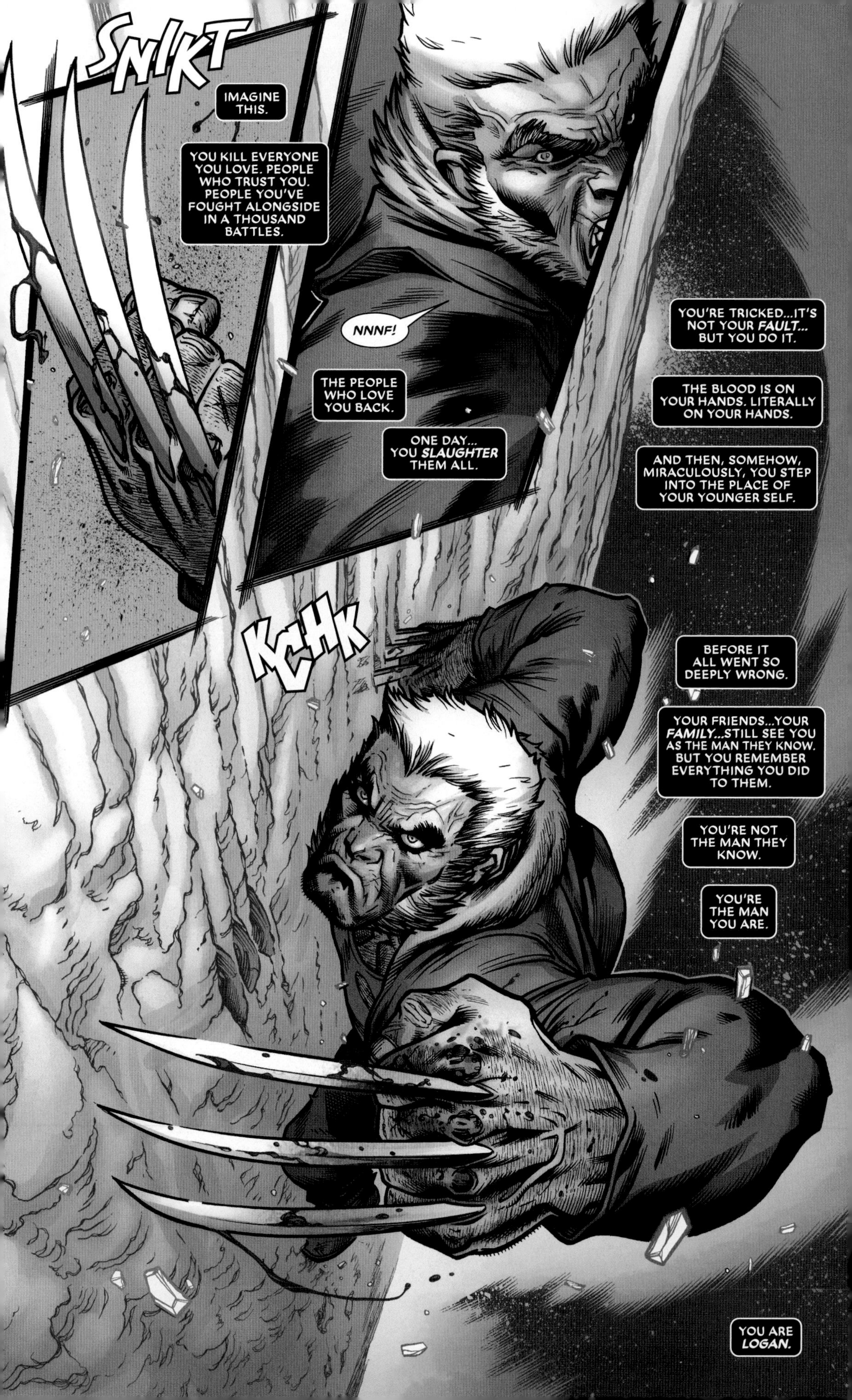
SNIKT
IMAGINE THIS.
YOU KILL EVERYONE YOU LOVE. PEOPLE WHO TRUST YOU. PEOPLE YOU'VE FOUGHT ALONGSIDE IN A THOUSAND BATTLES.
NNNF!
THE PEOPLE WHO LOVE YOU BACK.
ONE DAY... YOU SLAUGHTER THEM ALL.
YOU'RE TRICKED...IT'S NOT YOUR FAULT... BUT YOU DO IT.
THE BLOOD IS ON YOUR HANDS. LITERALLY ON YOUR HANDS.
AND THEN, SOMEHOW, MIRACULOUSLY, YOU STEP INTO THE PLACE OF YOUR YOUNGER SELF.
KCHK
BEFORE IT ALL WENT SO DEEPLY WRONG.
YOUR FRIENDS...YOUR FAMILY...STILL SEE YOU AS THE MAN THEY KNOW. BUT YOU REMEMBER EVERYTHING YOU DID TO THEM.
YOU'RE NOT THE MAN THEY KNOW.
YOU'RE THE MAN YOU ARE.
YOU ARE LOGAN.

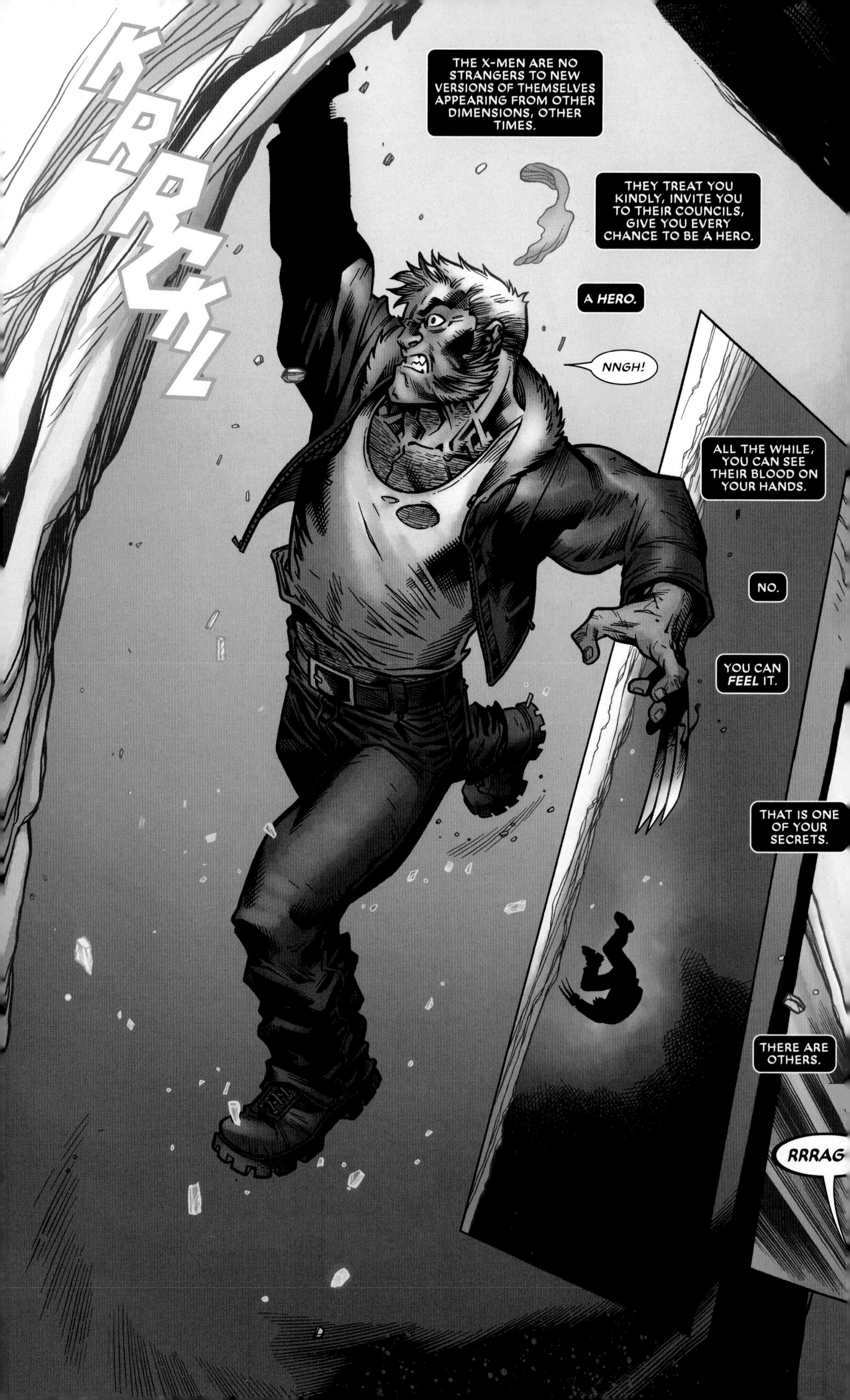
KRRCKL
THE X-MEN ARE NO STRANGERS TO NEW VERSIONS OF THEMSELVES APPEARING FROM OTHER DIMENSIONS, OTHER TIMES.
THEY TREAT YOU KINDLY, INVITE YOU TO THEIR COUNCILS, GIVE YOU EVERY CHANCE TO BE A HERO.
A *HERO.*
NNGH!
ALL THE WHILE, YOU CAN SEE THEIR BLOOD ON YOUR HANDS.
NO.
YOU CAN *FEEL* IT.
THAT IS ONE OF YOUR SECRETS.
THERE ARE OTHERS.
RRRAG

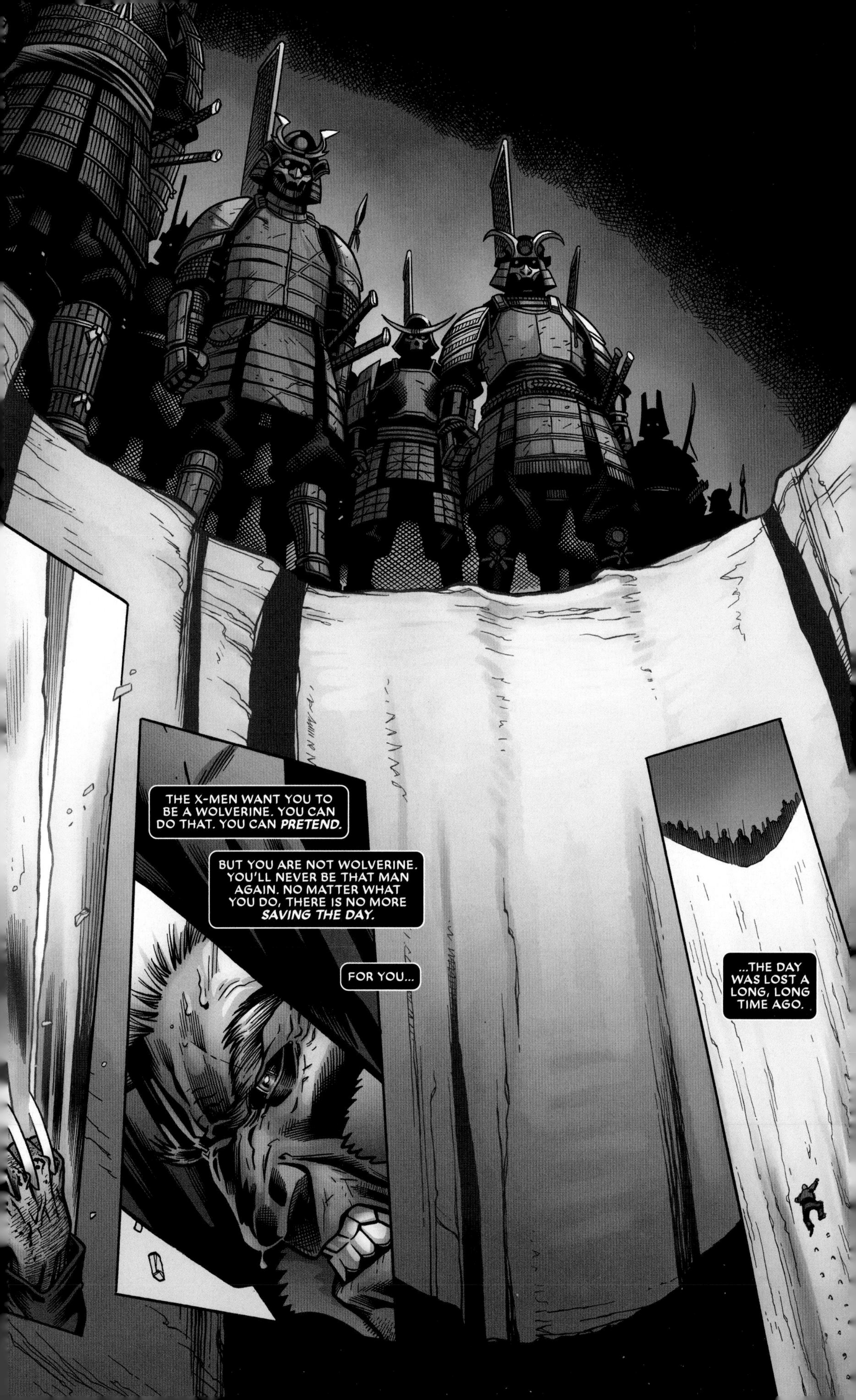
THE X-MEN WANT YOU TO BE A WOLVERINE. YOU CAN DO THAT. YOU CAN *PRETEND.*
BUT YOU ARE NOT WOLVERINE. YOU'LL NEVER BE THAT MAN AGAIN. NO MATTER WHAT YOU DO, THERE IS NO MORE *SAVING THE DAY.*
FOR YOU...
...THE DAY WAS LOST A LONG, LONG TIME AGO.

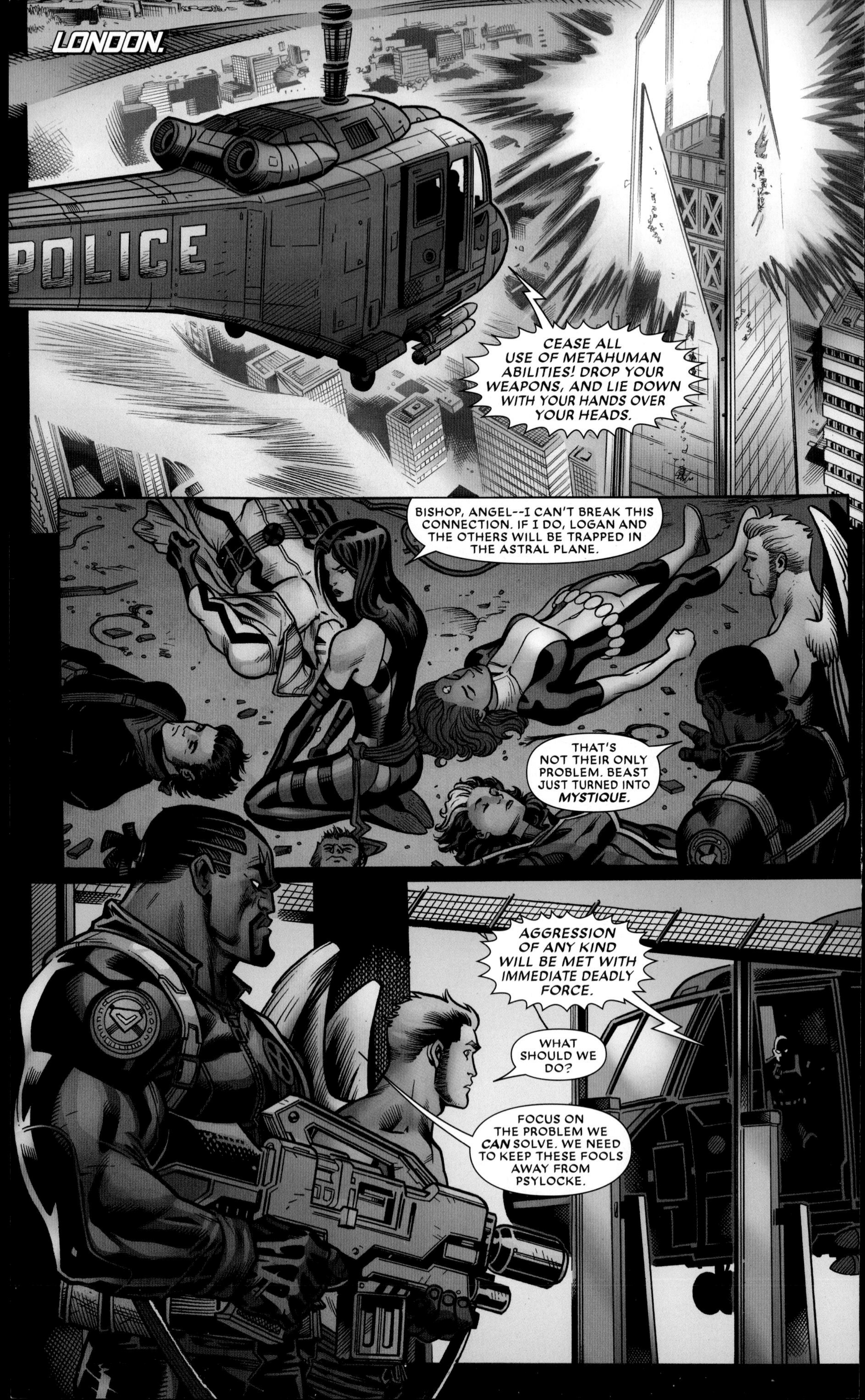
LONDON.
POLICE
CEASE ALL USE OF METAHUMAN ABILITIES! DROP YOUR WEAPONS, AND LIE DOWN WITH YOUR HANDS OVER YOUR HEADS.
BISHOP, ANGEL--I CAN'T BREAK THIS CONNECTION. IF I DO, LOGAN AND THE OTHERS WILL BE TRAPPED IN THE ASTRAL PLANE.
THAT'S NOT THEIR ONLY PROBLEM. BEAST JUST TURNED INTO MYSTIQUE.
AGGRESSION OF ANY KIND WILL BE MET WITH IMMEDIATE DEADLY FORCE.
WHAT SHOULD WE DO?
FOCUS ON THE PROBLEM WE CAN SOLVE. WE NEED TO KEEP THESE FOOLS AWAY FROM PSYLOCKE.

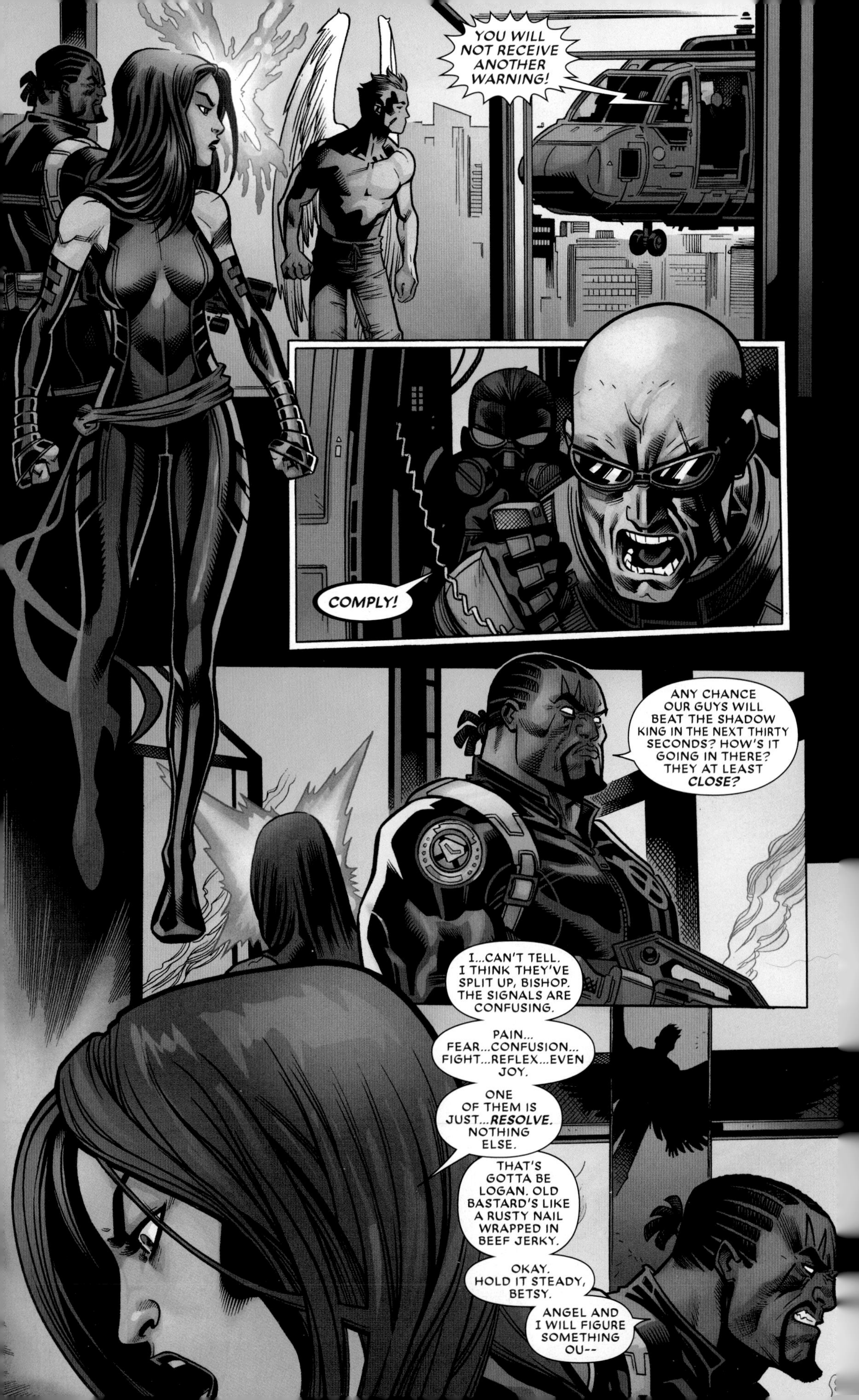
YOU WILL NOT RECEIVE ANOTHER WARNING!
COMPLY!
ANY CHANCE OUR GUYS WILL BEAT THE SHADOW KING IN THE NEXT THIRTY SECONDS? HOW'S IT GOING IN THERE? THEY AT LEAST CLOSE?
I...CAN'T TELL. I THINK THEY'VE SPLIT UP, BISHOP. THE SIGNALS ARE CONFUSING.
PAIN... FEAR...CONFUSION... FIGHT...REFLEX...EVEN JOY.
ONE OF THEM IS JUST...RESOLVE. NOTHING ELSE.
THAT'S GOTTA BE LOGAN. OLD BASTARD'S LIKE A RUSTY NAIL WRAPPED IN BEEF JERKY.
OKAY. HOLD IT STEADY, BETSY.
ANGEL AND I WILL FIGURE SOMETHING OU--

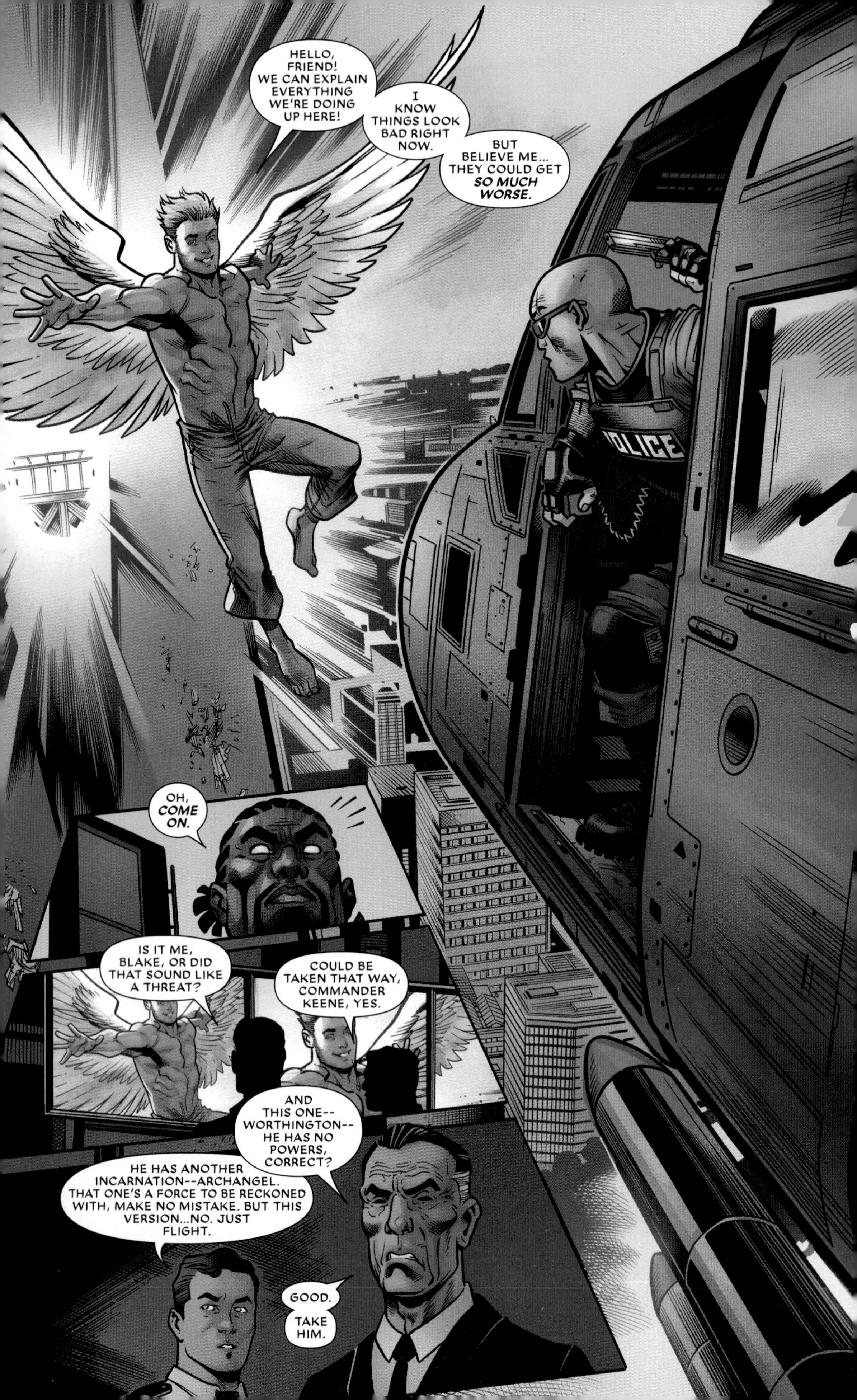
HELLO, FRIEND! WE CAN EXPLAIN EVERYTHING WE'RE DOING UP HERE!
I KNOW THINGS LOOK BAD RIGHT NOW.
BUT BELIEVE ME... THEY COULD GET ***SO MUCH WORSE.***
POLICE
OH, ***COME ON.***
IS IT ME, BLAKE, OR DID THAT SOUND LIKE A THREAT?
COULD BE TAKEN THAT WAY, COMMANDER KEENE, YES.
AND THIS ONE--WORTHINGTON--HE HAS NO POWERS, CORRECT?
HE HAS ANOTHER INCARNATION--ARCHANGEL. THAT ONE'S A FORCE TO BE RECKONED WITH, MAKE NO MISTAKE. BUT THIS VERSION...NO. JUST FLIGHT.
GOOD.
TAKE HIM.

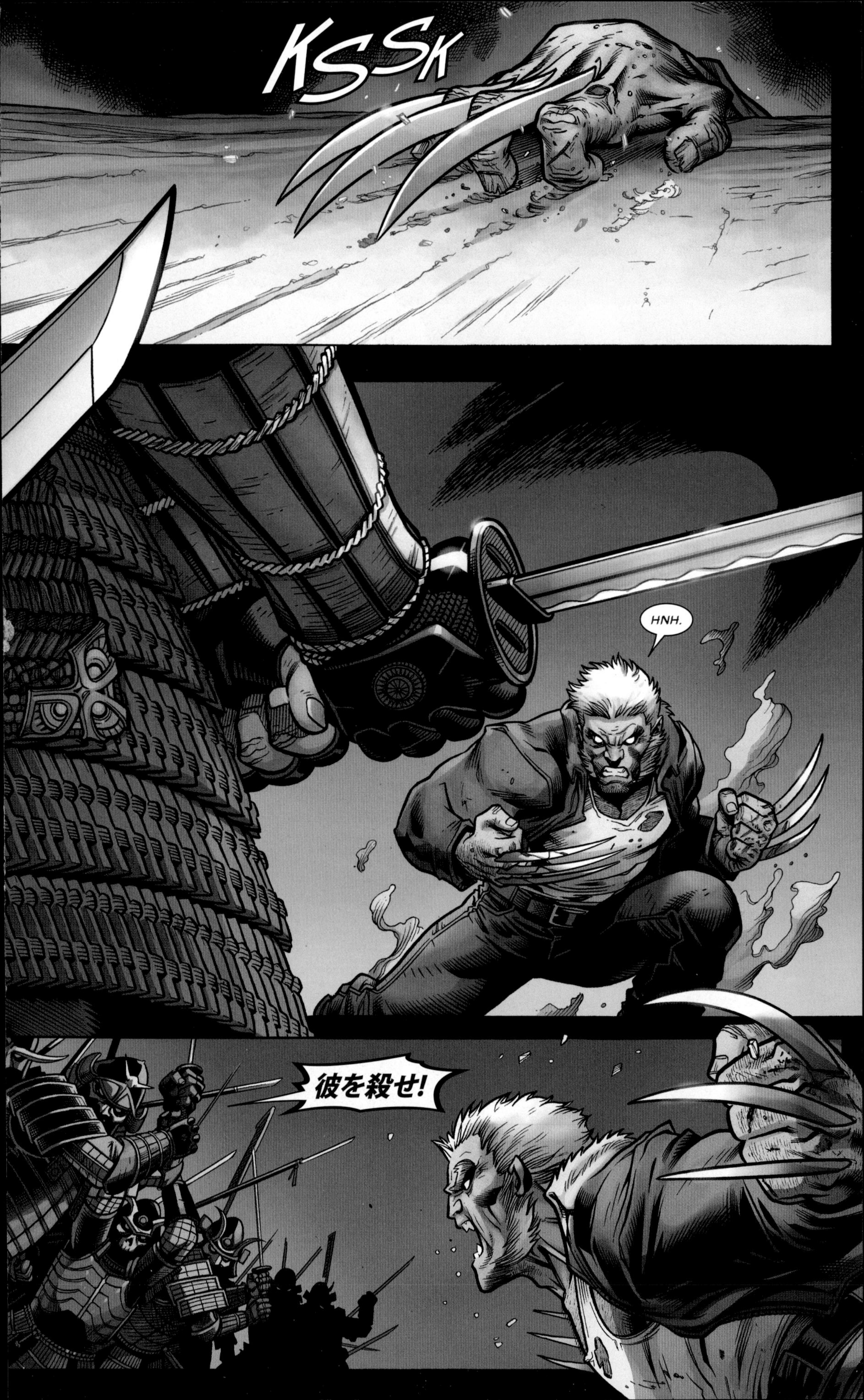
KSSK
HNH.
彼を殺せ!

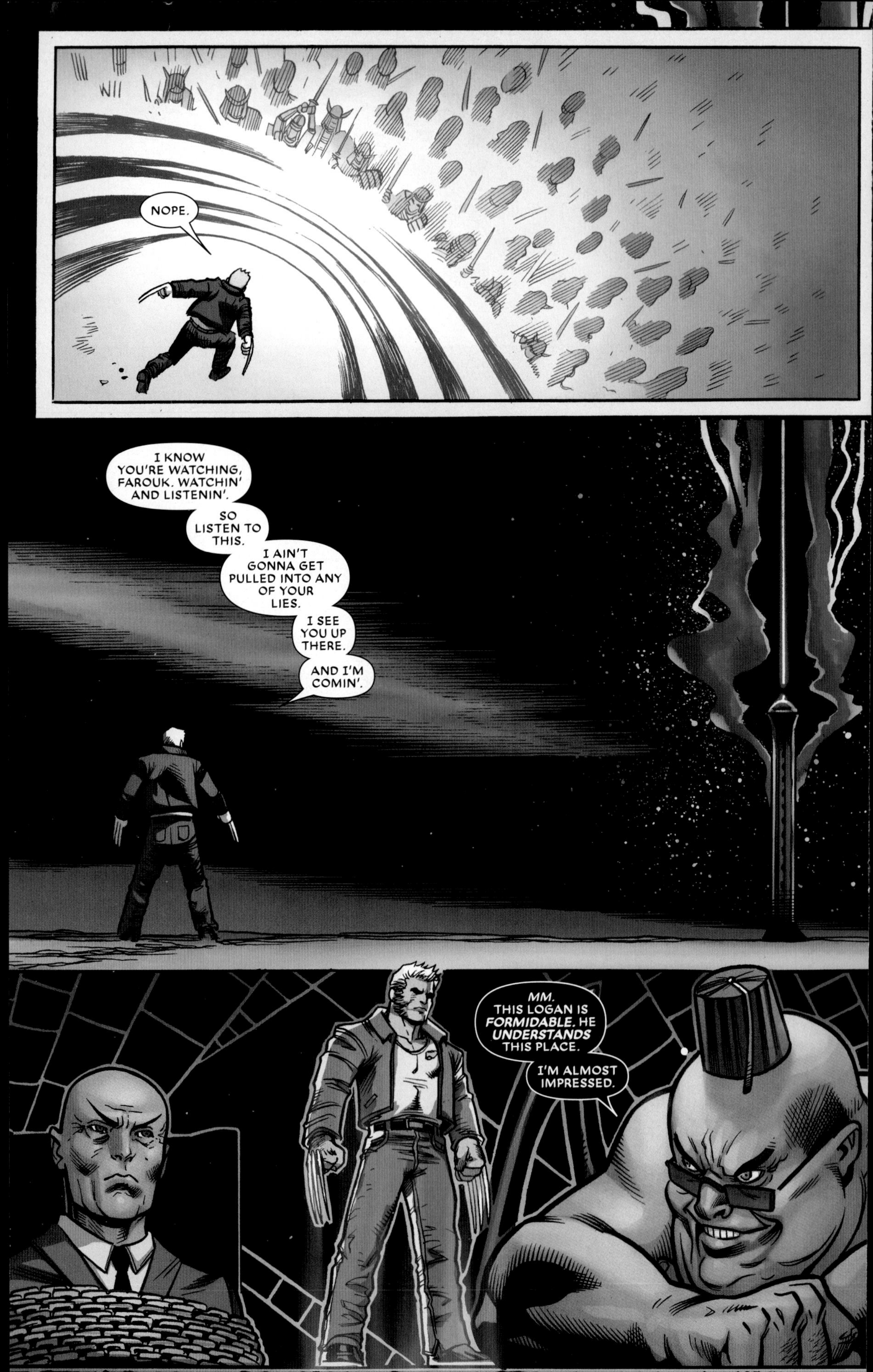
NOPE.
I KNOW YOU'RE WATCHING, FAROUK. WATCHIN' AND LISTENIN'.
SO LISTEN TO THIS.
I AIN'T GONNA GET PULLED INTO ANY OF YOUR LIES.
I SEE YOU UP THERE.
AND I'M COMIN'.
MM. THIS LOGAN IS *FORMIDABLE.* HE *UNDERSTANDS* THIS PLACE.
I'M ALMOST IMPRESSED.

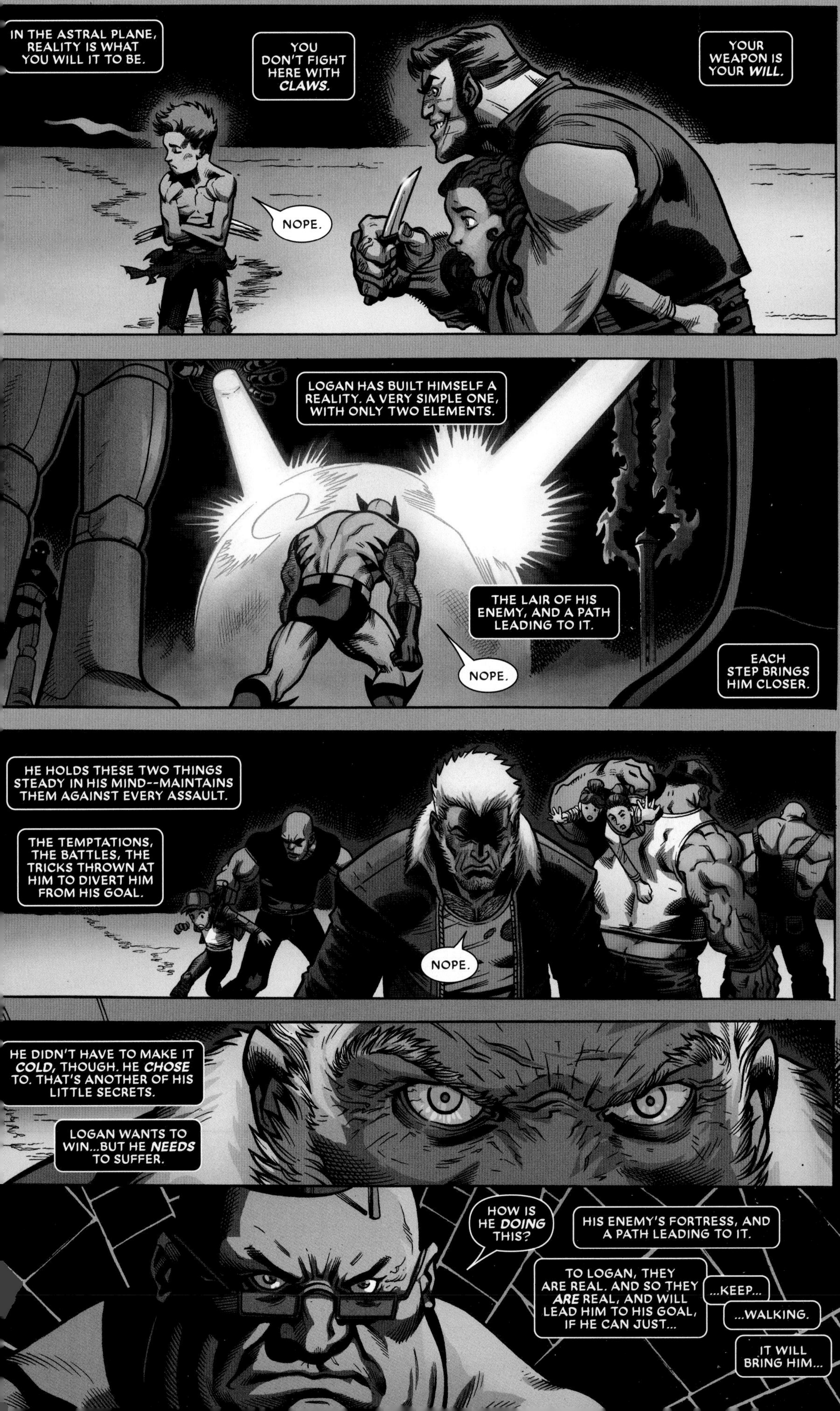
IN THE ASTRAL PLANE, REALITY IS WHAT YOU WILL IT TO BE.
YOU DON'T FIGHT HERE WITH *CLAWS.*
YOUR WEAPON IS YOUR *WILL.*
NOPE.
LOGAN HAS BUILT HIMSELF A REALITY. A VERY SIMPLE ONE, WITH ONLY TWO ELEMENTS.
THE LAIR OF HIS ENEMY, AND A PATH LEADING TO IT.
NOPE.
EACH STEP BRINGS HIM CLOSER.
HE HOLDS THESE TWO THINGS STEADY IN HIS MIND--MAINTAINS THEM AGAINST EVERY ASSAULT.
THE TEMPTATIONS, THE BATTLES, THE TRICKS THROWN AT HIM TO DIVERT HIM FROM HIS GOAL.
NOPE.
HE DIDN'T HAVE TO MAKE IT *COLD,* THOUGH. HE *CHOSE* TO. THAT'S ANOTHER OF HIS LITTLE SECRETS.
LOGAN WANTS TO WIN...BUT HE *NEEDS* TO SUFFER.
HOW IS HE *DOING* THIS?
HIS ENEMY'S FORTRESS, AND A PATH LEADING TO IT.
TO LOGAN, THEY ARE REAL. AND SO THEY *ARE* REAL, AND WILL LEAD HIM TO HIS GOAL, IF HE CAN JUST...
...KEEP...
...WALKING.
IT WILL BRING HIM...

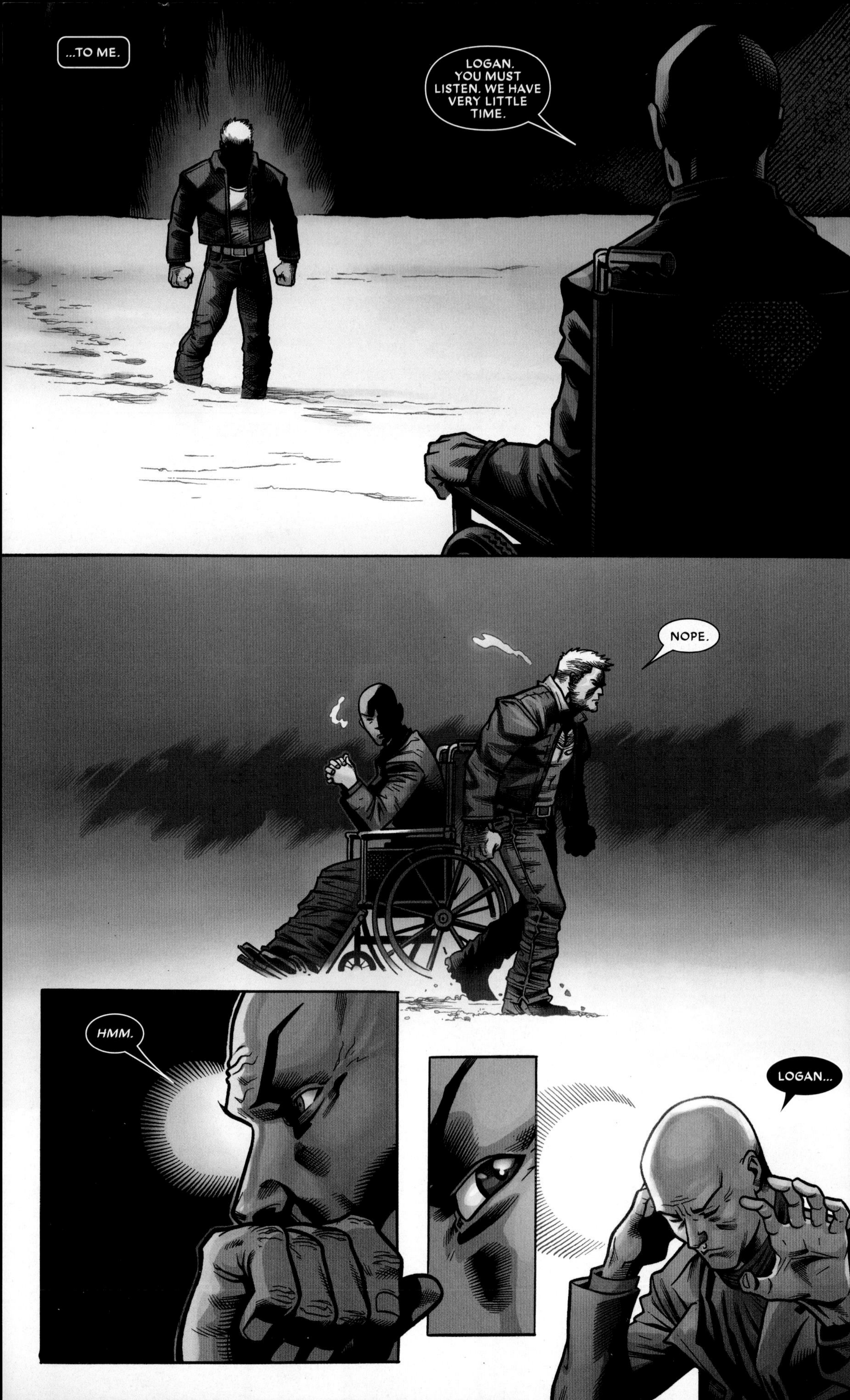
...TO ME.
LOGAN. YOU MUST LISTEN. WE HAVE VERY LITTLE TIME.
NOPE.
HMM.
LOGAN...

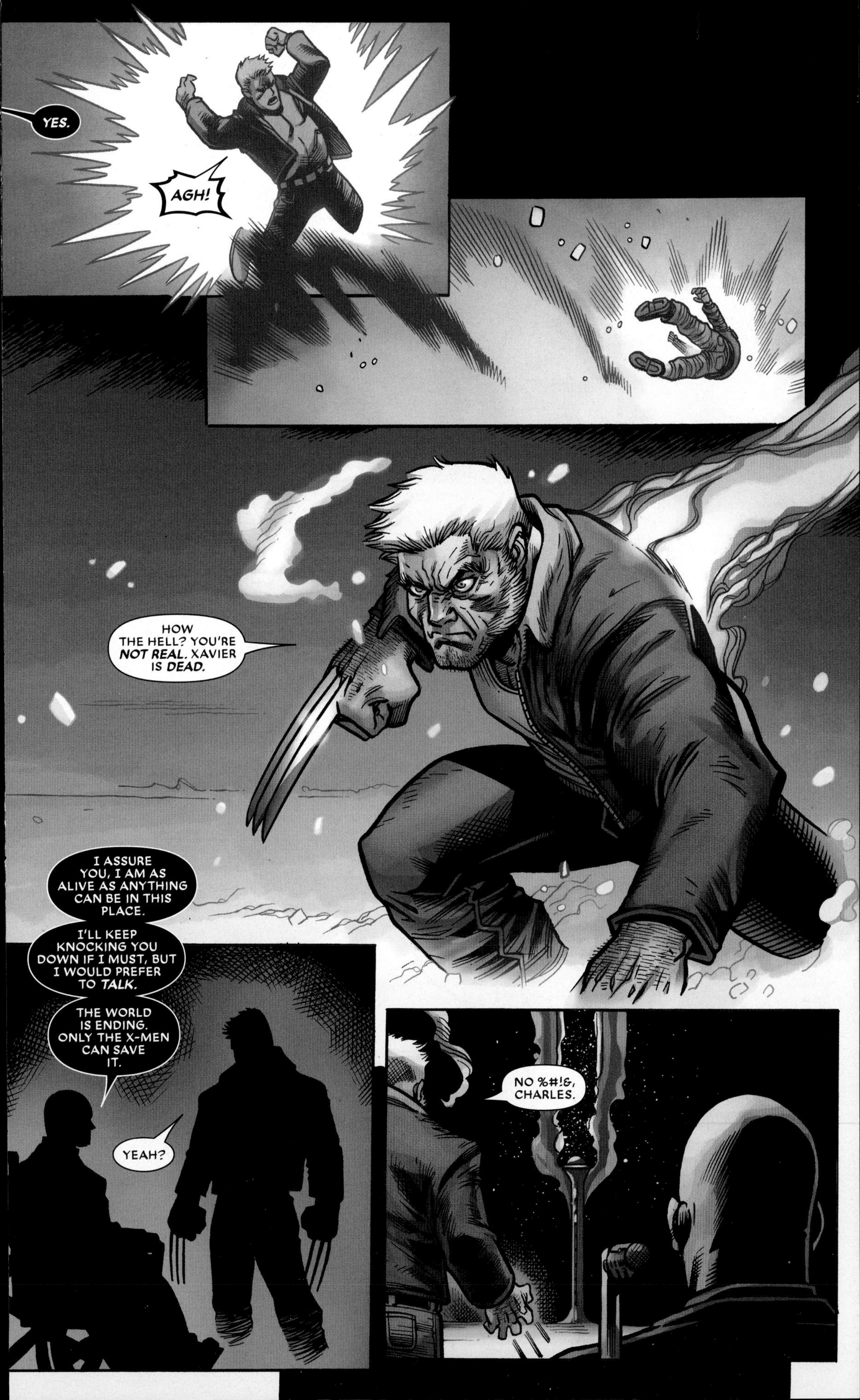
YES.
AGH!
HOW THE HELL? YOU'RE NOT REAL. XAVIER IS DEAD.
I ASSURE YOU, I AM AS ALIVE AS ANYTHING CAN BE IN THIS PLACE.
I'LL KEEP KNOCKING YOU DOWN IF I MUST, BUT I WOULD PREFER TO TALK.
THE WORLD IS ENDING. ONLY THE X-MEN CAN SAVE IT.
YEAH?
NO %#!&, CHARLES.

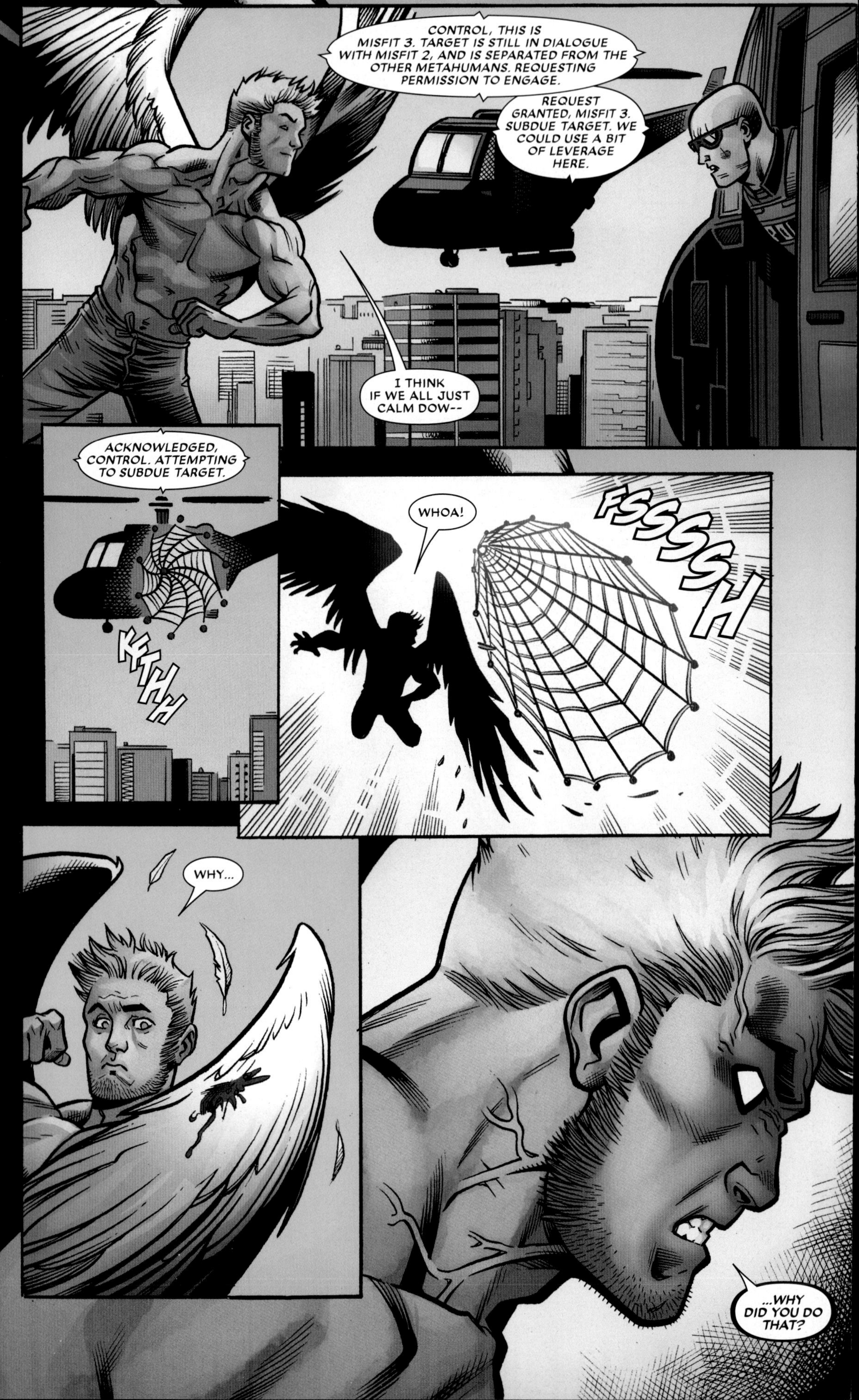
CONTROL, THIS IS MISFIT 3. TARGET IS STILL IN DIALOGUE WITH MISFIT 2, AND IS SEPARATED FROM THE OTHER METAHUMANS. REQUESTING PERMISSION TO ENGAGE.
REQUEST GRANTED, MISFIT 3. SUBDUE TARGET. WE COULD USE A BIT OF LEVERAGE HERE.
I THINK IF WE ALL JUST CALM DOW--
ACKNOWLEDGED, CONTROL. ATTEMPTING TO SUBDUE TARGET.
KKTHH
WHOA!
FSSSSH
WHY...
...WHY DID YOU DO THAT?

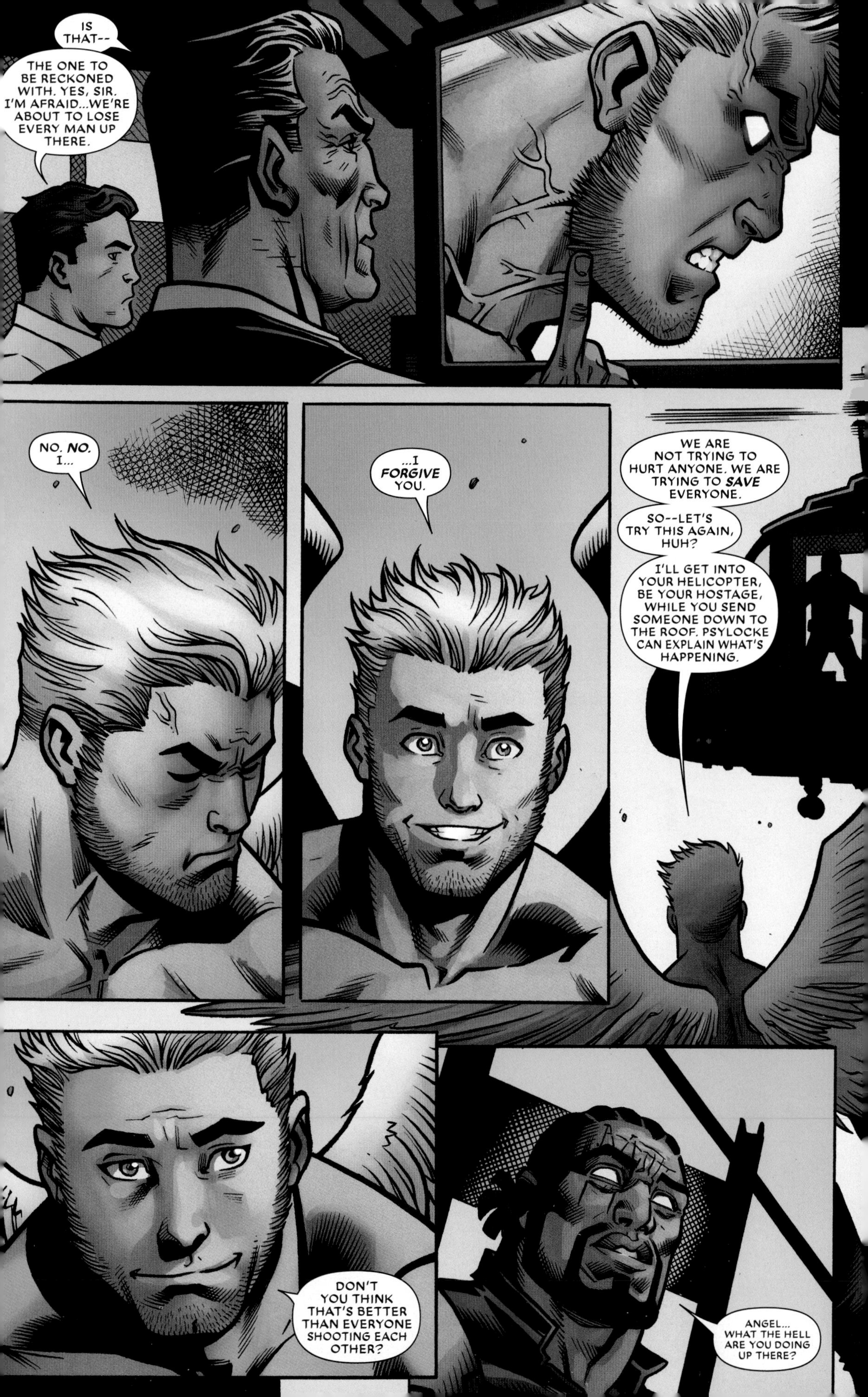
IS THAT--
THE ONE TO BE RECKONED WITH. YES, SIR. I'M AFRAID...WE'RE ABOUT TO LOSE EVERY MAN UP THERE.
NO. *NO.* I...
...I *FORGIVE* YOU.
WE ARE NOT TRYING TO HURT ANYONE. WE ARE TRYING TO *SAVE* EVERYONE.
SO--LET'S TRY THIS AGAIN, HUH?
I'LL GET INTO YOUR HELICOPTER, BE YOUR HOSTAGE, WHILE YOU SEND SOMEONE DOWN TO THE ROOF. PSYLOCKE CAN EXPLAIN WHAT'S HAPPENING.
DON'T YOU THINK THAT'S BETTER THAN EVERYONE SHOOTING EACH OTHER?
ANGEL... WHAT THE HELL ARE YOU DOING UP THERE?

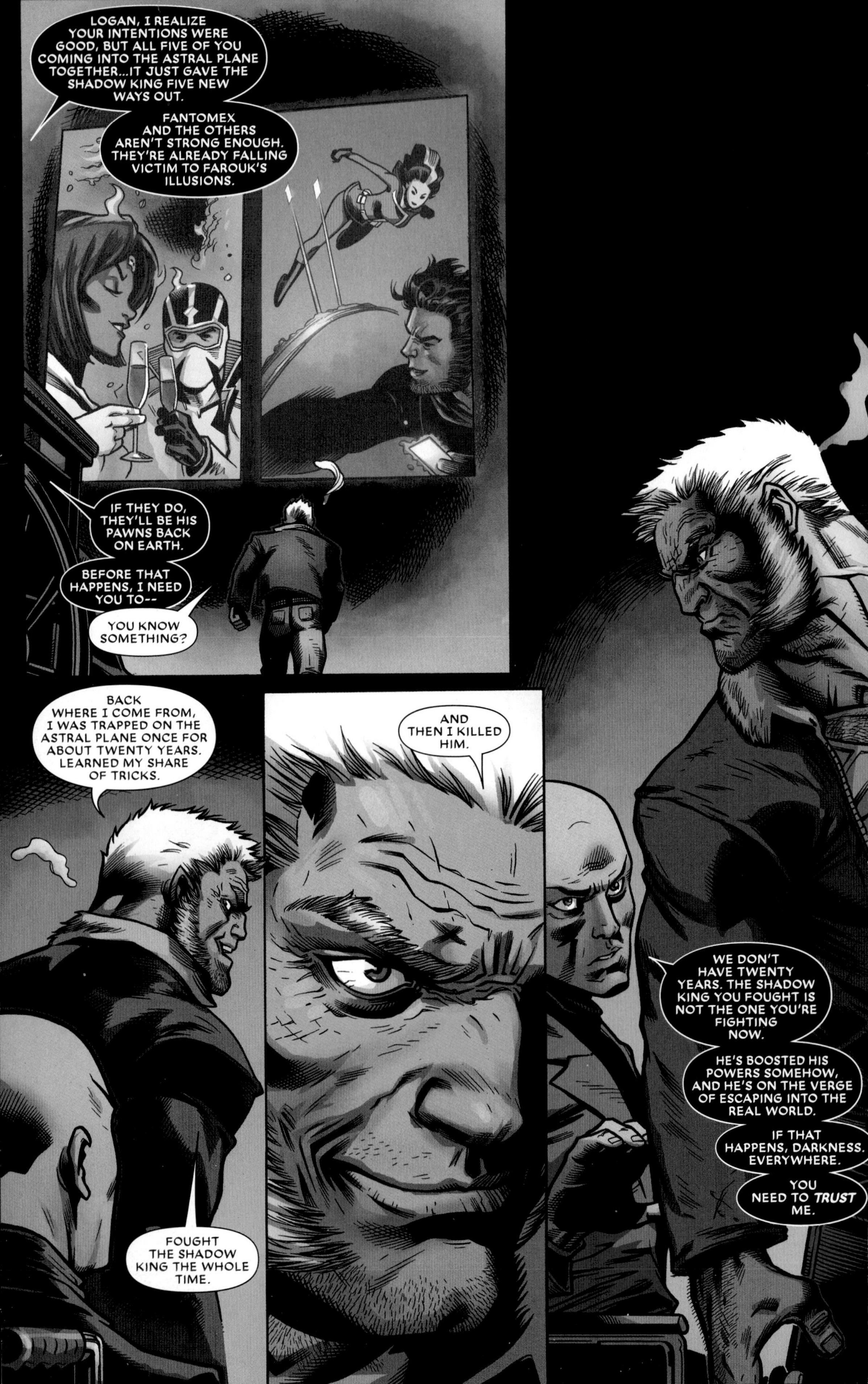
LOGAN, I REALIZE YOUR INTENTIONS WERE GOOD, BUT ALL FIVE OF YOU COMING INTO THE ASTRAL PLANE TOGETHER...IT JUST GAVE THE SHADOW KING FIVE NEW WAYS OUT.
FANTOMEX AND THE OTHERS AREN'T STRONG ENOUGH. THEY'RE ALREADY FALLING VICTIM TO FAROUK'S ILLUSIONS.
IF THEY DO, THEY'LL BE HIS PAWNS BACK ON EARTH.
BEFORE THAT HAPPENS, I NEED YOU TO--
YOU KNOW SOMETHING?
BACK WHERE I COME FROM, I WAS TRAPPED ON THE ASTRAL PLANE ONCE FOR ABOUT TWENTY YEARS. LEARNED MY SHARE OF TRICKS.
FOUGHT THE SHADOW KING THE WHOLE TIME.
AND THEN I KILLED HIM.
WE DON'T HAVE TWENTY YEARS. THE SHADOW KING YOU FOUGHT IS NOT THE ONE YOU'RE FIGHTING NOW.
HE'S BOOSTED HIS POWERS SOMEHOW, AND HE'S ON THE VERGE OF ESCAPING INTO THE REAL WORLD.
IF THAT HAPPENS, DARKNESS. EVERYWHERE.
YOU NEED TO *TRUST* ME.

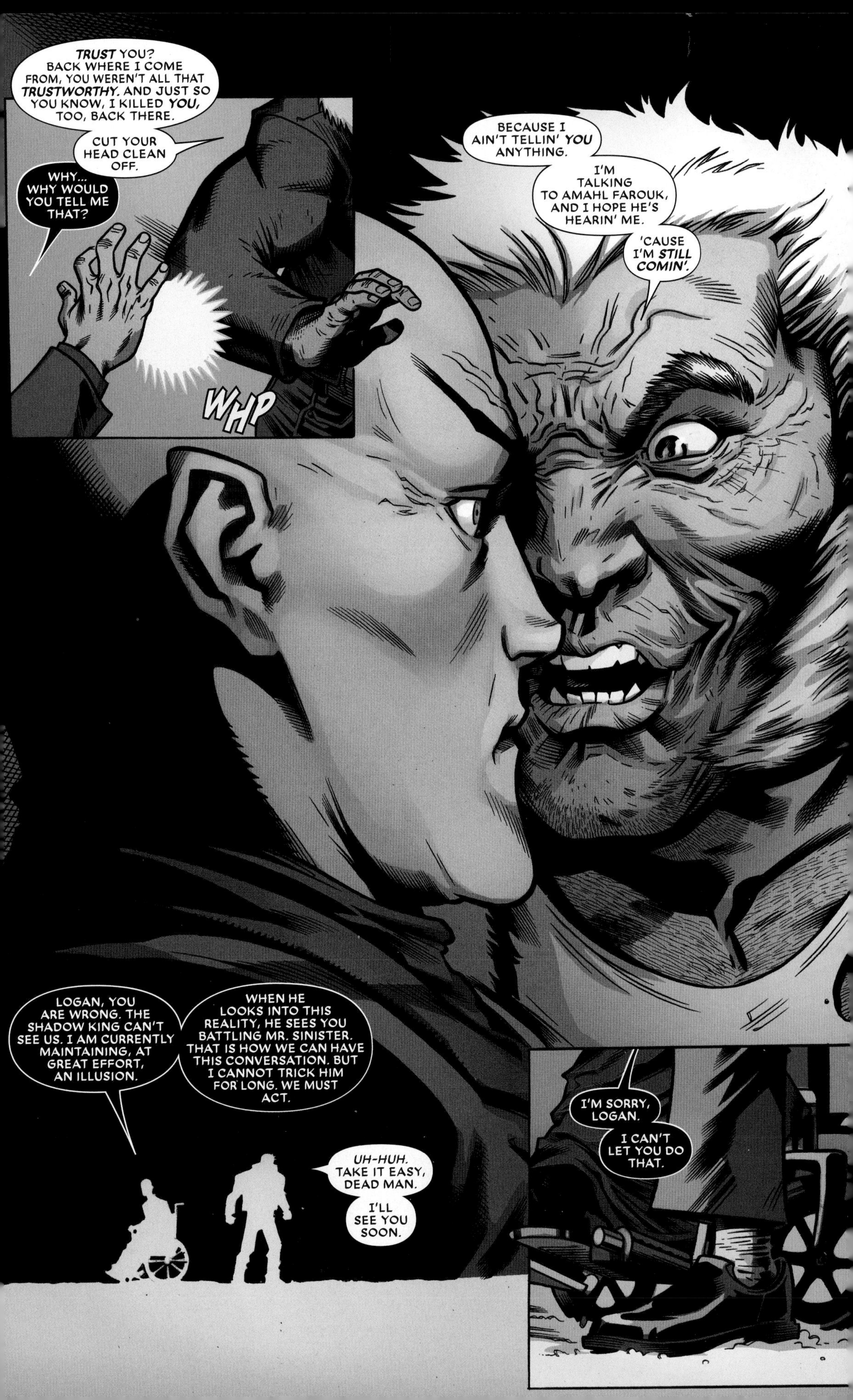
TRUST YOU? BACK WHERE I COME FROM, YOU WEREN'T ALL THAT TRUSTWORTHY. AND JUST SO YOU KNOW, I KILLED YOU, TOO, BACK THERE.
CUT YOUR HEAD CLEAN OFF.
WHY... WHY WOULD YOU TELL ME THAT?
WHP
BECAUSE I AIN'T TELLIN' YOU ANYTHING.
I'M TALKING TO AMAHL FAROUK, AND I HOPE HE'S HEARIN' ME.
'CAUSE I'M STILL COMIN'.
LOGAN, YOU ARE WRONG. THE SHADOW KING CAN'T SEE US. I AM CURRENTLY MAINTAINING, AT GREAT EFFORT, AN ILLUSION.
WHEN HE LOOKS INTO THIS REALITY, HE SEES YOU BATTLING MR. SINISTER. THAT IS HOW WE CAN HAVE THIS CONVERSATION. BUT I CANNOT TRICK HIM FOR LONG. WE MUST ACT.
UH-HUH. TAKE IT EASY, DEAD MAN.
I'LL SEE YOU SOON.
I'M SORRY, LOGAN.
I CAN'T LET YOU DO THAT.

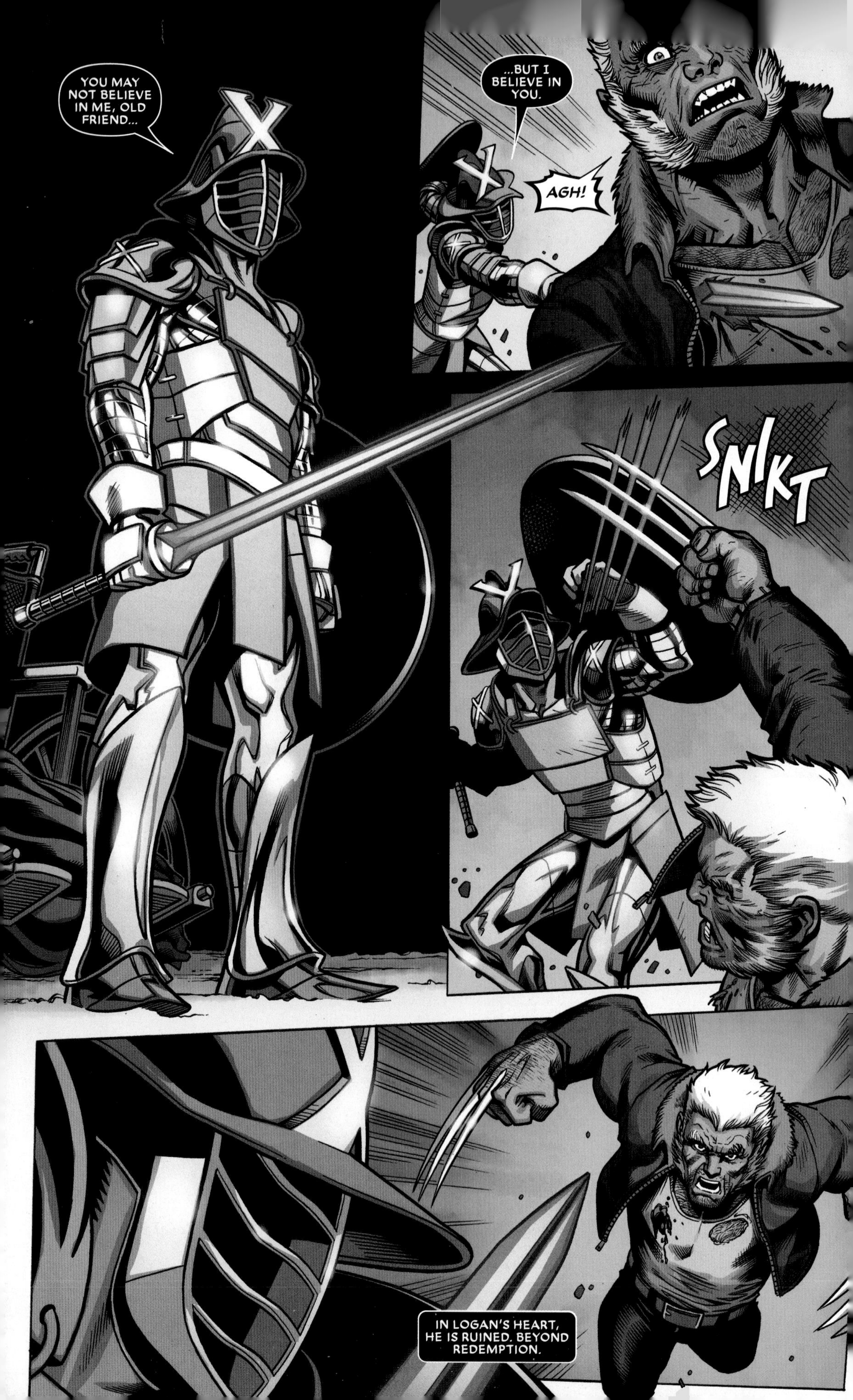
YOU MAY NOT BELIEVE IN ME, OLD FRIEND...
...BUT I BELIEVE IN YOU.
AGH!
SNIKT
IN LOGAN'S HEART, HE IS RUINED. BEYOND REDEMPTION.

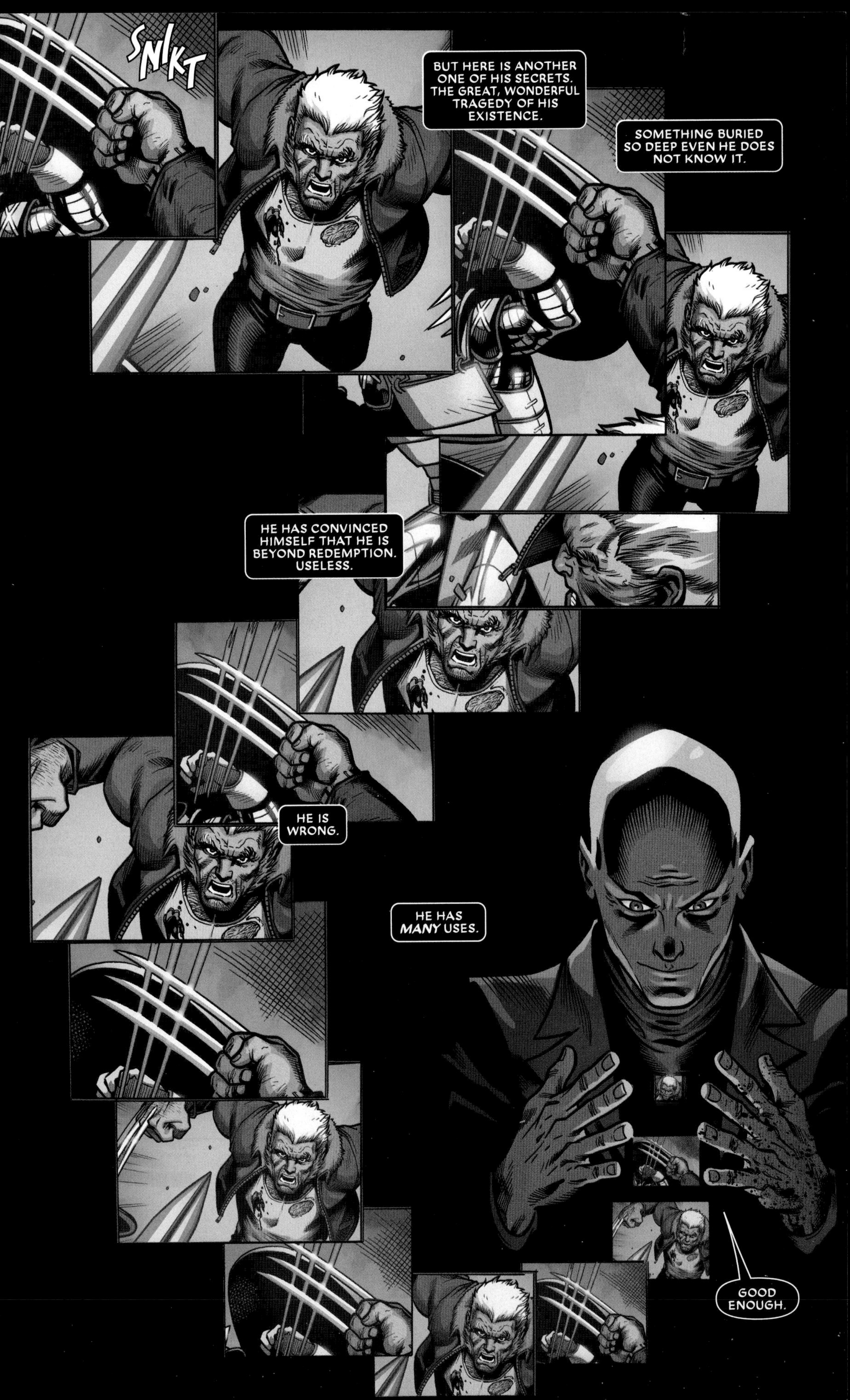
SNIKT
BUT HERE IS ANOTHER ONE OF HIS SECRETS. THE GREAT, WONDERFUL TRAGEDY OF HIS EXISTENCE.
SOMETHING BURIED SO DEEP EVEN HE DOES NOT KNOW IT.
HE HAS CONVINCED HIMSELF THAT HE IS BEYOND REDEMPTION. USELESS.
HE IS WRONG.
HE HAS *MANY* USES.
GOOD ENOUGH.

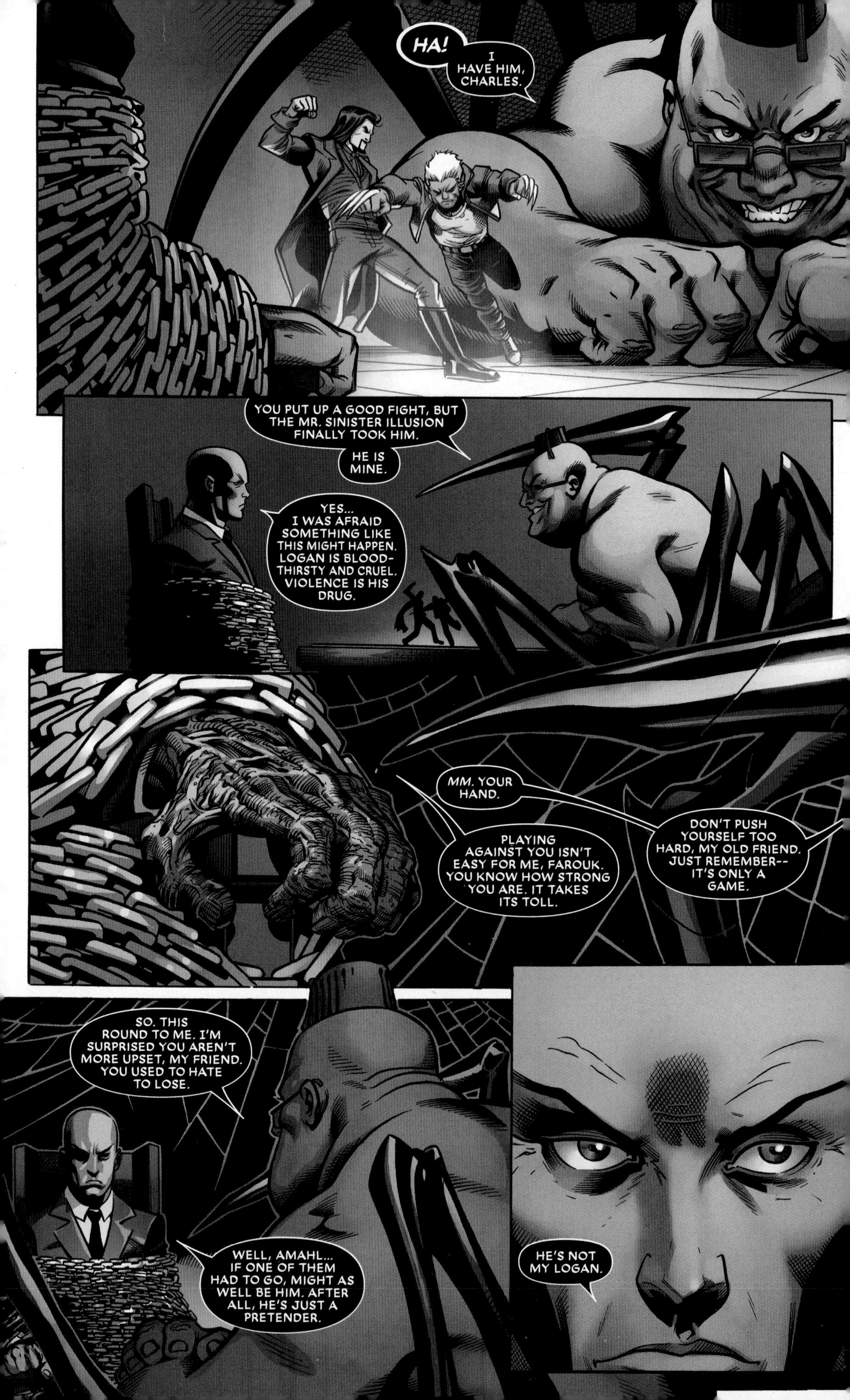
HA!
I HAVE HIM, CHARLES.
YOU PUT UP A GOOD FIGHT, BUT THE MR. SINISTER ILLUSION FINALLY TOOK HIM.
HE IS MINE.
YES... I WAS AFRAID SOMETHING LIKE THIS MIGHT HAPPEN. LOGAN IS BLOOD-THIRSTY AND CRUEL. VIOLENCE IS HIS DRUG.
MM. YOUR HAND.
PLAYING AGAINST YOU ISN'T EASY FOR ME, FAROUK. YOU KNOW HOW STRONG YOU ARE. IT TAKES ITS TOLL.
DON'T PUSH YOURSELF TOO HARD, MY OLD FRIEND. JUST REMEMBER-- IT'S ONLY A GAME.
SO. THIS ROUND TO ME. I'M SURPRISED YOU AREN'T MORE UPSET, MY FRIEND. YOU USED TO HATE TO LOSE.
WELL, AMAHL... IF ONE OF THEM HAD TO GO, MIGHT AS WELL BE HIM. AFTER ALL, HE'S JUST A PRETENDER.
HE'S NOT MY LOGAN.

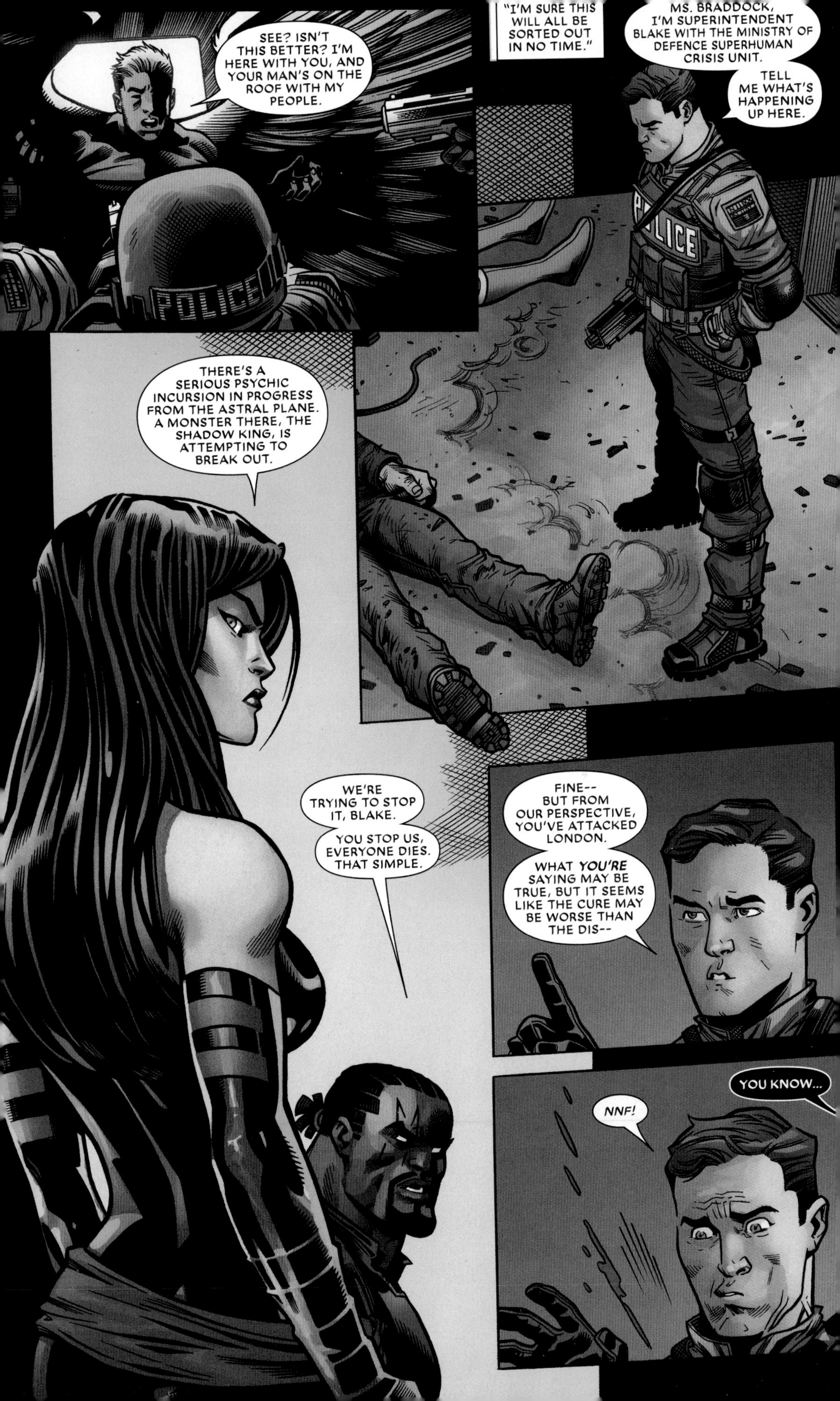
SEE? ISN'T THIS BETTER? I'M HERE WITH YOU, AND YOUR MAN'S ON THE ROOF WITH MY PEOPLE.
"I'M SURE THIS WILL ALL BE SORTED OUT IN NO TIME."
MS. BRADDOCK, I'M SUPERINTENDENT BLAKE WITH THE MINISTRY OF DEFENCE SUPERHUMAN CRISIS UNIT.
TELL ME WHAT'S HAPPENING UP HERE.
POLICE
POLICE
THERE'S A SERIOUS PSYCHIC INCURSION IN PROGRESS FROM THE ASTRAL PLANE. A MONSTER THERE, THE SHADOW KING, IS ATTEMPTING TO BREAK OUT.
WE'RE TRYING TO STOP IT, BLAKE.
YOU STOP US, EVERYONE DIES. THAT SIMPLE.
FINE-- BUT FROM OUR PERSPECTIVE, YOU'VE ATTACKED LONDON.
WHAT *YOU'RE* SAYING MAY BE TRUE, BUT IT SEEMS LIKE THE CURE MAY BE WORSE THAN THE DIS--
YOU KNOW...
NNF!

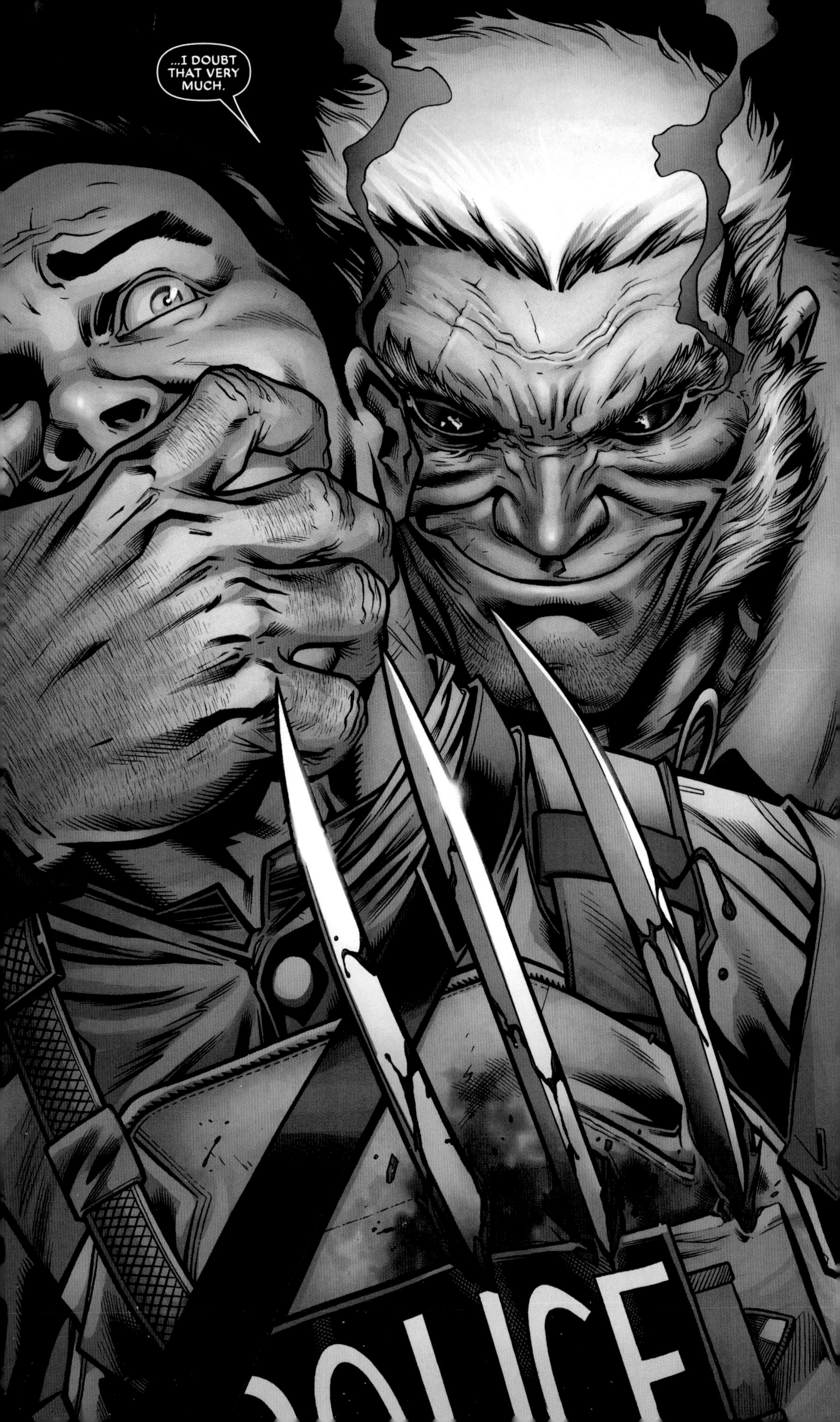
...I DOUBT THAT VERY MUCH.
POLICE

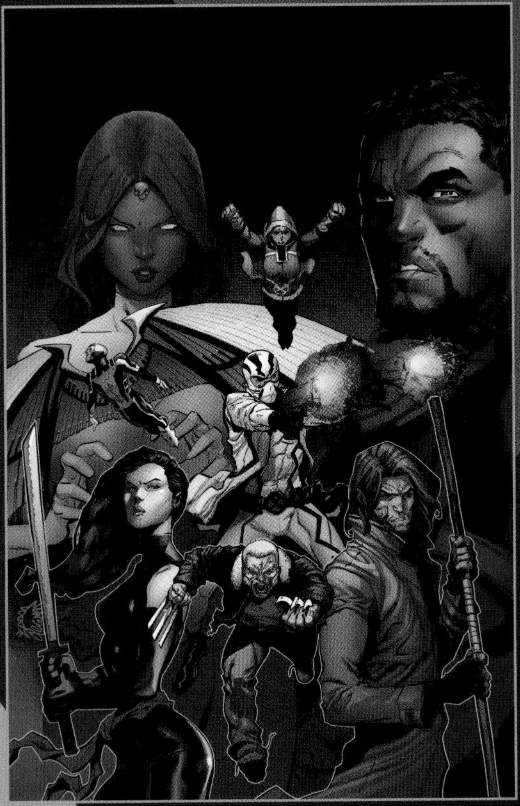

#2 VARIANT
BY **RYAN STEGMAN**
& **MARTE GRACIA**

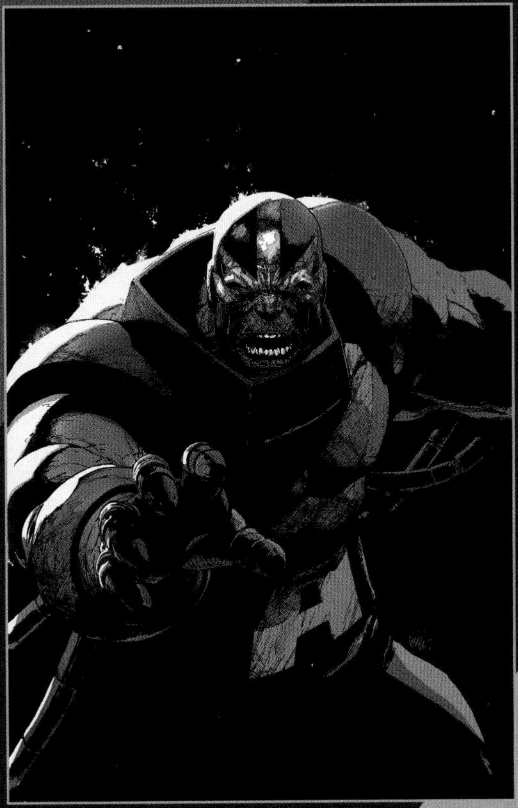

#2 VILLAIN VARIANT
BY **LEINIL FRANCIS YU**

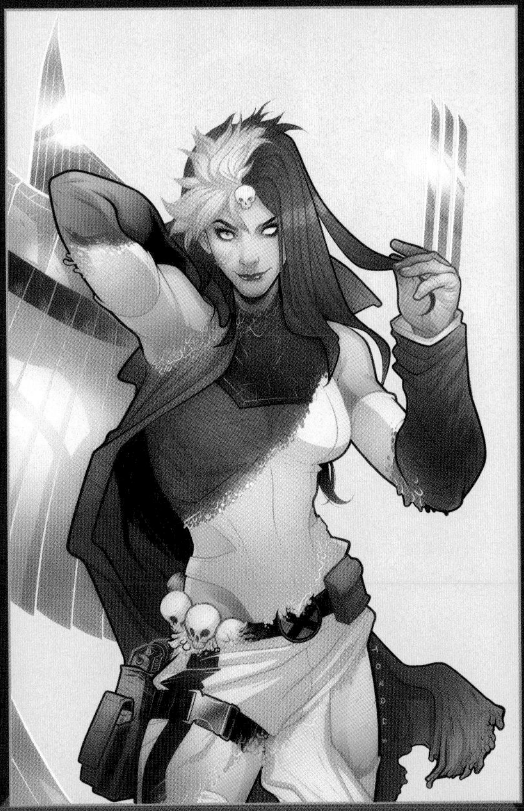

#2 VARIANT
BY **ELIZABETH TORQUE**

4

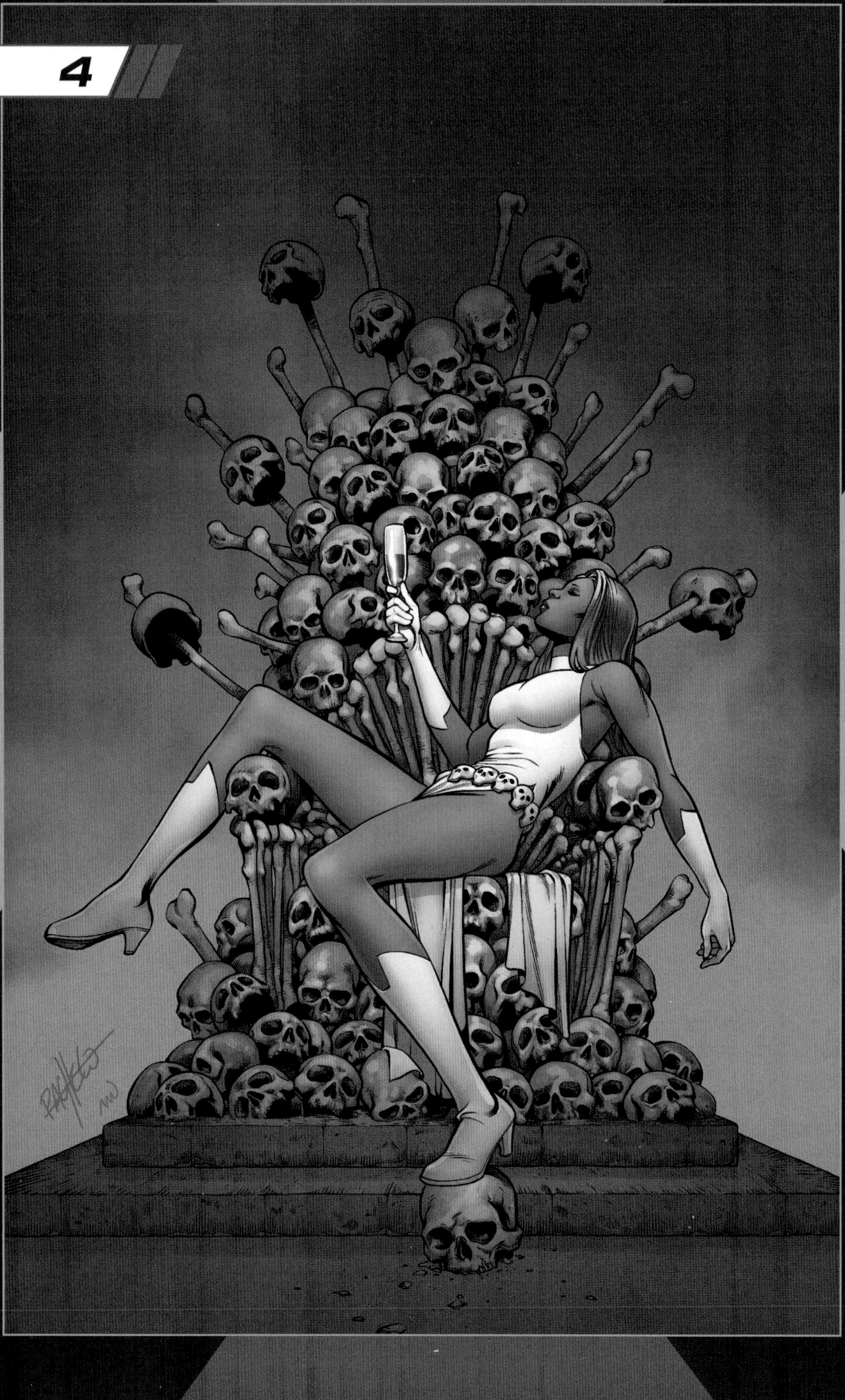

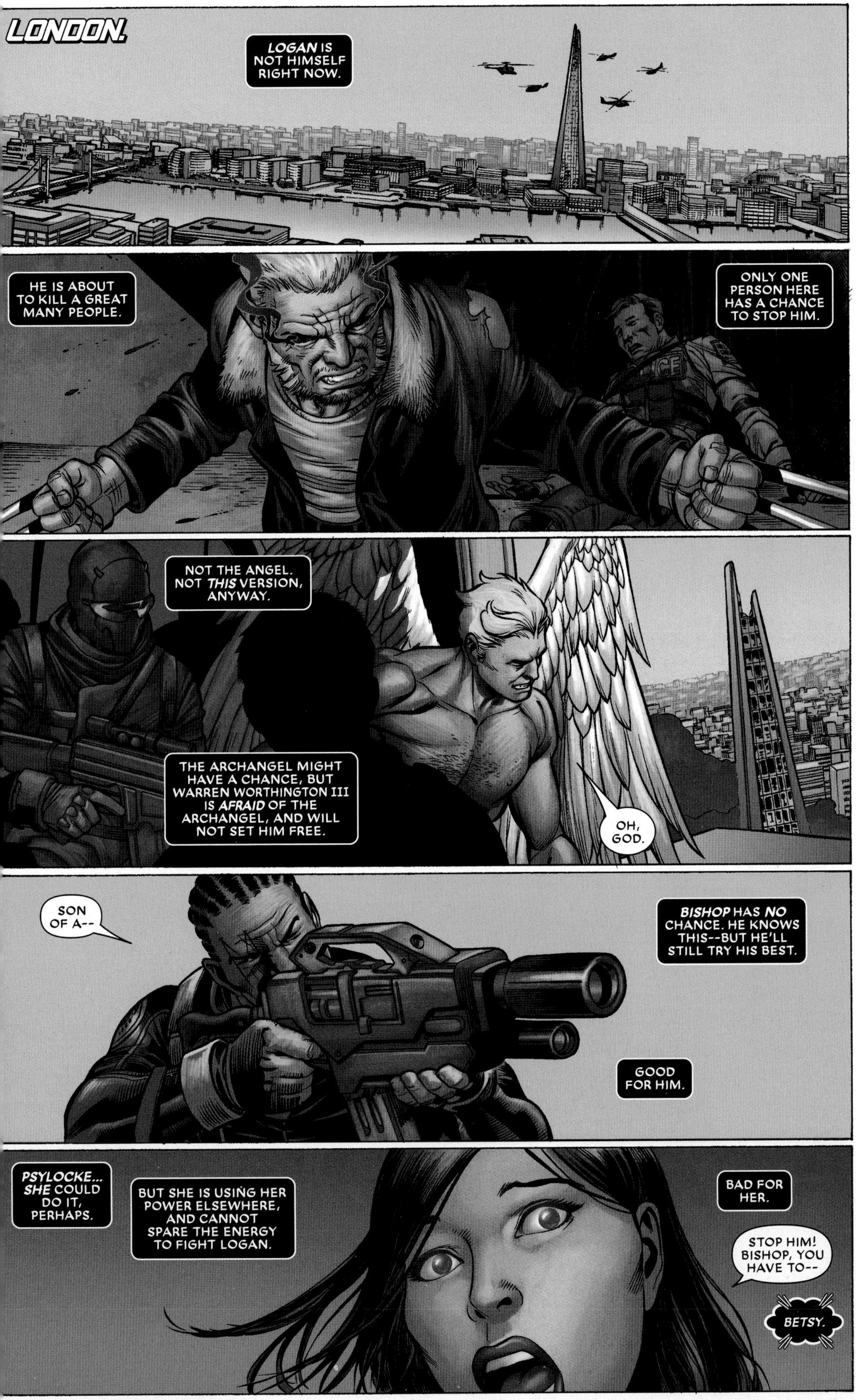
LONDON.
LOGAN IS NOT HIMSELF RIGHT NOW.
HE IS ABOUT TO KILL A GREAT MANY PEOPLE.
ONLY ONE PERSON HERE HAS A CHANCE TO STOP HIM.
NOT THE ANGEL. NOT THIS VERSION, ANYWAY.
THE ARCHANGEL MIGHT HAVE A CHANCE, BUT WARREN WORTHINGTON III IS AFRAID OF THE ARCHANGEL, AND WILL NOT SET HIM FREE.
OH, GOD.
SON OF A--
BISHOP HAS NO CHANCE. HE KNOWS THIS--BUT HE'LL STILL TRY HIS BEST.
GOOD FOR HIM.
PSYLOCKE... SHE COULD DO IT, PERHAPS.
BUT SHE IS USING HER POWER ELSEWHERE, AND CANNOT SPARE THE ENERGY TO FIGHT LOGAN.
BAD FOR HER.
STOP HIM! BISHOP, YOU HAVE TO--
BETSY.

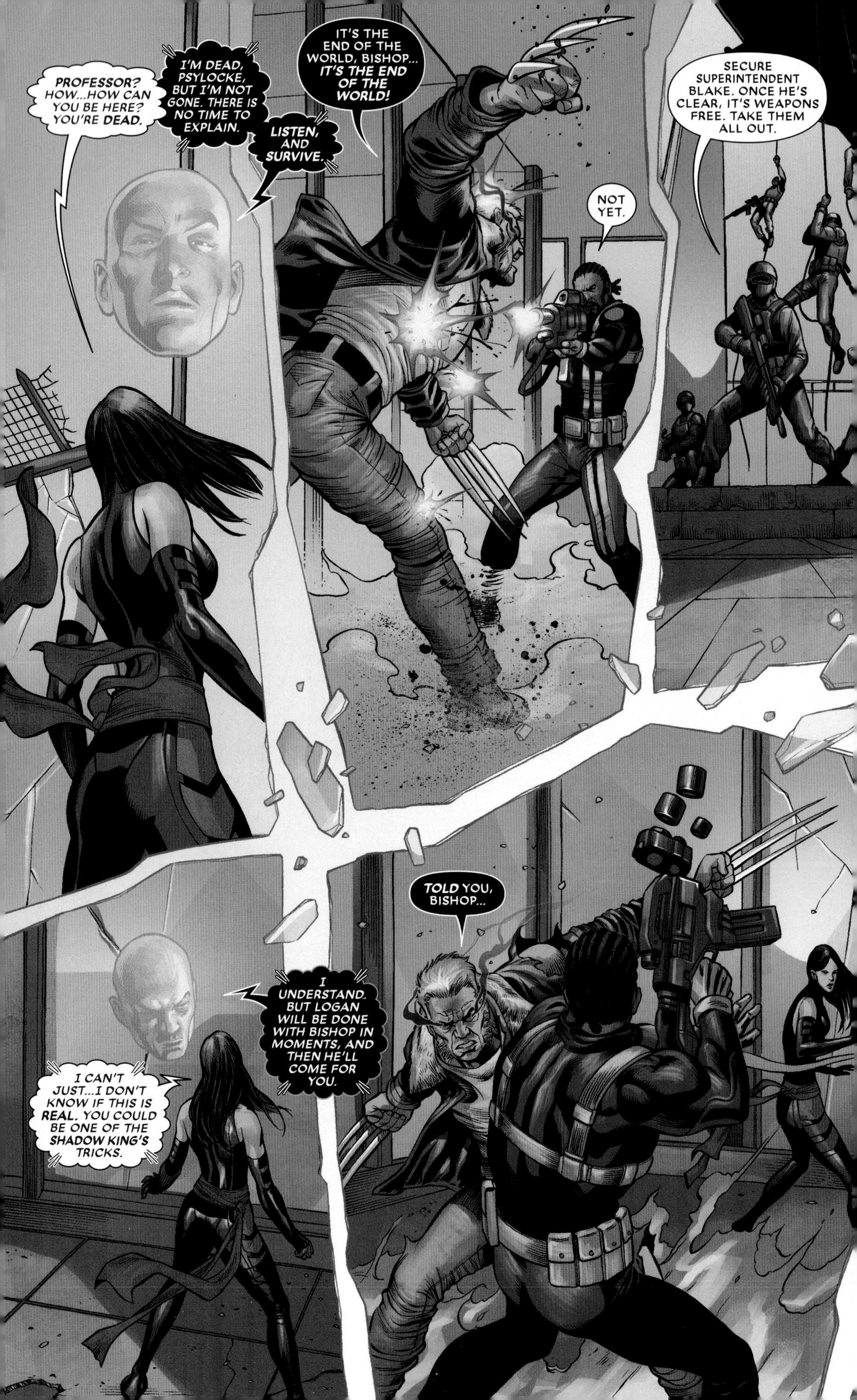
PROFESSOR? HOW...HOW CAN YOU BE HERE? YOU'RE DEAD.
I'M DEAD, PSYLOCKE, BUT I'M NOT GONE. THERE IS NO TIME TO EXPLAIN.
LISTEN, AND SURVIVE.
IT'S THE END OF THE WORLD, BISHOP... IT'S THE END OF THE WORLD!
SECURE SUPERINTENDENT BLAKE. ONCE HE'S CLEAR, IT'S WEAPONS FREE. TAKE THEM ALL OUT.
NOT YET.
TOLD YOU, BISHOP...
I UNDERSTAND. BUT LOGAN WILL BE DONE WITH BISHOP IN MOMENTS, AND THEN HE'LL COME FOR YOU.
I CAN'T JUST...I DON'T KNOW IF THIS IS REAL. YOU COULD BE ONE OF THE SHADOW KING'S TRICKS.

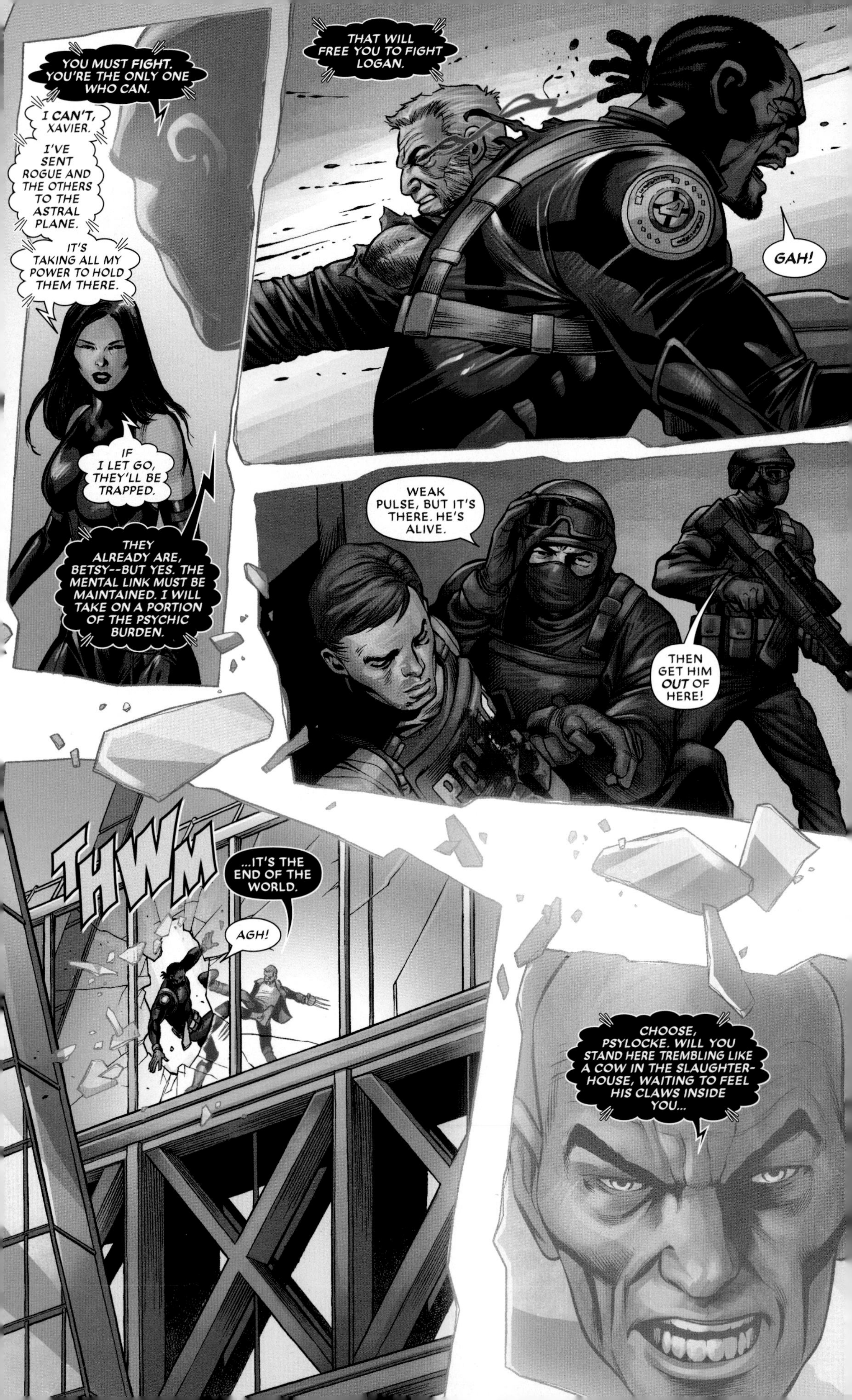
YOU MUST FIGHT. YOU'RE THE ONLY ONE WHO CAN.
I CAN'T, XAVIER.
I'VE SENT ROGUE AND THE OTHERS TO THE ASTRAL PLANE.
IT'S TAKING ALL MY POWER TO HOLD THEM THERE.
IF I LET GO, THEY'LL BE TRAPPED.
THEY ALREADY ARE, BETSY--BUT YES. THE MENTAL LINK MUST BE MAINTAINED. I WILL TAKE ON A PORTION OF THE PSYCHIC BURDEN.
THAT WILL FREE YOU TO FIGHT LOGAN.
GAH!
WEAK PULSE, BUT IT'S THERE. HE'S ALIVE.
THEN GET HIM OUT OF HERE!
THWM
...IT'S THE END OF THE WORLD.
AGH!
CHOOSE, PSYLOCKE. WILL YOU STAND HERE TREMBLING LIKE A COW IN THE SLAUGHTER-HOUSE, WAITING TO FEEL HIS CLAWS INSIDE YOU...

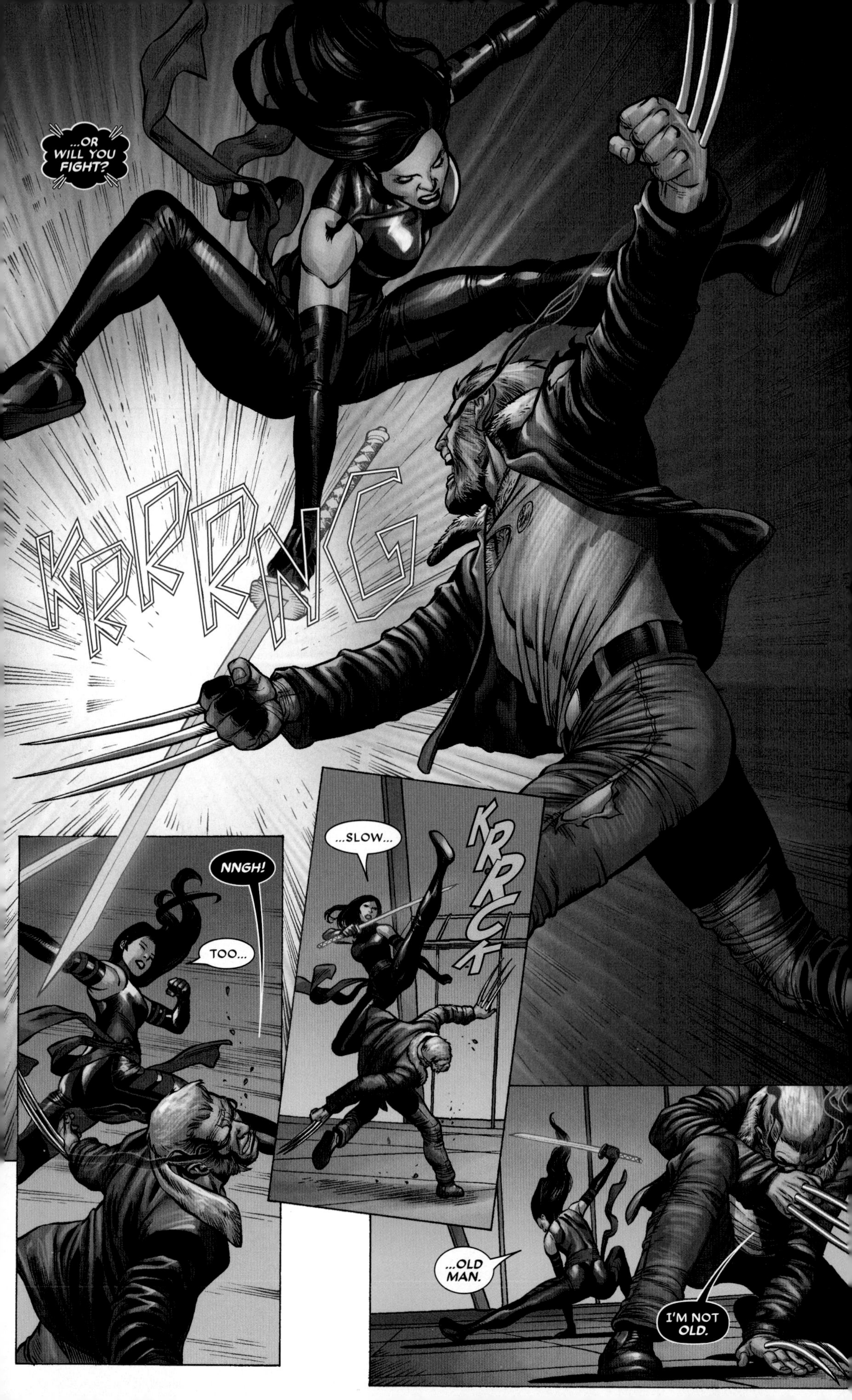
...OR WILL YOU FIGHT?
KRRRNG
NNGH!
TOO...
...SLOW...
KRRCK
...OLD MAN.
I'M NOT OLD.

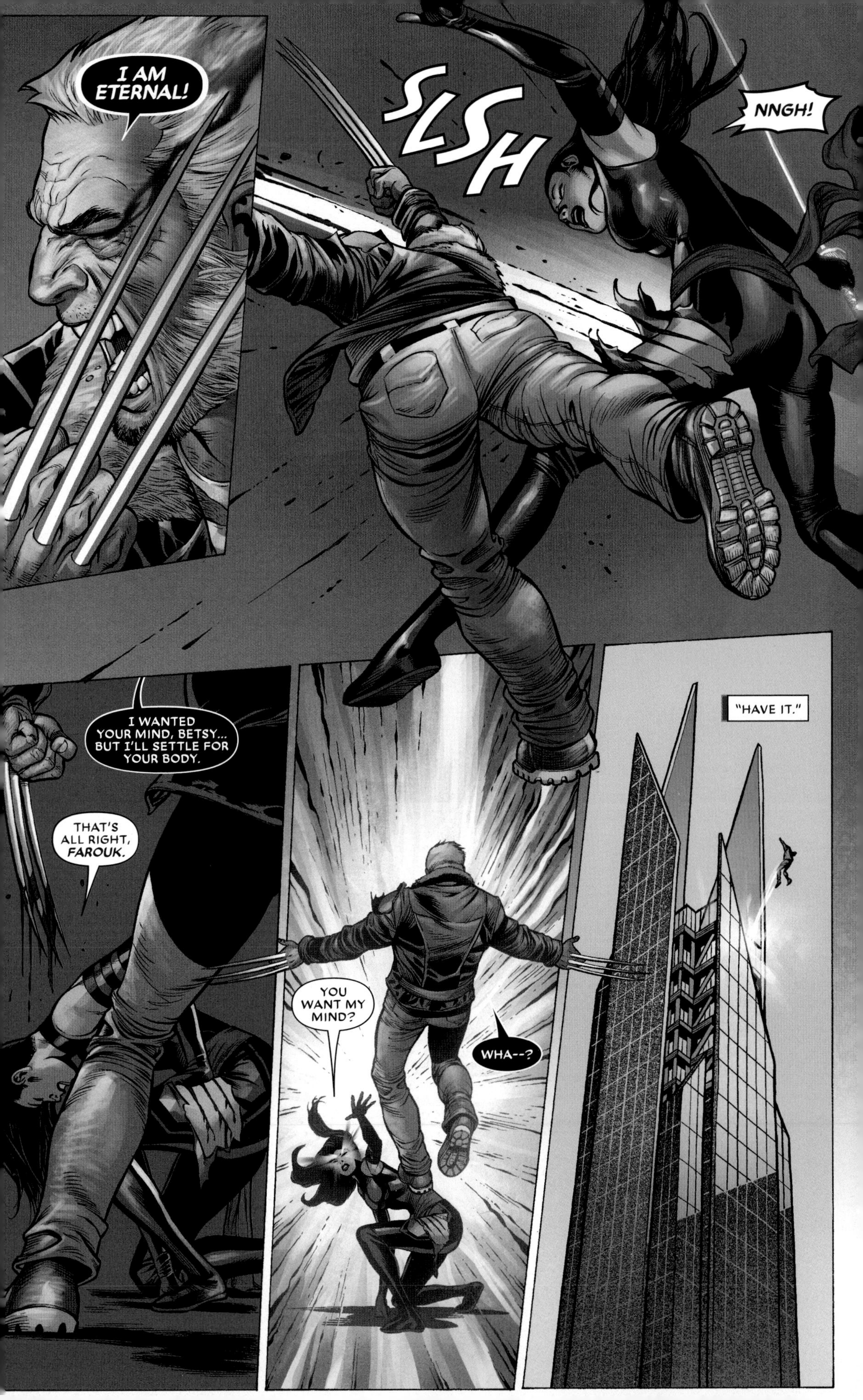
I AM ETERNAL!
SLSH
NNGH!
I WANTED YOUR MIND, BETSY... BUT I'LL SETTLE FOR YOUR BODY.
THAT'S ALL RIGHT, FAROUK.
YOU WANT MY MIND?
WHA--?
"HAVE IT."

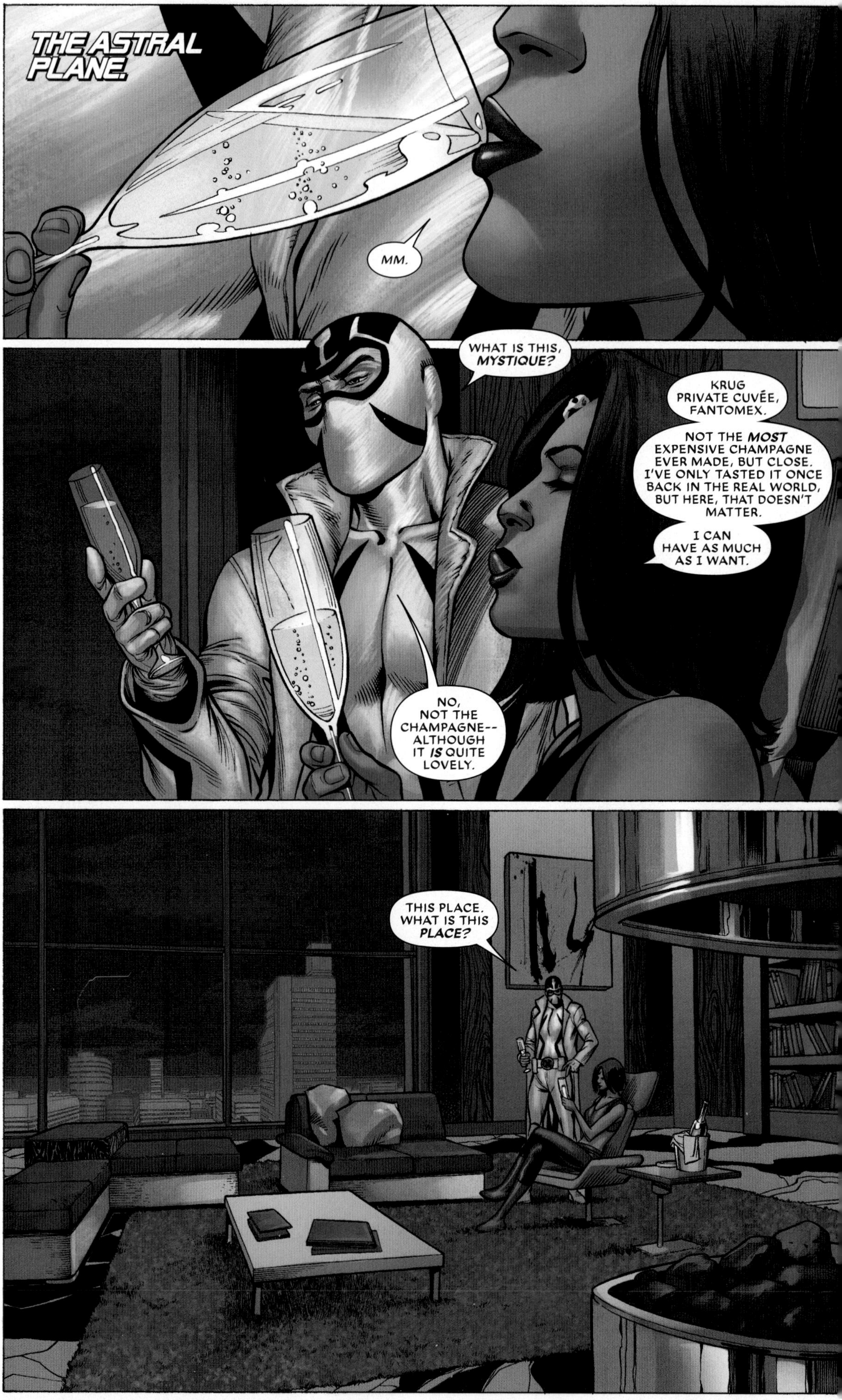
THE ASTRAL PLANE.
MM.
WHAT IS THIS, MYSTIQUE?
KRUG PRIVATE CUVÉE, FANTOMEX.
NOT THE MOST EXPENSIVE CHAMPAGNE EVER MADE, BUT CLOSE. I'VE ONLY TASTED IT ONCE BACK IN THE REAL WORLD, BUT HERE, THAT DOESN'T MATTER.
I CAN HAVE AS MUCH AS I WANT.
NO, NOT THE CHAMPAGNE-- ALTHOUGH IT IS QUITE LOVELY.
THIS PLACE. WHAT IS THIS PLACE?

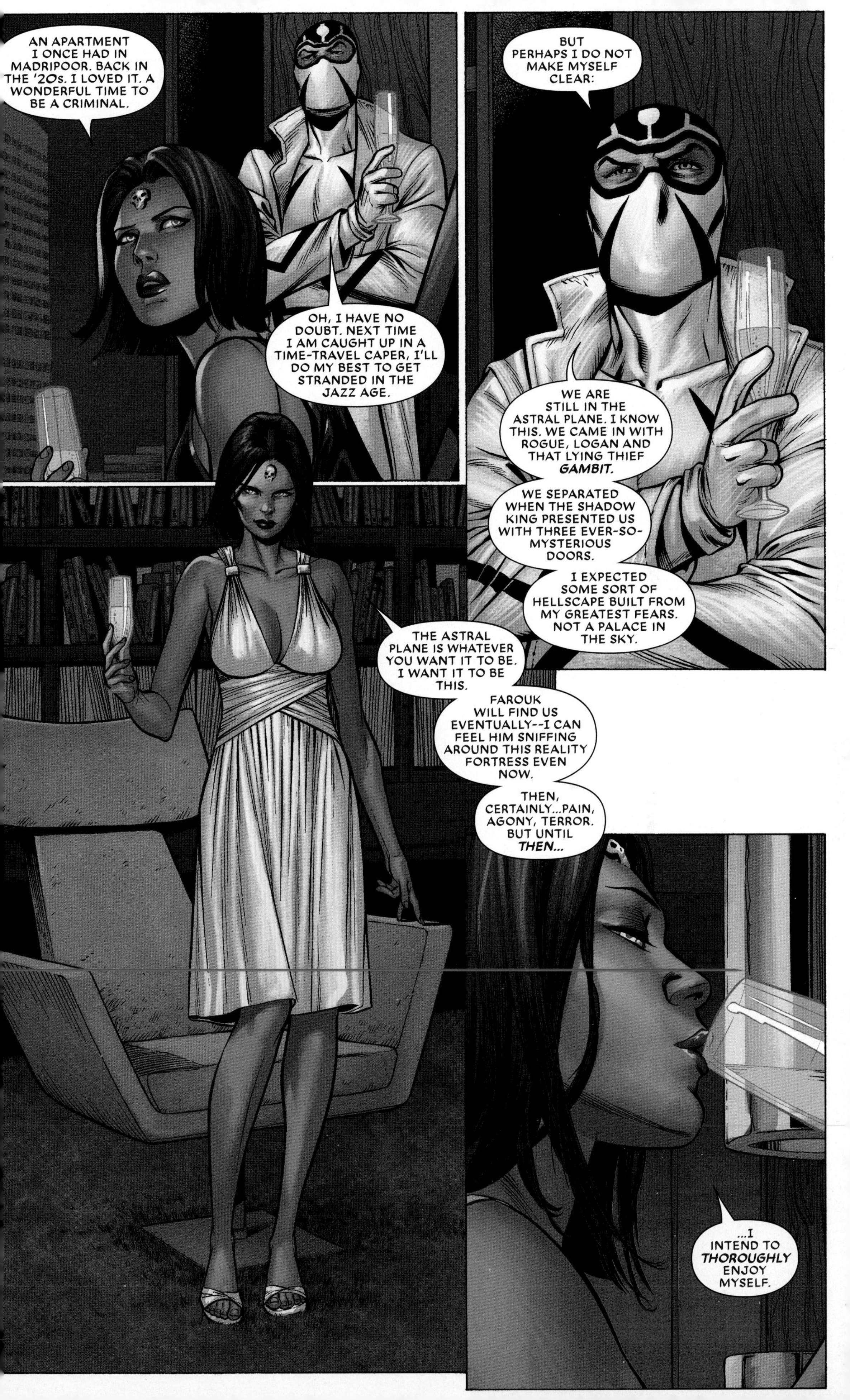

AN APARTMENT I ONCE HAD IN MADRIPOOR. BACK IN THE '20s. I LOVED IT. A WONDERFUL TIME TO BE A CRIMINAL.
OH, I HAVE NO DOUBT. NEXT TIME I AM CAUGHT UP IN A TIME-TRAVEL CAPER, I'LL DO MY BEST TO GET STRANDED IN THE JAZZ AGE.
BUT PERHAPS I DO NOT MAKE MYSELF CLEAR:
WE ARE STILL IN THE ASTRAL PLANE. I KNOW THIS. WE CAME IN WITH ROGUE, LOGAN AND THAT LYING THIEF *GAMBIT.*
WE SEPARATED WHEN THE SHADOW KING PRESENTED US WITH THREE EVER-SO-MYSTERIOUS DOORS.
I EXPECTED SOME SORT OF HELLSCAPE BUILT FROM MY GREATEST FEARS. NOT A PALACE IN THE SKY.
THE ASTRAL PLANE IS WHATEVER YOU WANT IT TO BE. I WANT IT TO BE THIS.
FAROUK WILL FIND US EVENTUALLY--I CAN FEEL HIM SNIFFING AROUND THIS REALITY FORTRESS EVEN NOW.
THEN, CERTAINLY...PAIN, AGONY, TERROR. BUT UNTIL *THEN...*
...I INTEND TO *THOROUGHLY* ENJOY MYSELF.

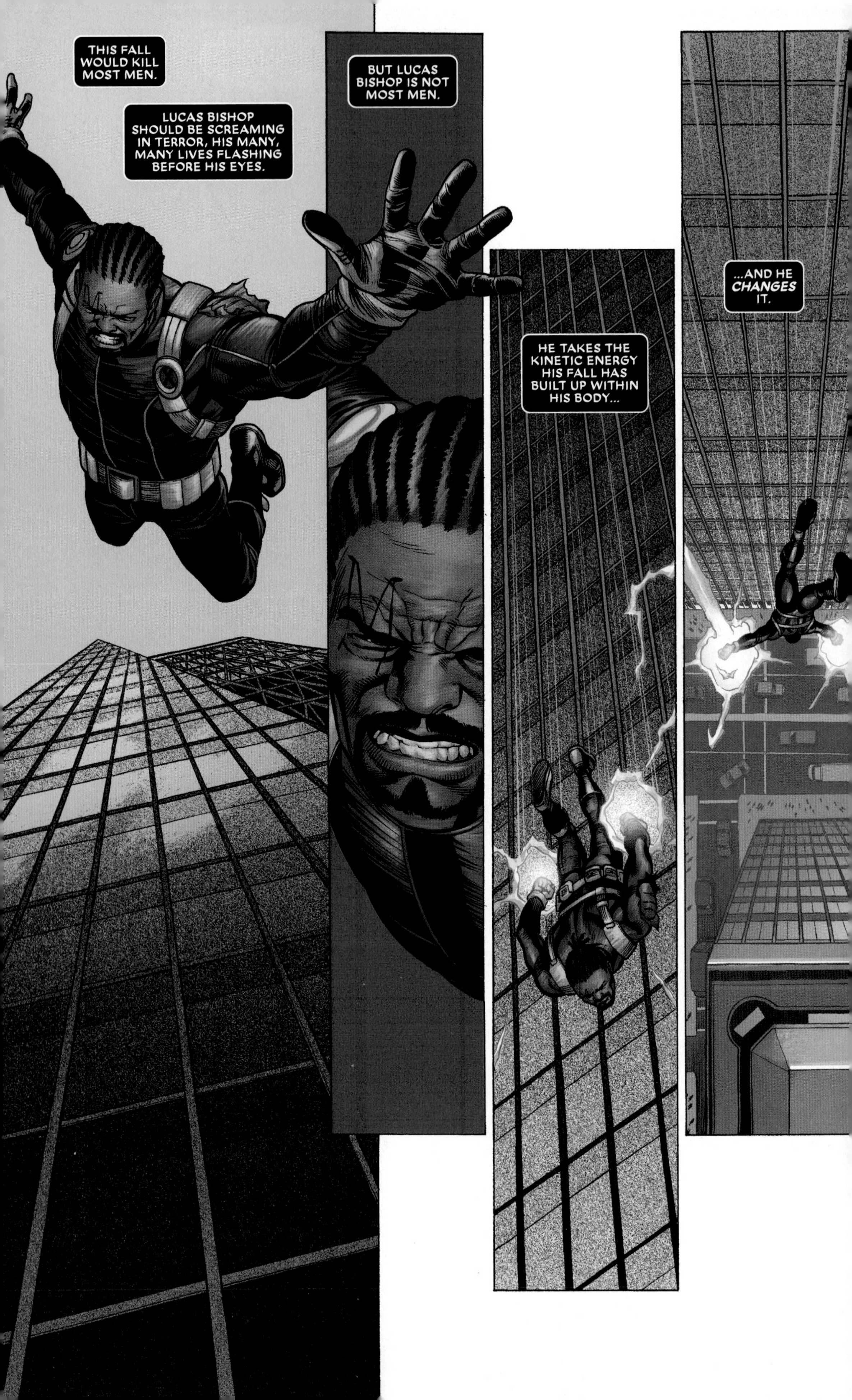
THIS FALL WOULD KILL MOST MEN.
LUCAS BISHOP SHOULD BE SCREAMING IN TERROR, HIS MANY, MANY LIVES FLASHING BEFORE HIS EYES.
BUT LUCAS BISHOP IS NOT MOST MEN.
HE TAKES THE KINETIC ENERGY HIS FALL HAS BUILT UP WITHIN HIS BODY...
...AND HE *CHANGES* IT.

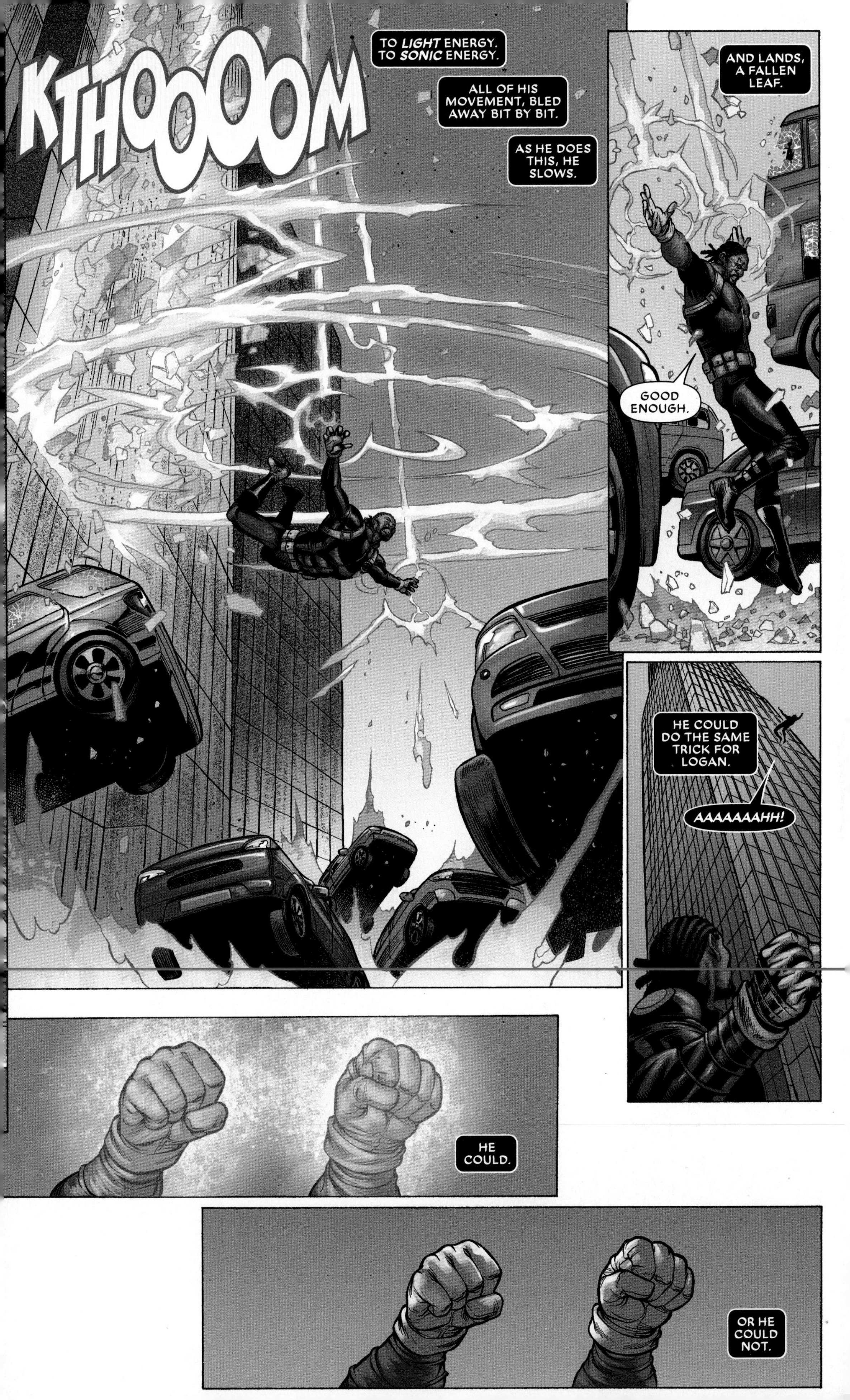
KTHOOOOOM
TO LIGHT ENERGY. TO SONIC ENERGY.
ALL OF HIS MOVEMENT, BLED AWAY BIT BY BIT.
AS HE DOES THIS, HE SLOWS.
AND LANDS, A FALLEN LEAF.
GOOD ENOUGH.
HE COULD DO THE SAME TRICK FOR LOGAN.
AAAAAAAHH!
HE COULD.
OR HE COULD NOT.

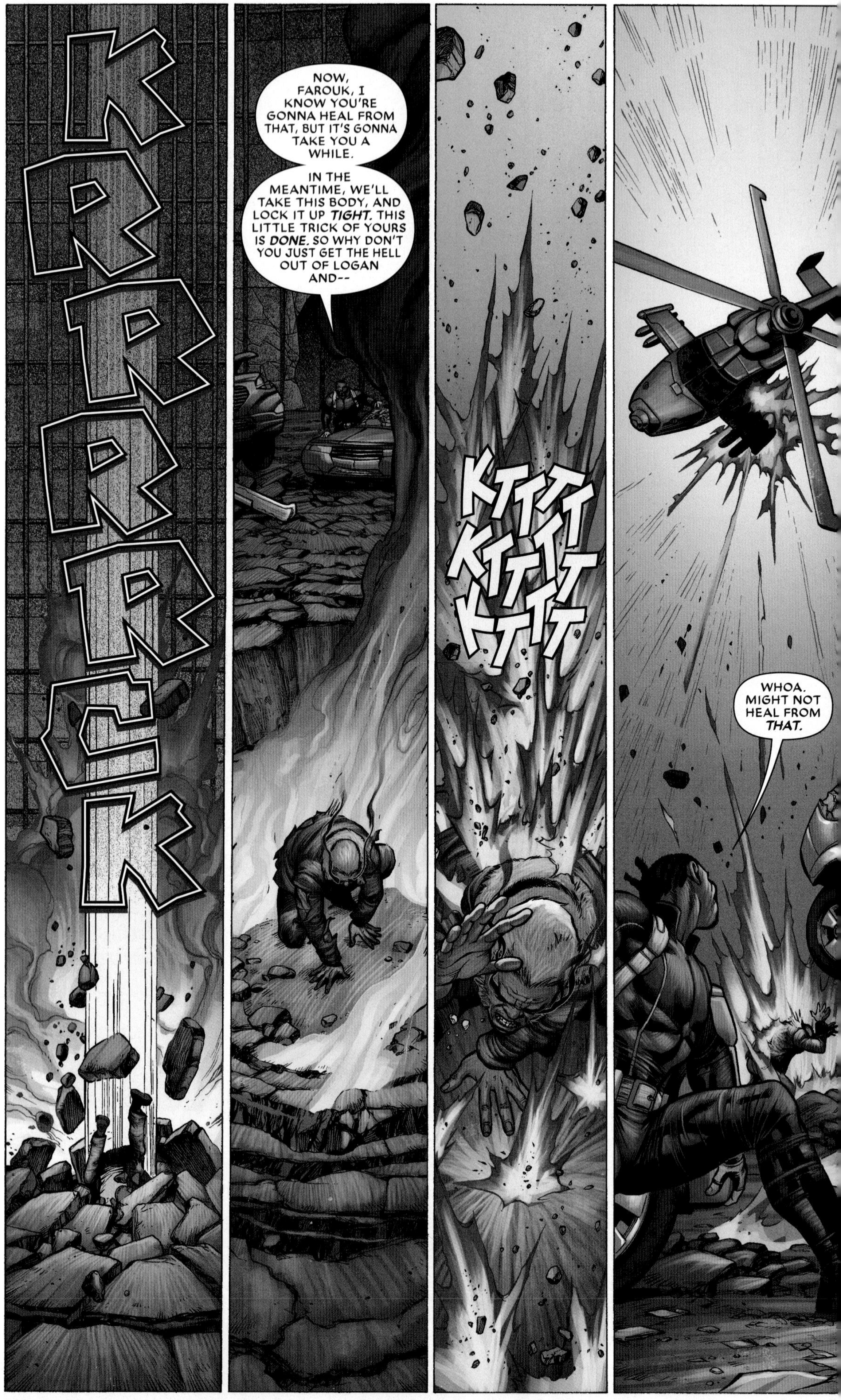
KRRRCK
NOW, FAROUK, I KNOW YOU'RE GONNA HEAL FROM THAT, BUT IT'S GONNA TAKE YOU A WHILE.
IN THE MEANTIME, WE'LL TAKE THIS BODY, AND LOCK IT UP TIGHT. THIS LITTLE TRICK OF YOURS IS DONE. SO WHY DON'T YOU JUST GET THE HELL OUT OF LOGAN AND--
KTTT KTTTT KTTT
WHOA. MIGHT NOT HEAL FROM THAT.

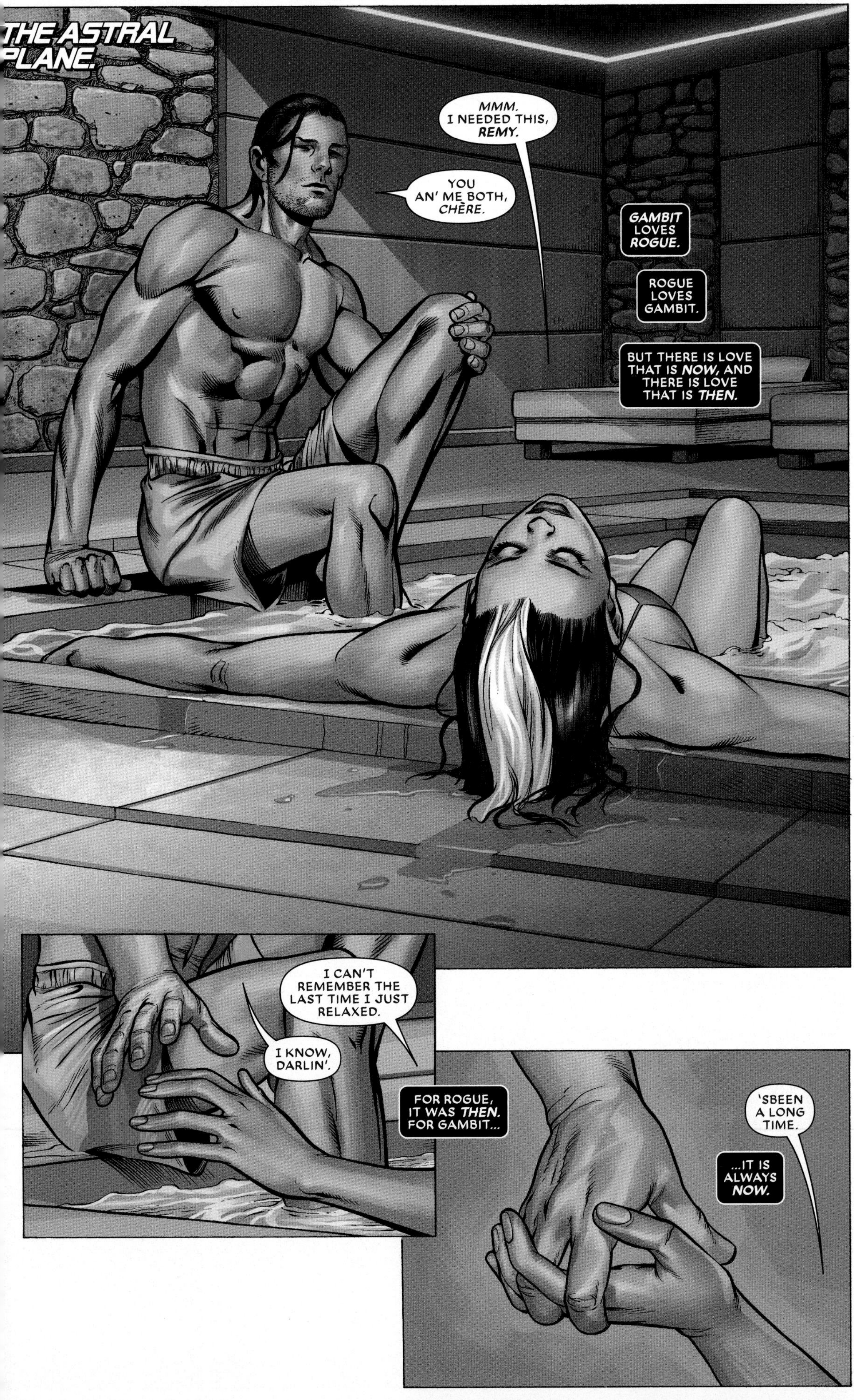
THE ASTRAL PLANE.
MMM. I NEEDED THIS, REMY.
YOU AN' ME BOTH, CHÈRE.
GAMBIT LOVES ROGUE.
ROGUE LOVES GAMBIT.
BUT THERE IS LOVE THAT IS NOW, AND THERE IS LOVE THAT IS THEN.
I CAN'T REMEMBER THE LAST TIME I JUST RELAXED.
I KNOW, DARLIN'.
FOR ROGUE, IT WAS THEN. FOR GAMBIT...
'SBEEN A LONG TIME.
...IT IS ALWAYS NOW.

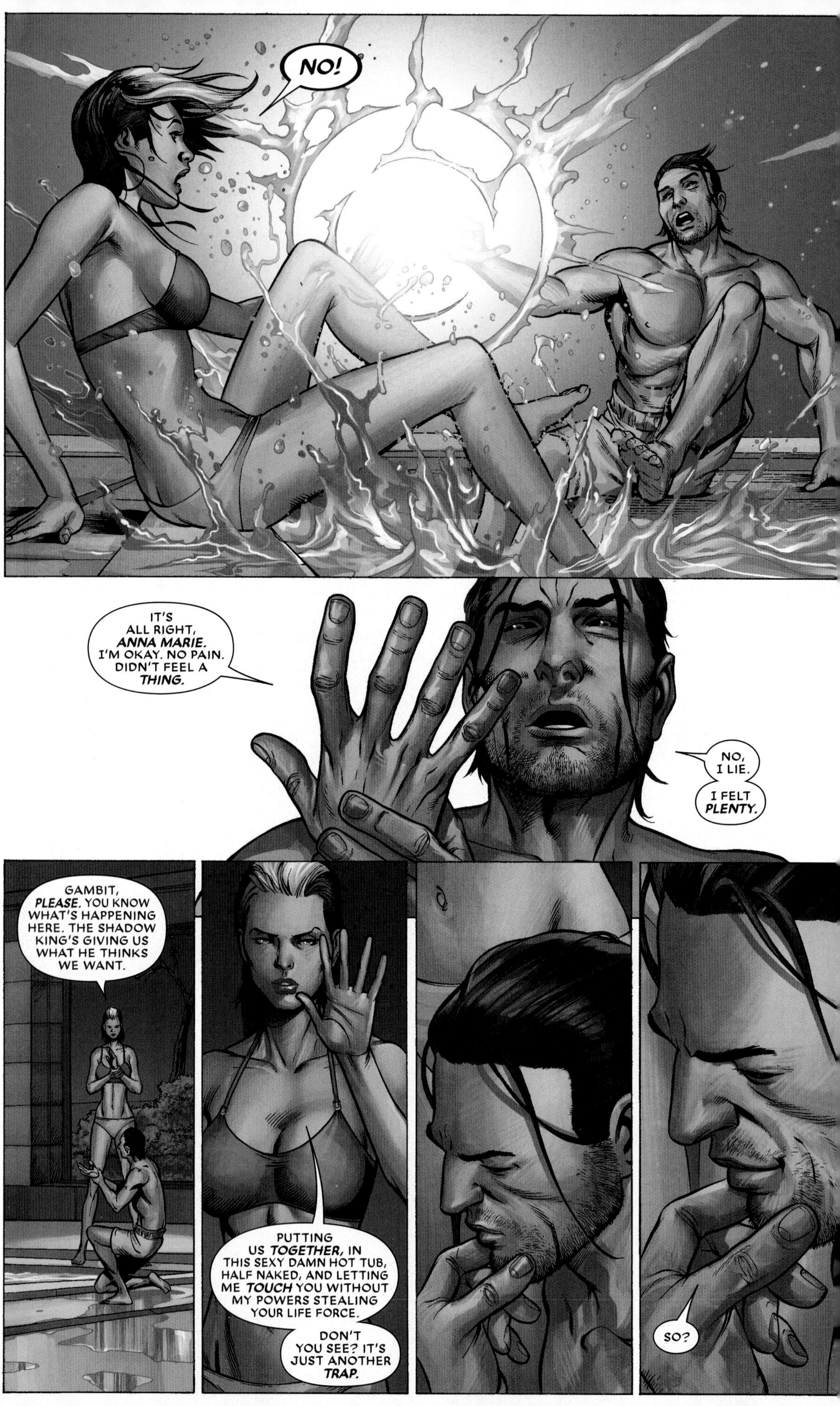
NO!
IT'S ALL RIGHT, ANNA MARIE. I'M OKAY. NO PAIN. DIDN'T FEEL A THING.
NO, I LIE.
I FELT PLENTY.
GAMBIT, PLEASE. YOU KNOW WHAT'S HAPPENING HERE. THE SHADOW KING'S GIVING US WHAT HE THINKS WE WANT.
PUTTING US TOGETHER, IN THIS SEXY DAMN HOT TUB, HALF NAKED, AND LETTING ME TOUCH YOU WITHOUT MY POWERS STEALING YOUR LIFE FORCE.
DON'T YOU SEE? IT'S JUST ANOTHER TRAP.
SO?

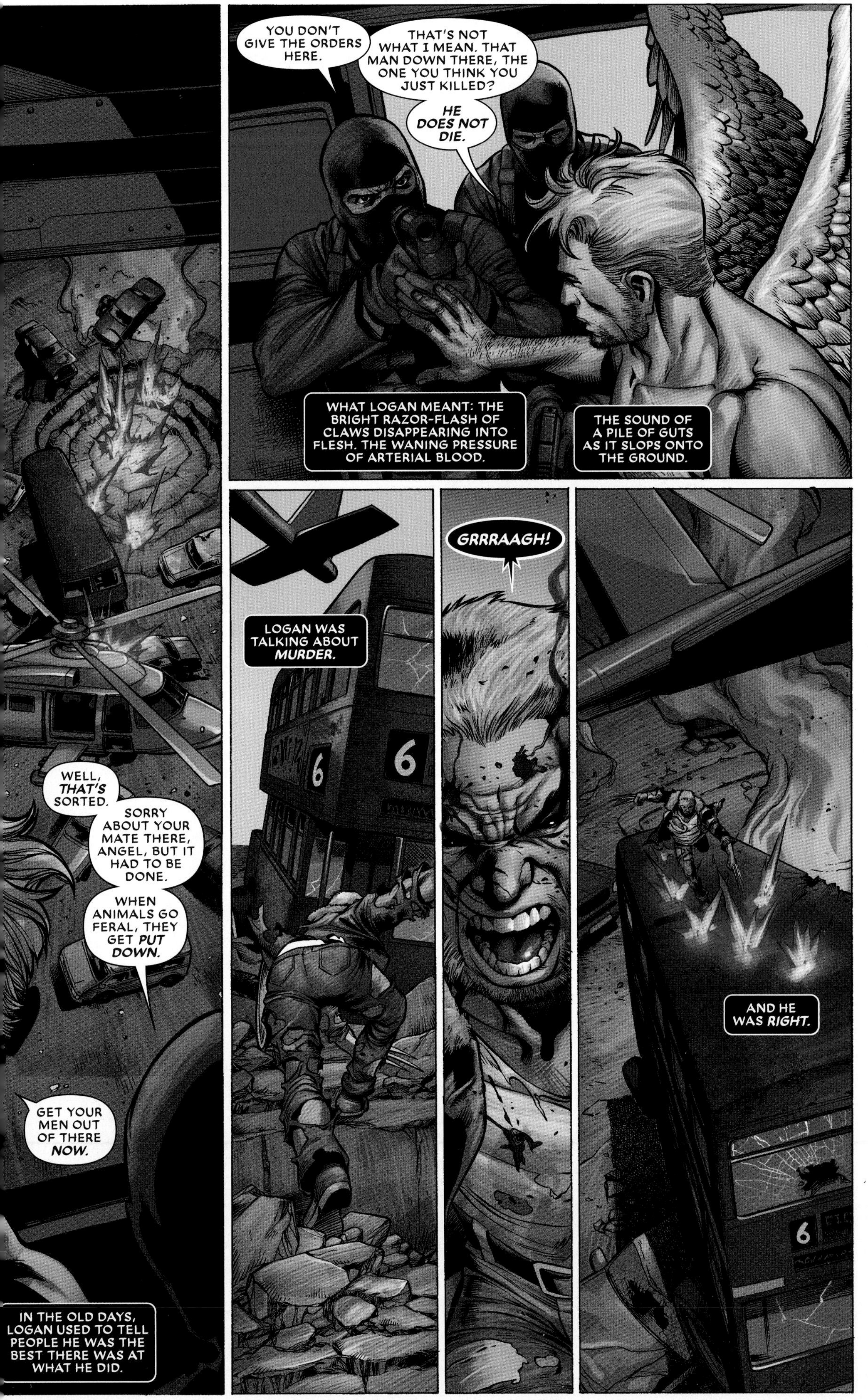
YOU DON'T GIVE THE ORDERS HERE.
THAT'S NOT WHAT I MEAN. THAT MAN DOWN THERE, THE ONE YOU THINK YOU JUST KILLED?
HE DOES NOT DIE.
WHAT LOGAN MEANT: THE BRIGHT RAZOR-FLASH OF CLAWS DISAPPEARING INTO FLESH. THE WANING PRESSURE OF ARTERIAL BLOOD.
THE SOUND OF A PILE OF GUTS AS IT SLOPS ONTO THE GROUND.
WELL, THAT'S SORTED.
SORRY ABOUT YOUR MATE THERE, ANGEL, BUT IT HAD TO BE DONE.
WHEN ANIMALS GO FERAL, THEY GET PUT DOWN.
GET YOUR MEN OUT OF THERE NOW.
IN THE OLD DAYS, LOGAN USED TO TELL PEOPLE HE WAS THE BEST THERE WAS AT WHAT HE DID.
LOGAN WAS TALKING ABOUT MURDER.
GRRRAAGH!
AND HE WAS RIGHT.

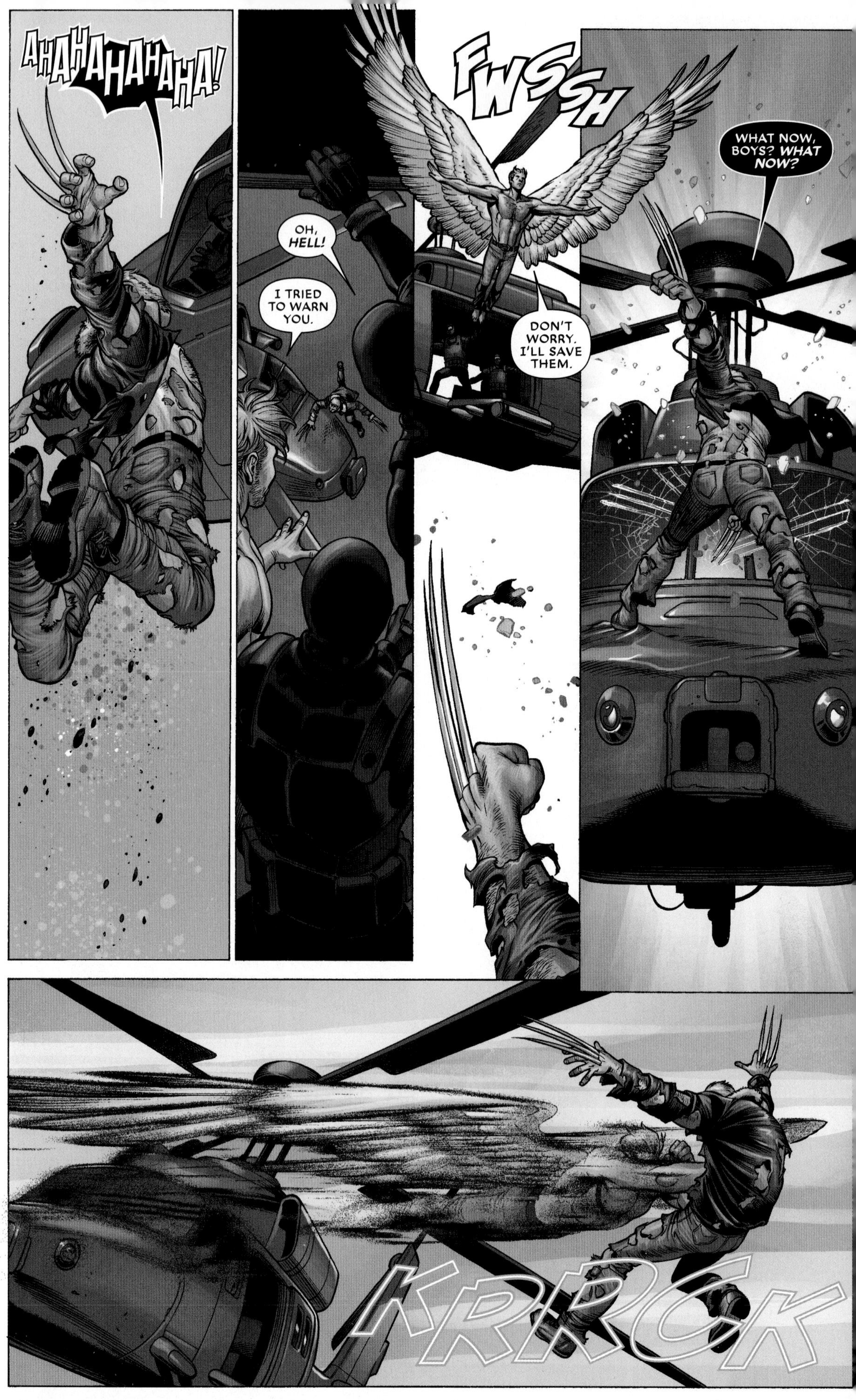
AHAHAHAHAHA!
OH, HELL!
I TRIED TO WARN YOU.
FWSSH
DON'T WORRY. I'LL SAVE THEM.
WHAT NOW, BOYS? WHAT NOW?
KRRCK

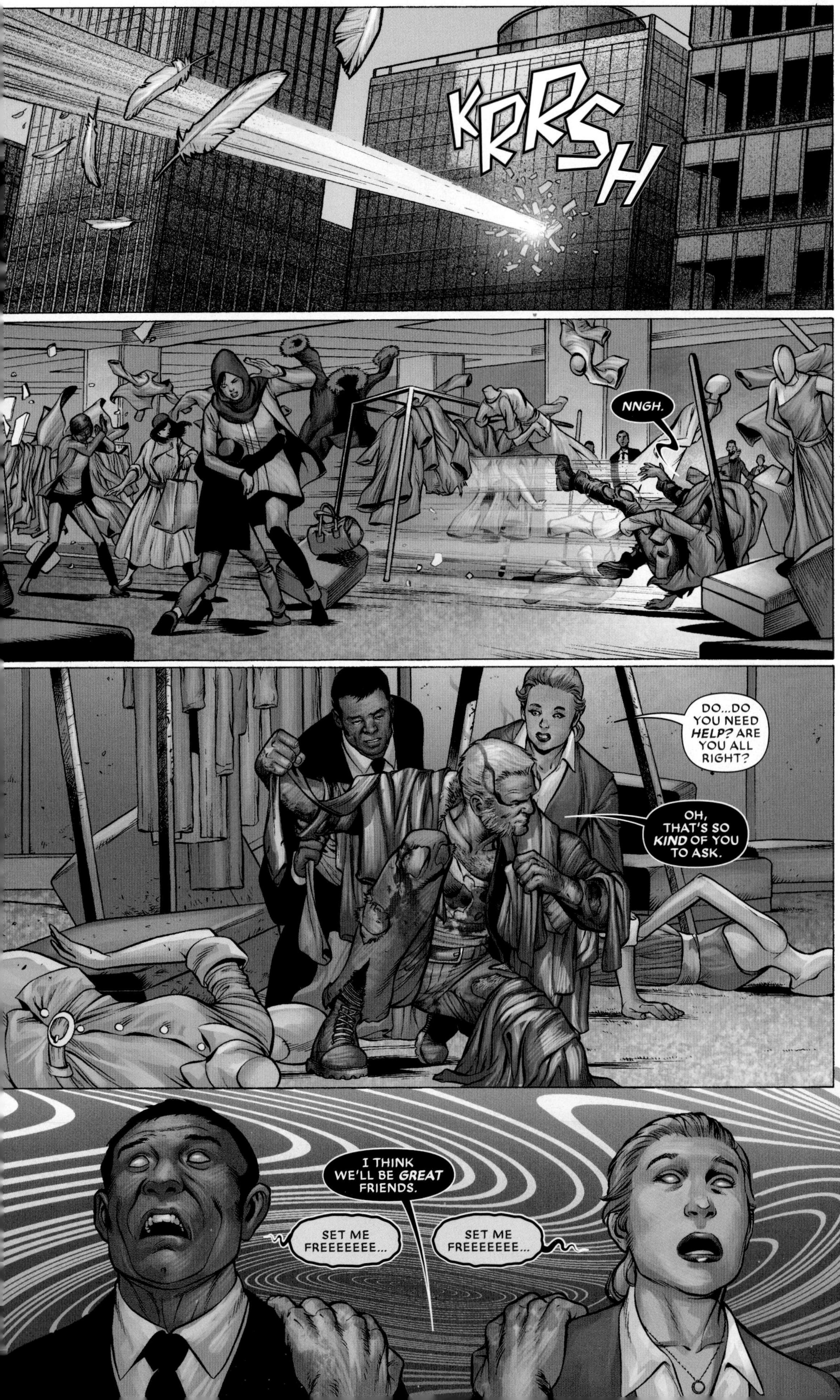
KRRSH
NNGH.
DO...DO YOU NEED HELP? ARE YOU ALL RIGHT?
OH, THAT'S SO KIND OF YOU TO ASK.
I THINK WE'LL BE GREAT FRIENDS.
SET ME FREEEEEEE...
SET ME FREEEEEEE...

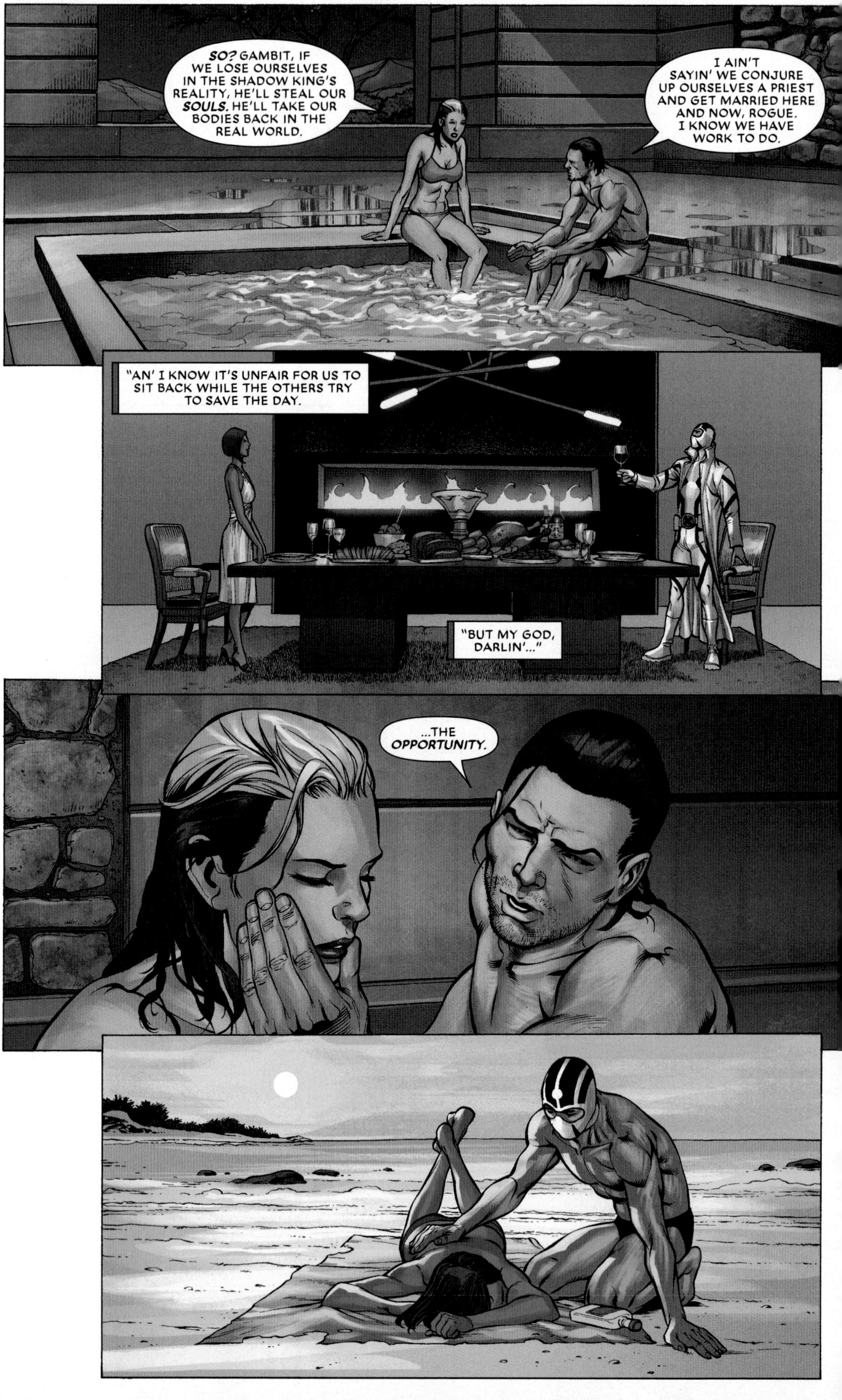
SO? GAMBIT, IF WE LOSE OURSELVES IN THE SHADOW KING'S REALITY, HE'LL STEAL OUR SOULS. HE'LL TAKE OUR BODIES BACK IN THE REAL WORLD.
I AIN'T SAYIN' WE CONJURE UP OURSELVES A PRIEST AND GET MARRIED HERE AND NOW, ROGUE. I KNOW WE HAVE WORK TO DO.
"AN' I KNOW IT'S UNFAIR FOR US TO SIT BACK WHILE THE OTHERS TRY TO SAVE THE DAY.
"BUT MY GOD, DARLIN'..."
...THE OPPORTUNITY.

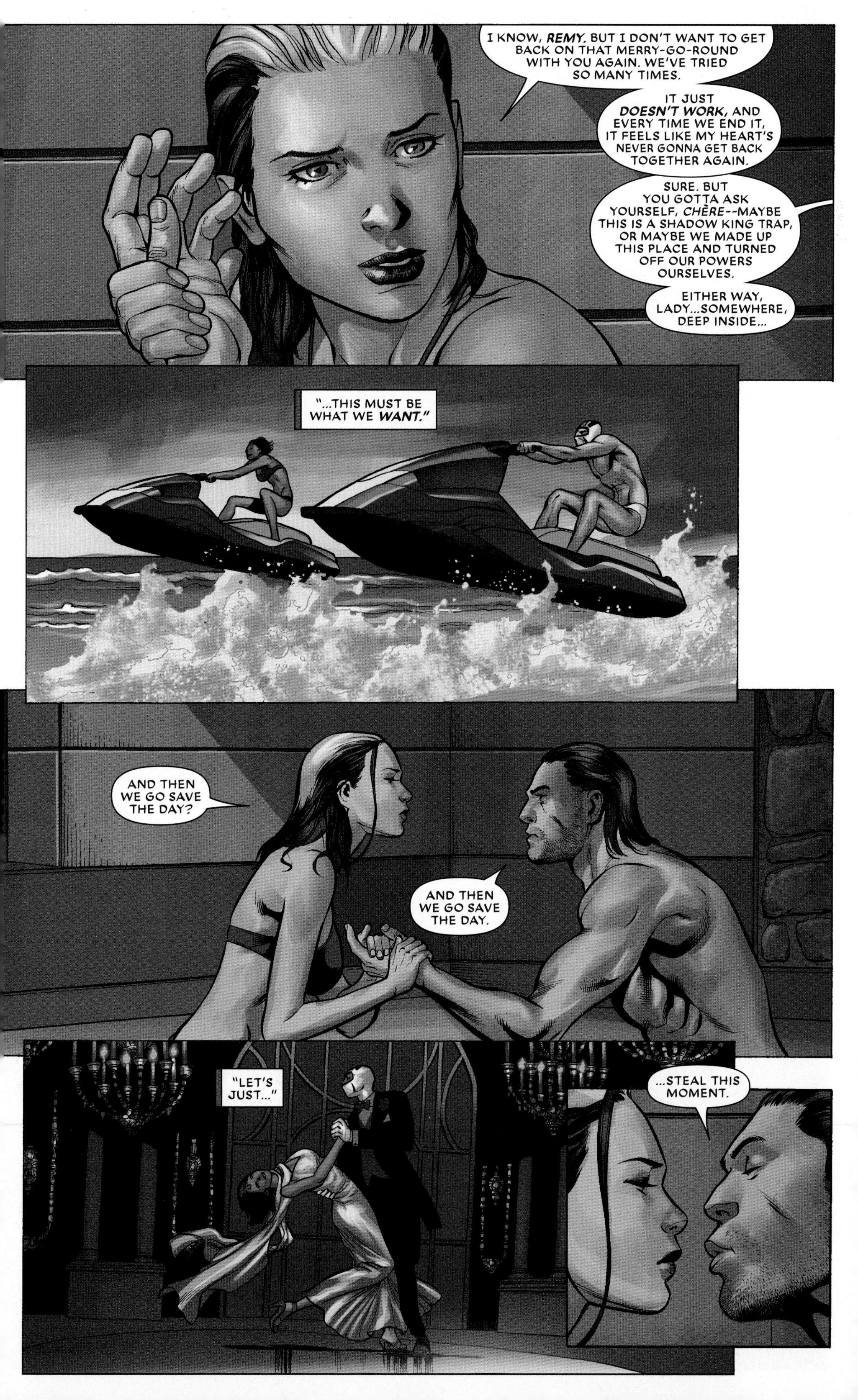
I KNOW, REMY. BUT I DON'T WANT TO GET BACK ON THAT MERRY-GO-ROUND WITH YOU AGAIN. WE'VE TRIED SO MANY TIMES.
IT JUST DOESN'T WORK, AND EVERY TIME WE END IT, IT FEELS LIKE MY HEART'S NEVER GONNA GET BACK TOGETHER AGAIN.
SURE. BUT YOU GOTTA ASK YOURSELF, CHÈRE--MAYBE THIS IS A SHADOW KING TRAP, OR MAYBE WE MADE UP THIS PLACE AND TURNED OFF OUR POWERS OURSELVES.
EITHER WAY, LADY...SOMEWHERE, DEEP INSIDE...
"...THIS MUST BE WHAT WE WANT."
AND THEN WE GO SAVE THE DAY?
AND THEN WE GO SAVE THE DAY.
"LET'S JUST..."
...STEAL THIS MOMENT.

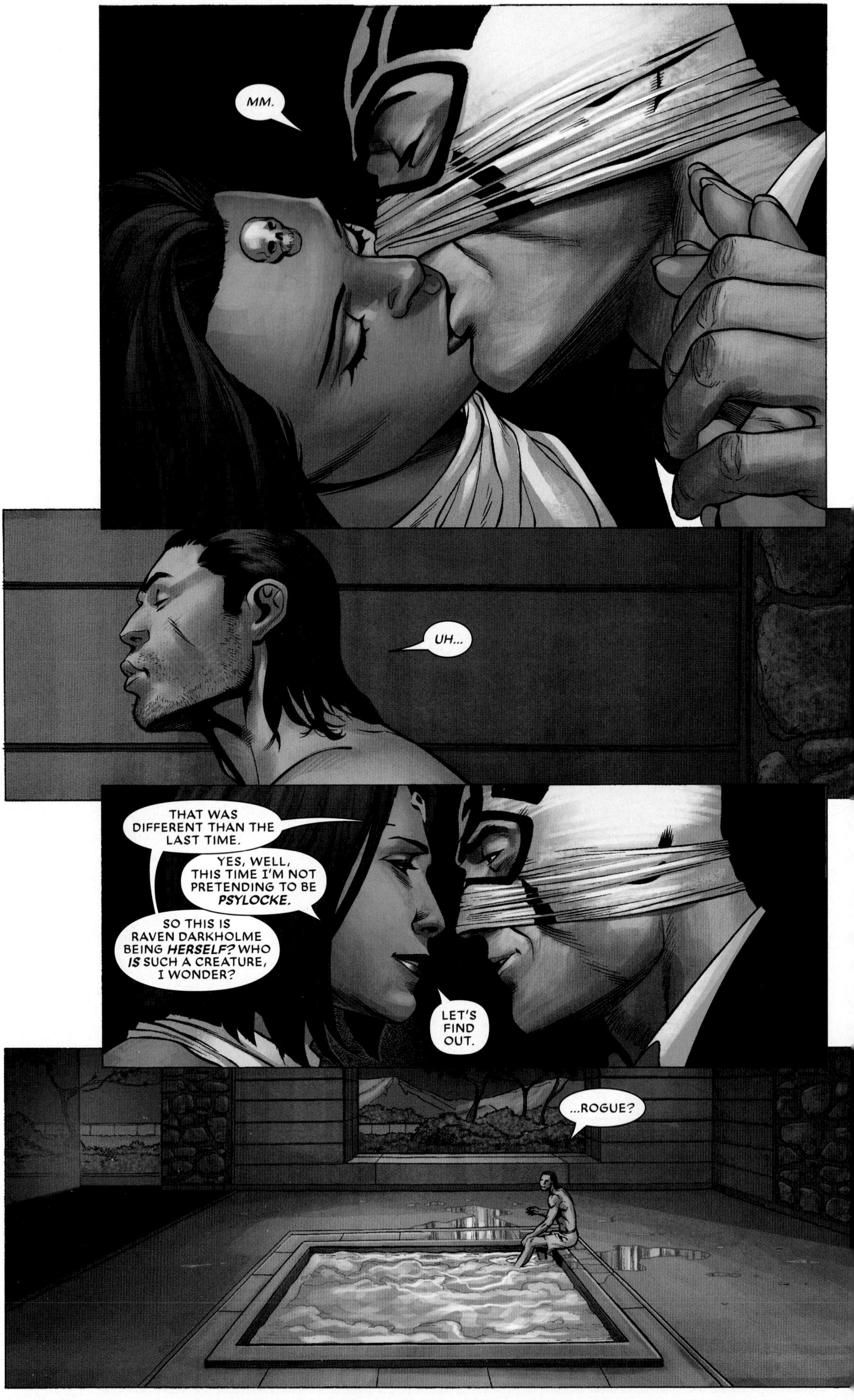
MM.
UH...
THAT WAS DIFFERENT THAN THE LAST TIME.
YES, WELL, THIS TIME I'M NOT PRETENDING TO BE PSYLOCKE.
SO THIS IS RAVEN DARKHOLME BEING HERSELF? WHO IS SUCH A CREATURE, I WONDER?
LET'S FIND OUT.
...ROGUE?

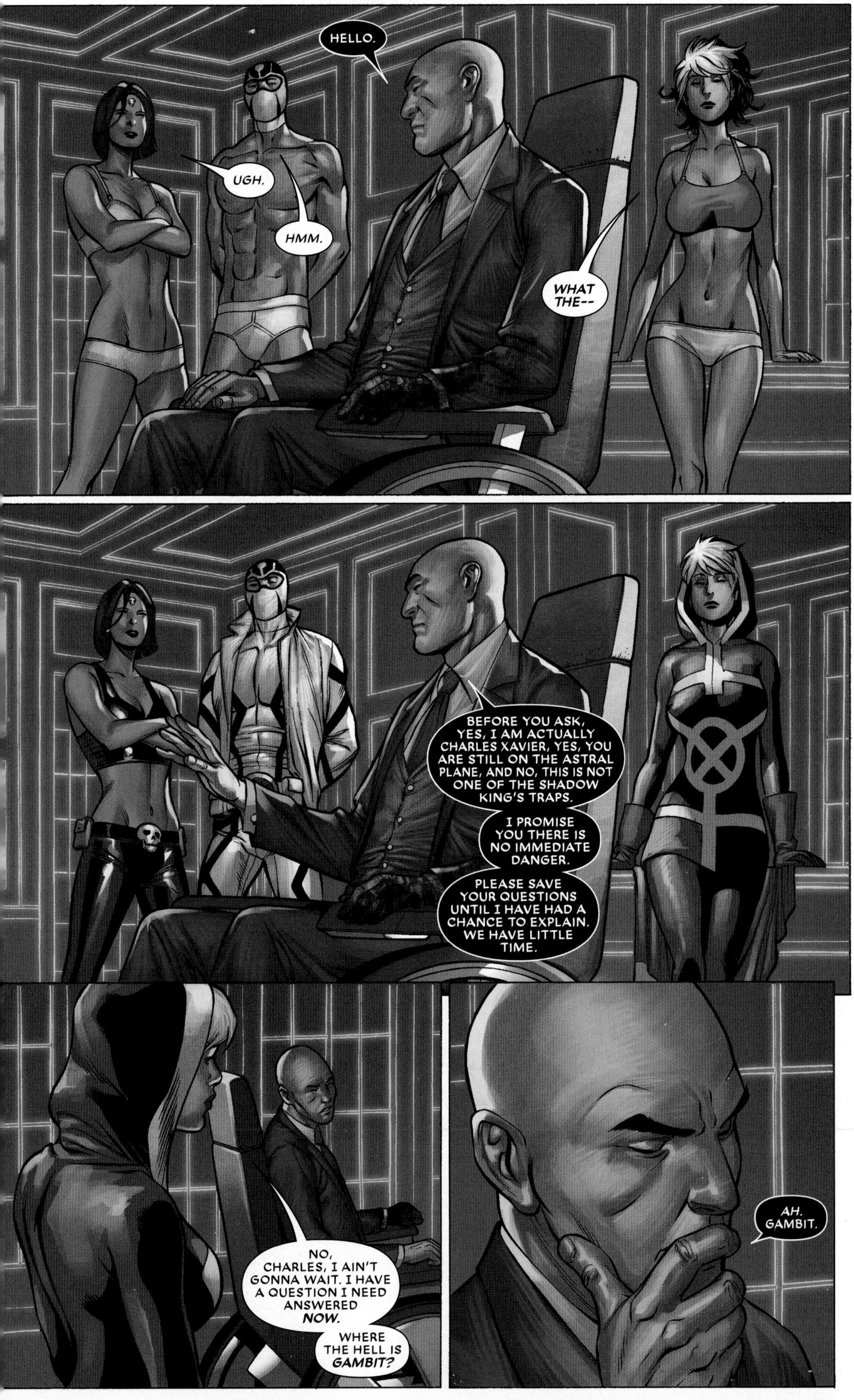
HELLO.
UGH.
HMM.
WHAT THE--
BEFORE YOU ASK, YES, I AM ACTUALLY CHARLES XAVIER, YES, YOU ARE STILL ON THE ASTRAL PLANE, AND NO, THIS IS NOT ONE OF THE SHADOW KING'S TRAPS.
I PROMISE YOU THERE IS NO IMMEDIATE DANGER.
PLEASE SAVE YOUR QUESTIONS UNTIL I HAVE HAD A CHANCE TO EXPLAIN. WE HAVE LITTLE TIME.
NO, CHARLES, I AIN'T GONNA WAIT. I HAVE A QUESTION I NEED ANSWERED *NOW.*
WHERE THE HELL IS *GAMBIT?*
AH. GAMBIT.

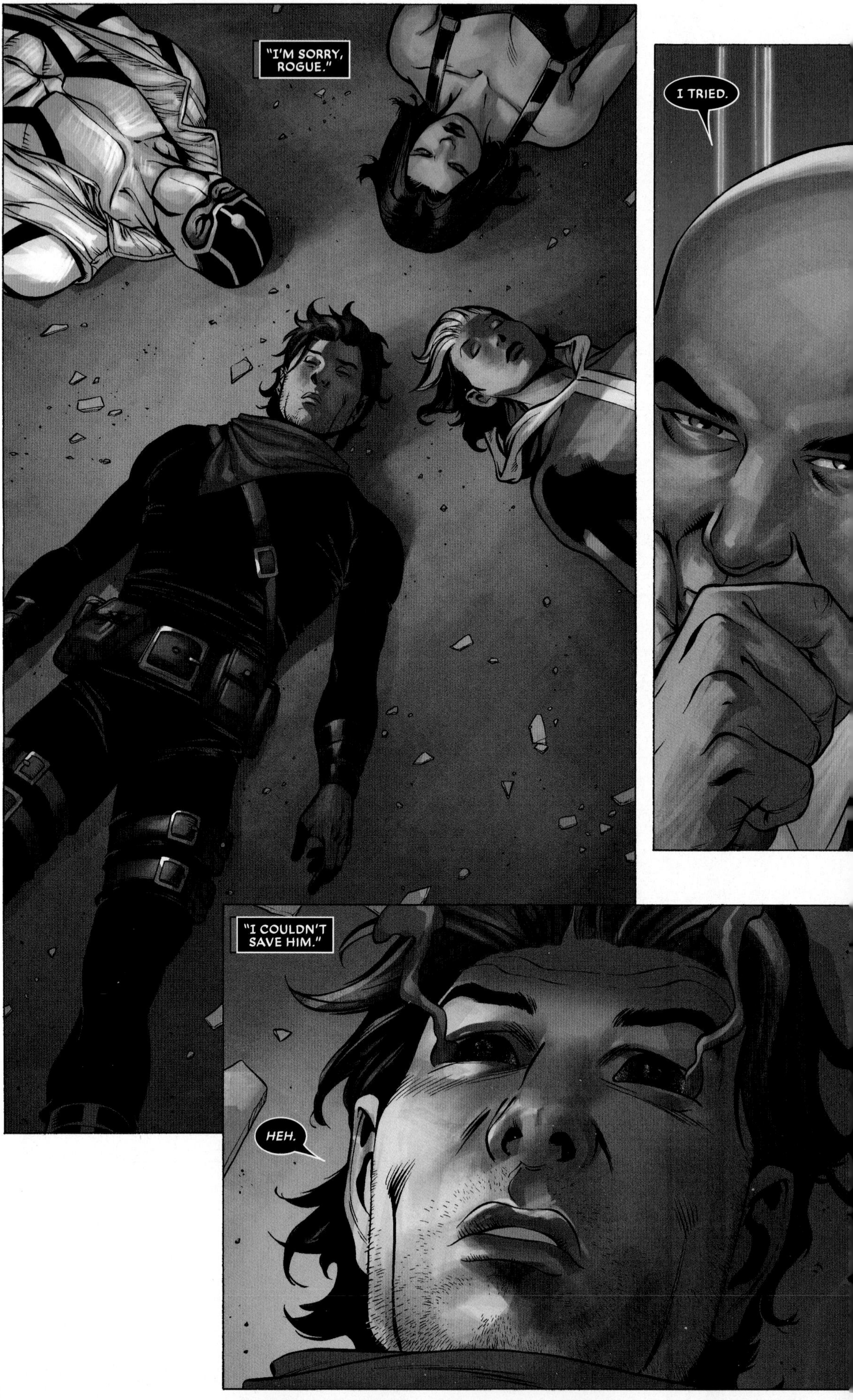
"I'M SORRY, ROGUE."
I TRIED.
"I COULDN'T SAVE HIM."
HEH.

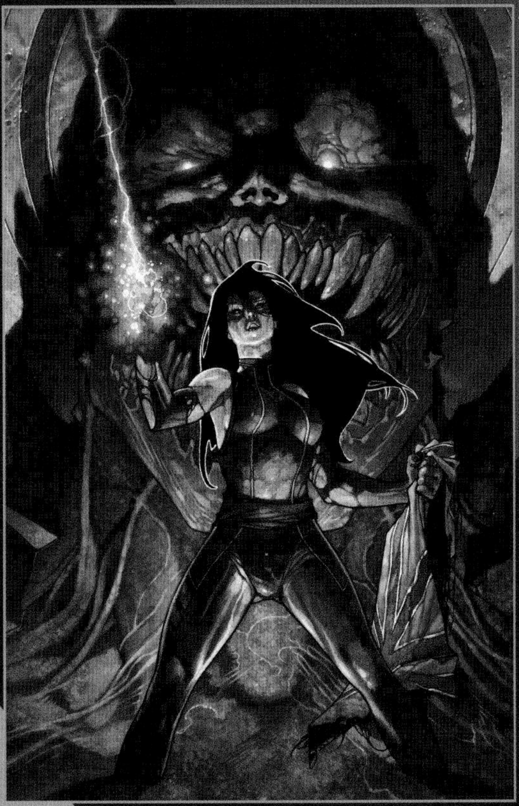

#3 VARIANT
BY **SIMONE BIANCHI**

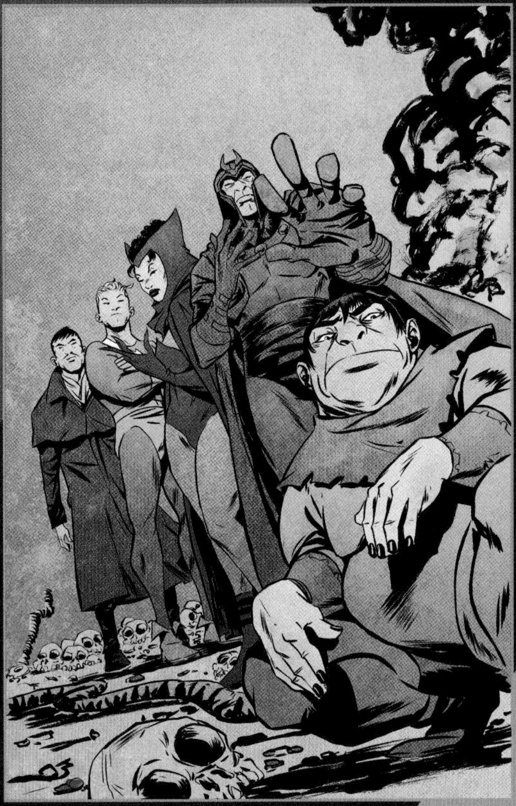

#3 VARIANT
BY **SANFORD GREENE**

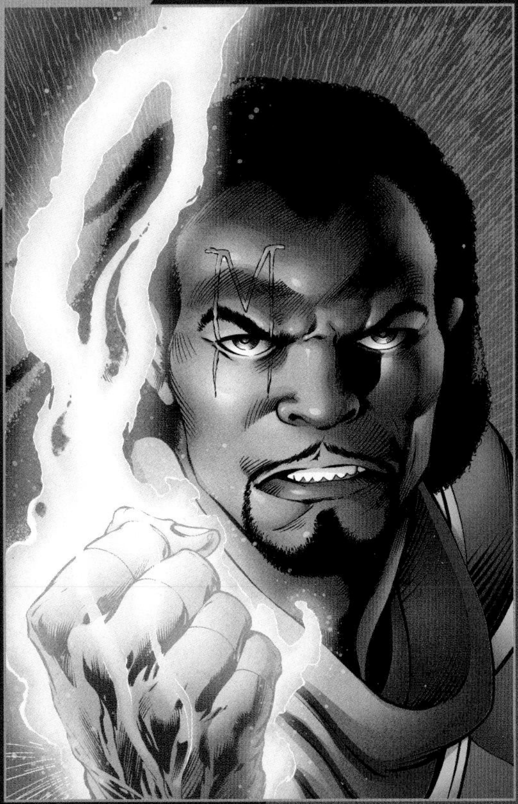

#3 VARIANT
BY **ALAN DAVIS, MARK FARMER**
& **MATT YACKEY**

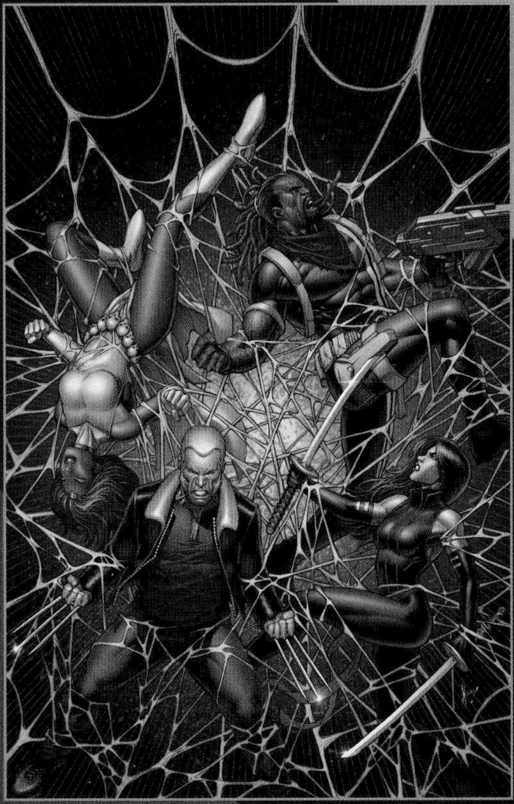

#3 VARIANT
BY **DALE KEOWN**

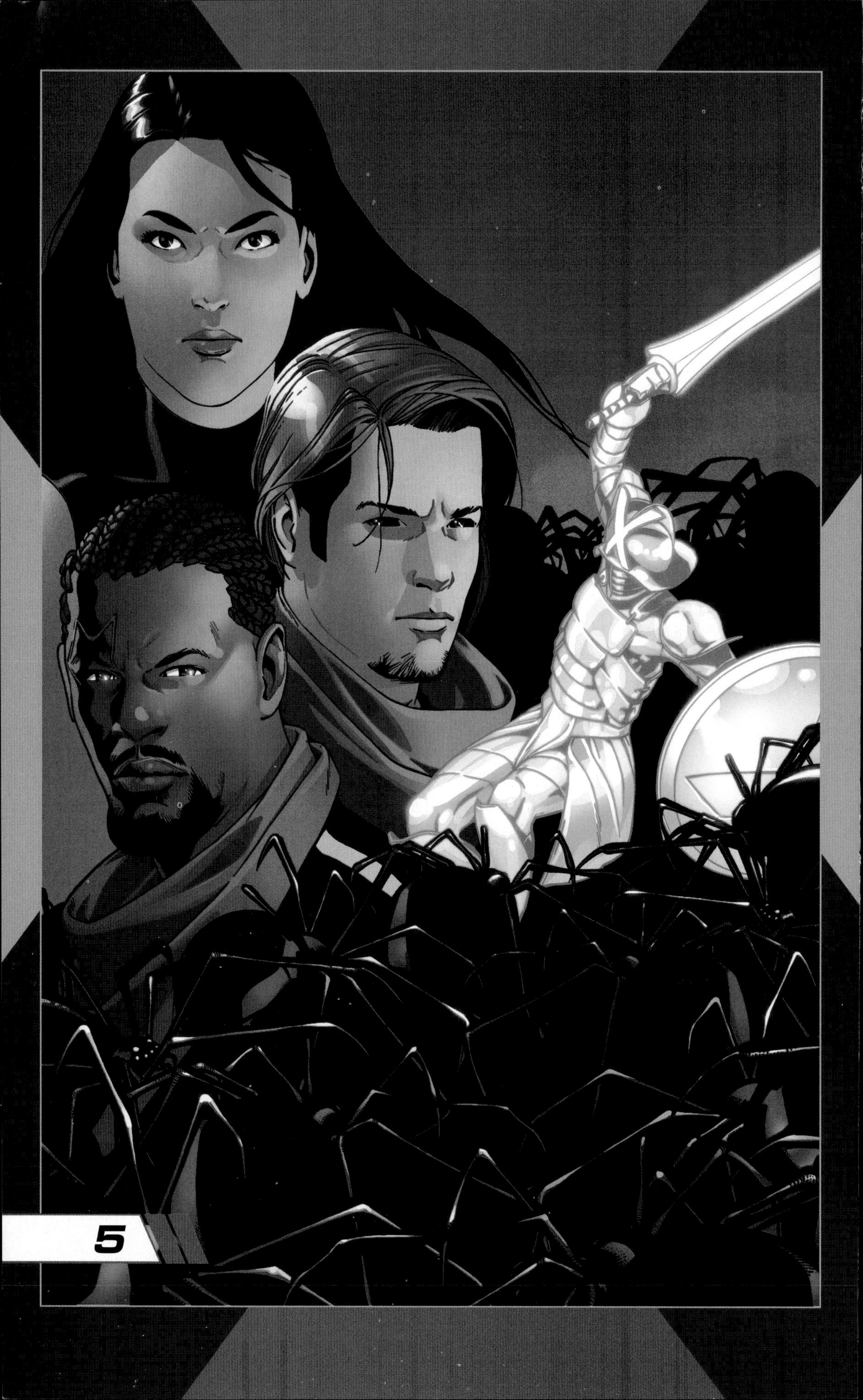

5

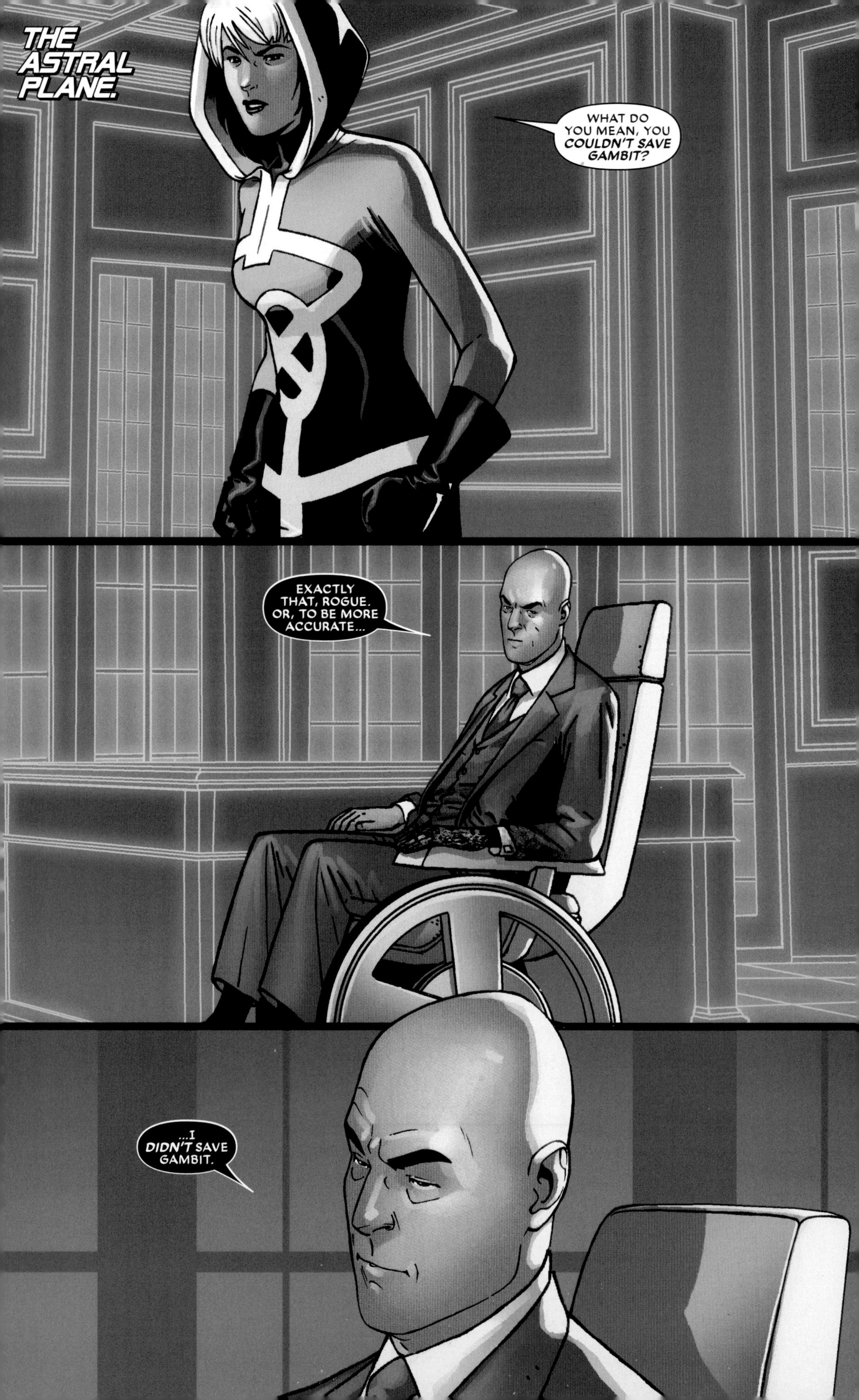
THE ASTRAL PLANE.
WHAT DO YOU MEAN, YOU COULDN'T SAVE GAMBIT?
EXACTLY THAT, ROGUE. OR, TO BE MORE ACCURATE...
...I DIDN'T SAVE GAMBIT.

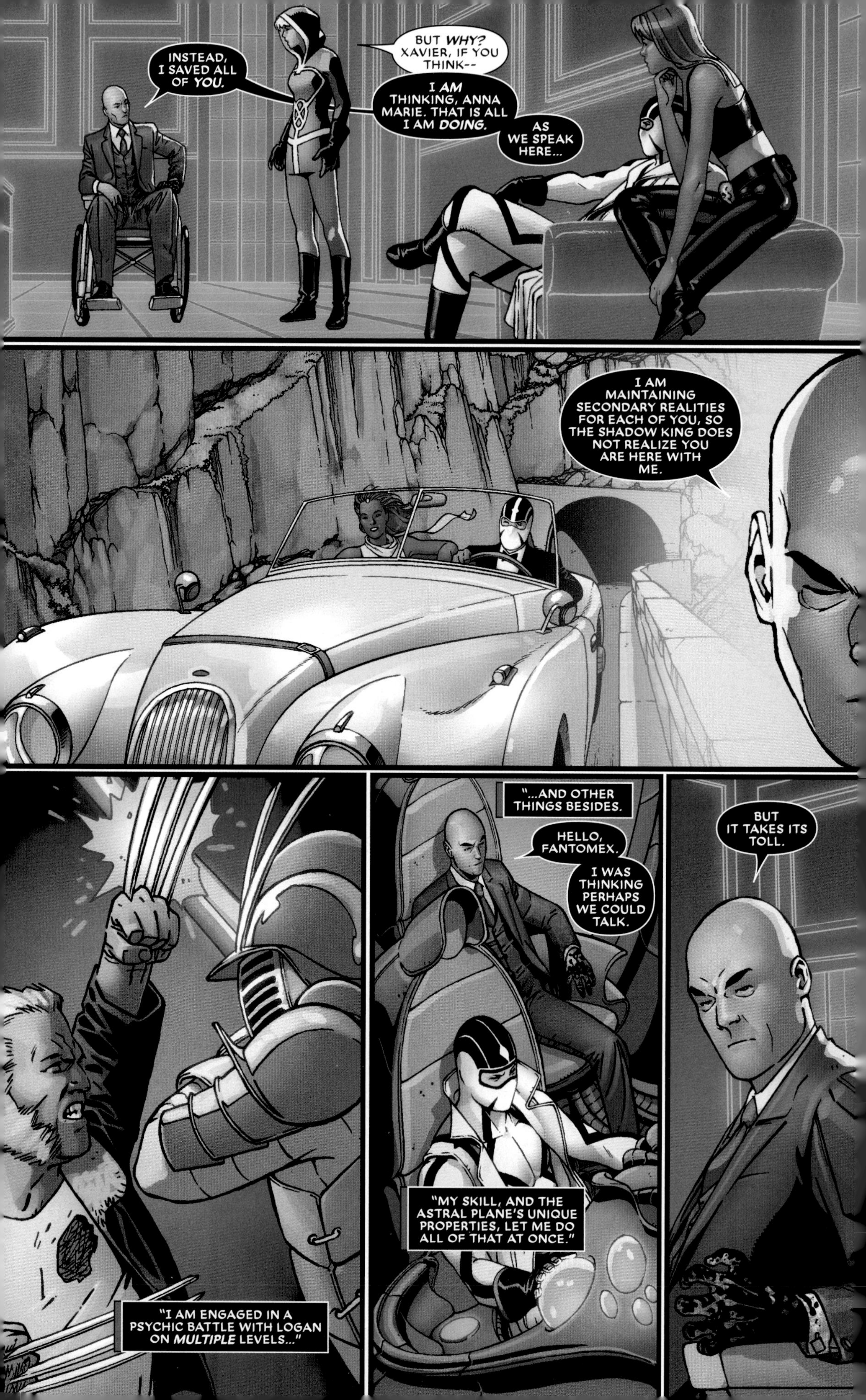
INSTEAD, I SAVED ALL OF YOU.
BUT WHY? XAVIER, IF YOU THINK--
I AM THINKING, ANNA MARIE. THAT IS ALL I AM DOING.
AS WE SPEAK HERE...
I AM MAINTAINING SECONDARY REALITIES FOR EACH OF YOU, SO THE SHADOW KING DOES NOT REALIZE YOU ARE HERE WITH ME.
"I AM ENGAGED IN A PSYCHIC BATTLE WITH LOGAN ON MULTIPLE LEVELS..."
"...AND OTHER THINGS BESIDES.
HELLO, FANTOMEX.
I WAS THINKING PERHAPS WE COULD TALK.
"MY SKILL, AND THE ASTRAL PLANE'S UNIQUE PROPERTIES, LET ME DO ALL OF THAT AT ONCE."
BUT IT TAKES ITS TOLL.

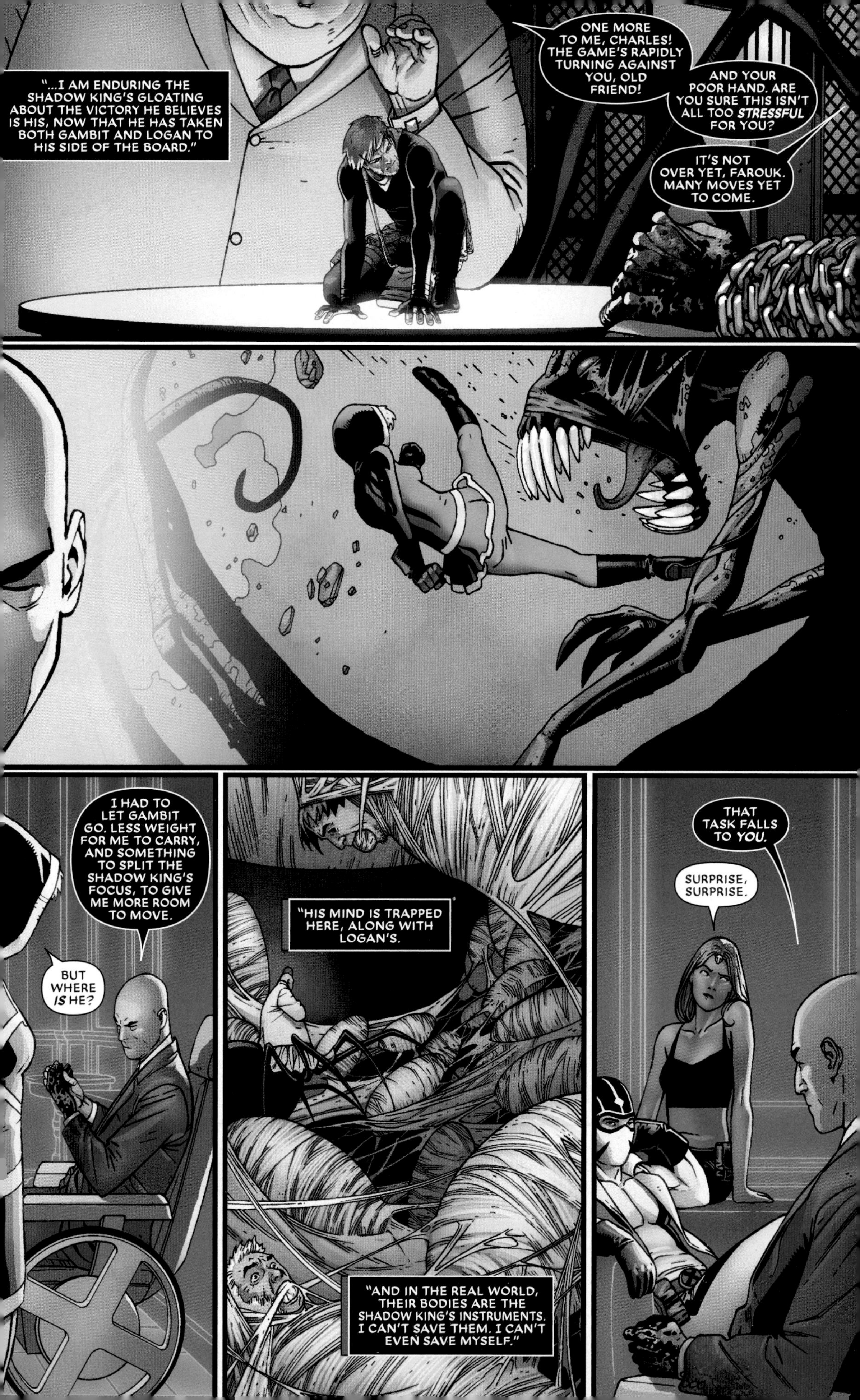
"...I AM ENDURING THE SHADOW KING'S GLOATING ABOUT THE VICTORY HE BELIEVES IS HIS, NOW THAT HE HAS TAKEN BOTH GAMBIT AND LOGAN TO HIS SIDE OF THE BOARD."
ONE MORE TO ME, CHARLES! THE GAME'S RAPIDLY TURNING AGAINST YOU, OLD FRIEND!
AND YOUR POOR HAND. ARE YOU SURE THIS ISN'T ALL TOO *STRESSFUL* FOR YOU?
IT'S NOT OVER YET, FAROUK. MANY MOVES YET TO COME.
I HAD TO LET GAMBIT GO. LESS WEIGHT FOR ME TO CARRY, AND SOMETHING TO SPLIT THE SHADOW KING'S FOCUS, TO GIVE ME MORE ROOM TO MOVE.
BUT WHERE *IS* HE?
"HIS MIND IS TRAPPED HERE, ALONG WITH LOGAN'S.
"AND IN THE REAL WORLD, THEIR BODIES ARE THE SHADOW KING'S INSTRUMENTS. I CAN'T SAVE THEM. I CAN'T EVEN SAVE MYSELF."
THAT TASK FALLS TO *YOU.*
SURPRISE, SURPRISE.

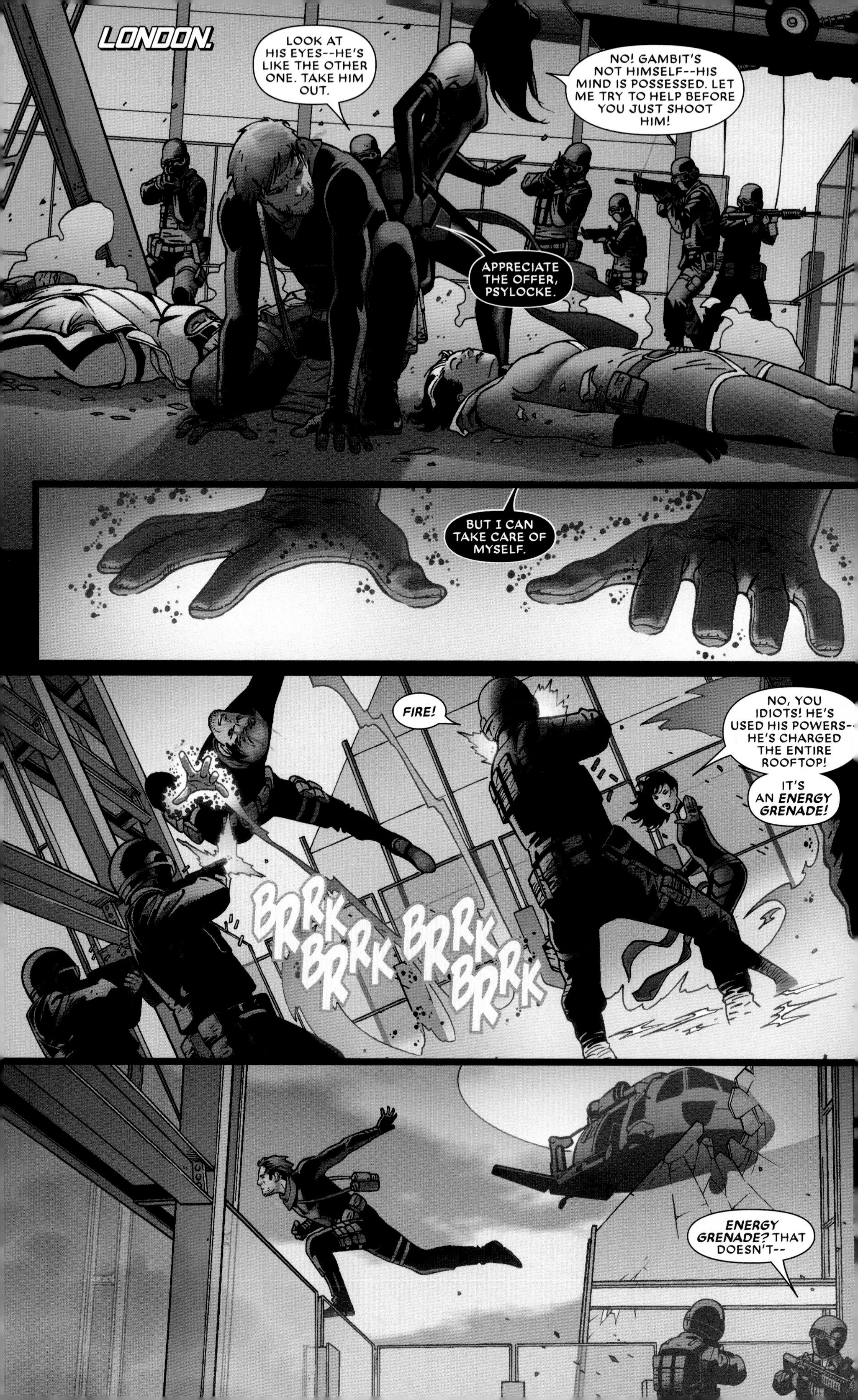
LONDON.
LOOK AT HIS EYES--HE'S LIKE THE OTHER ONE. TAKE HIM OUT.
NO! GAMBIT'S NOT HIMSELF--HIS MIND IS POSSESSED. LET ME TRY TO HELP BEFORE YOU JUST SHOOT HIM!
APPRECIATE THE OFFER, PSYLOCKE.
BUT I CAN TAKE CARE OF MYSELF.
FIRE!
NO, YOU IDIOTS! HE'S USED HIS POWERS-- HE'S CHARGED THE ENTIRE ROOFTOP!
IT'S AN ENERGY GRENADE!
BRRK BRRK BRRK BRRK
ENERGY GRENADE? THAT DOESN'T--

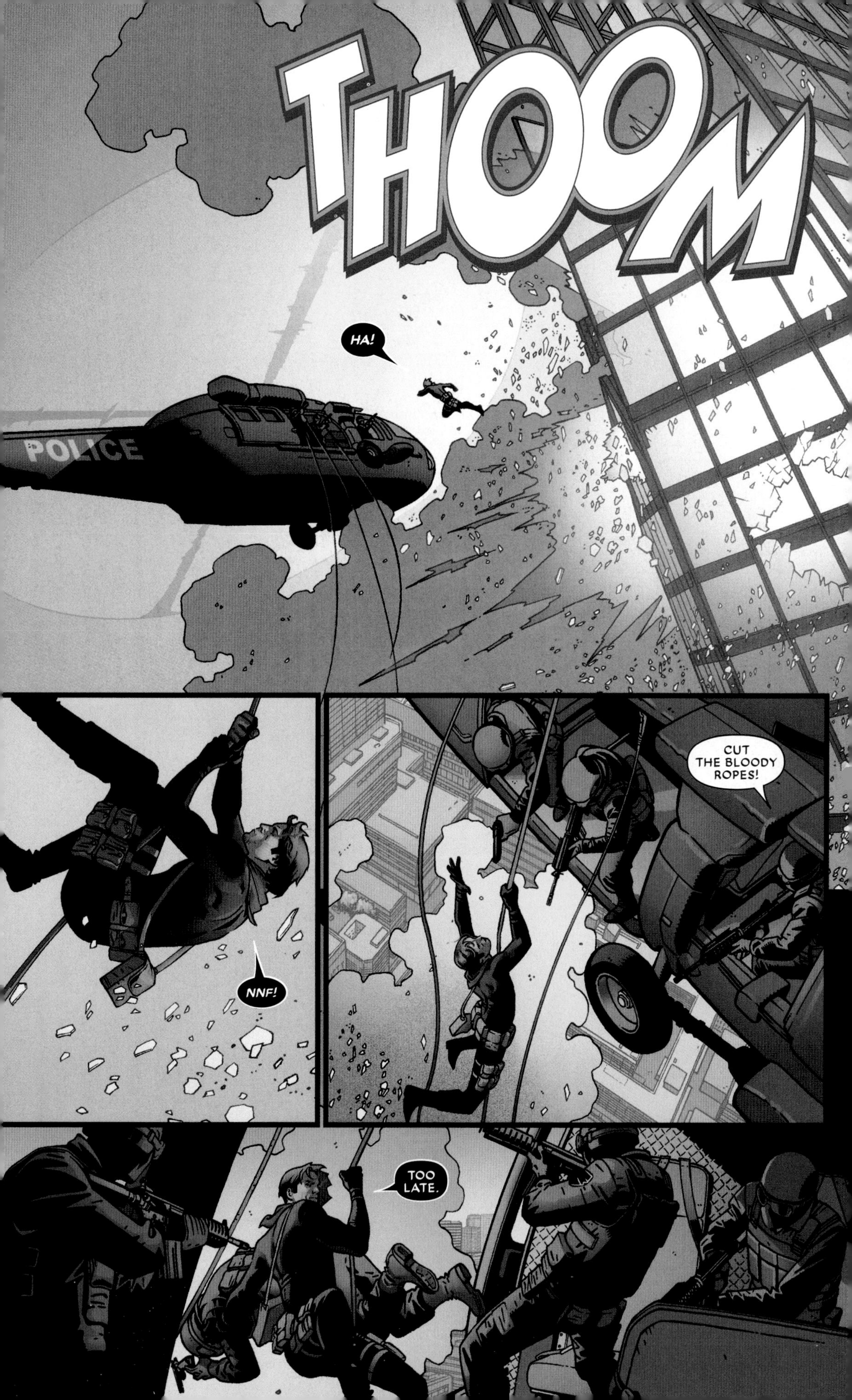
THOOM
HA!
POLICE
NNF!
CUT THE BLOODY ROPES!
TOO LATE.

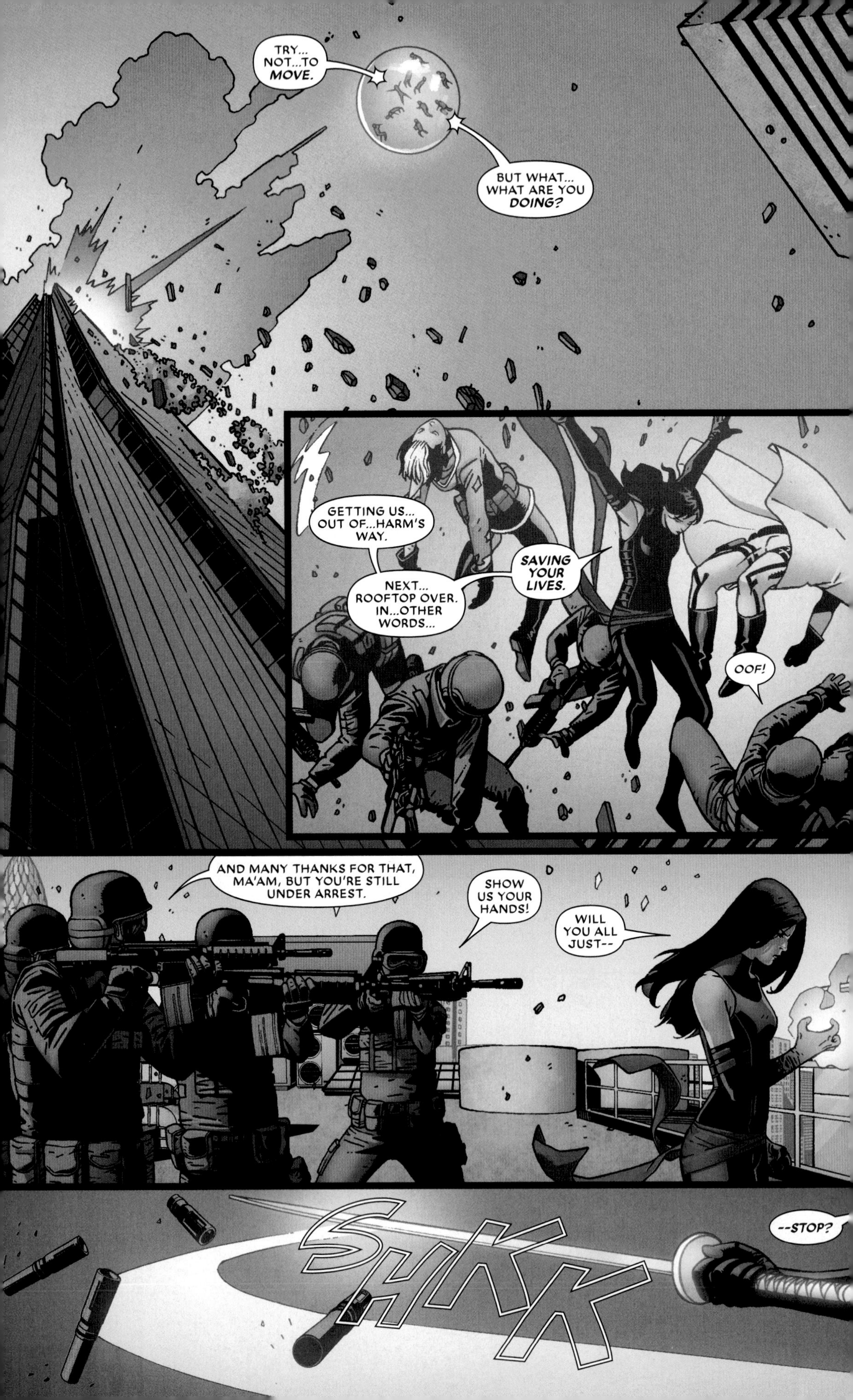

TRY... NOT...TO MOVE.
BUT WHAT... WHAT ARE YOU DOING?
GETTING US... OUT OF...HARM'S WAY.
NEXT... ROOFTOP OVER. IN...OTHER WORDS...
SAVING YOUR LIVES.
OOF!
AND MANY THANKS FOR THAT, MA'AM, BUT YOU'RE STILL UNDER ARREST.
SHOW US YOUR HANDS!
WILL YOU ALL JUST--
SHINK
--STOP?

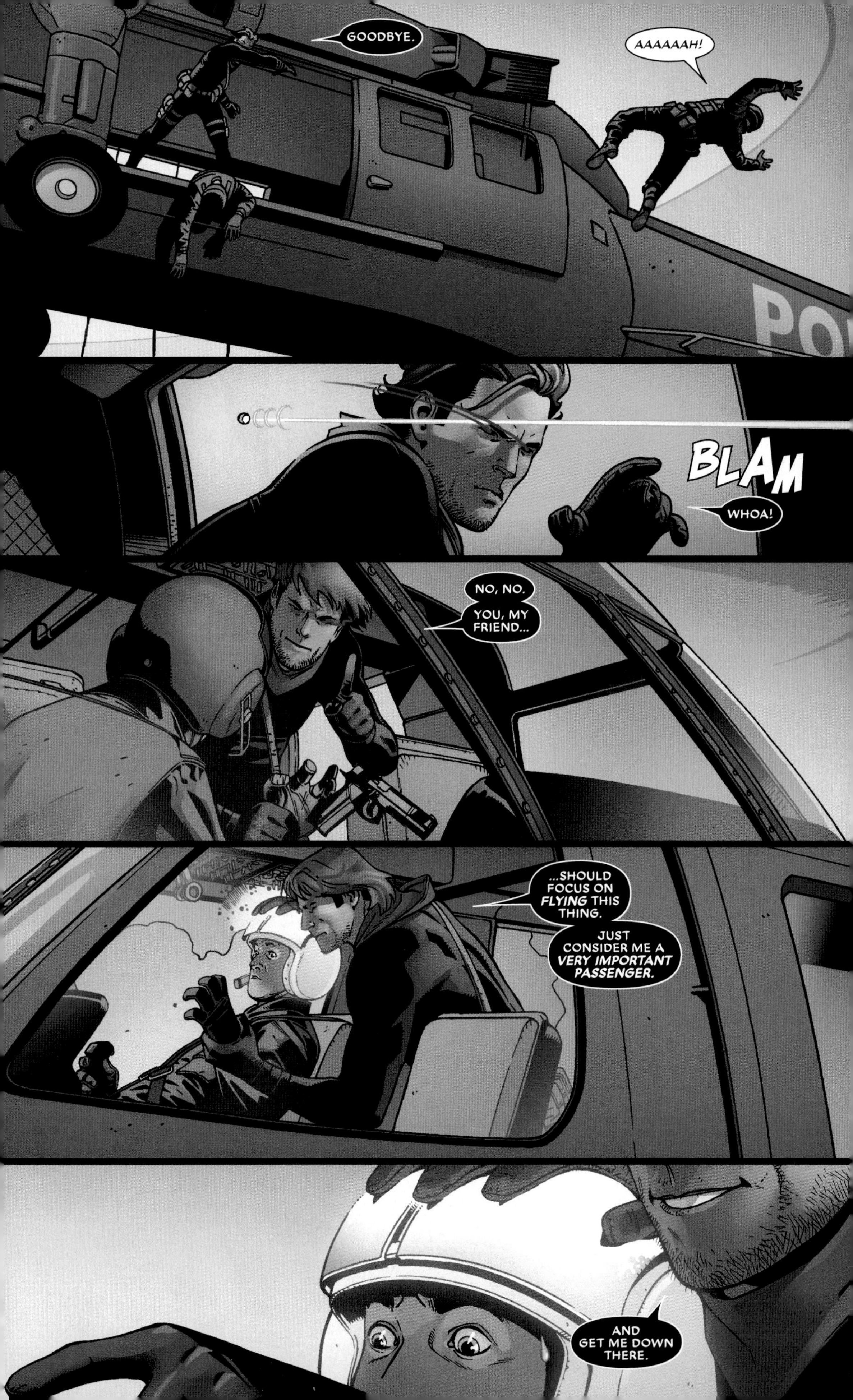
GOODBYE.
AAAAAAH!
BLAM
WHOA!
NO, NO.
YOU, MY FRIEND...
...SHOULD FOCUS ON FLYING THIS THING.
JUST CONSIDER ME A VERY IMPORTANT PASSENGER.
AND GET ME DOWN THERE.

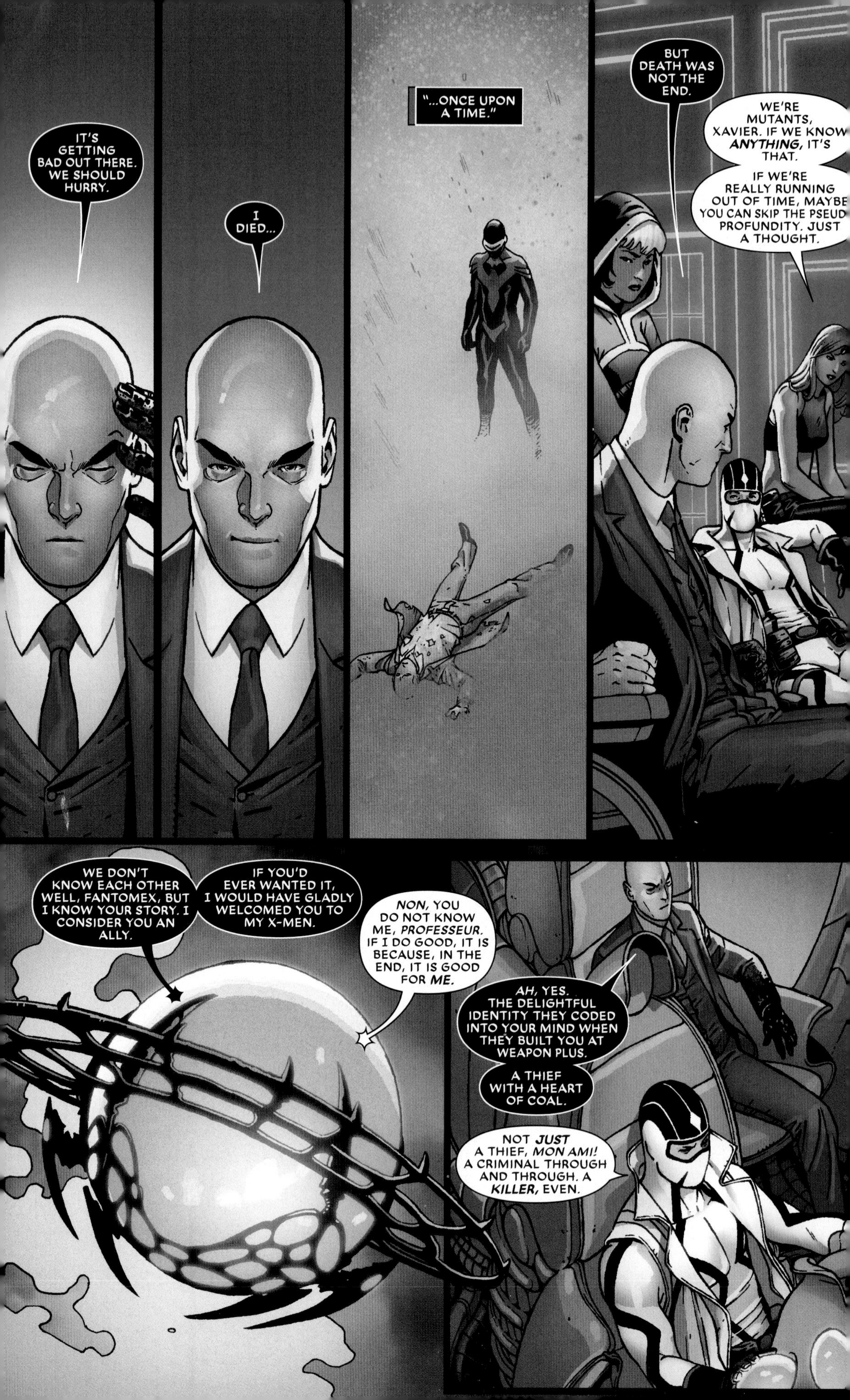
IT'S GETTING BAD OUT THERE. WE SHOULD HURRY.
I DIED...
"...ONCE UPON A TIME."
BUT DEATH WAS NOT THE END.
WE'RE MUTANTS, XAVIER. IF WE KNOW ANYTHING, IT'S THAT.
IF WE'RE REALLY RUNNING OUT OF TIME, MAYBE YOU CAN SKIP THE PSEUDO-PROFUNDITY. JUST A THOUGHT.
WE DON'T KNOW EACH OTHER WELL, FANTOMEX, BUT I KNOW YOUR STORY. I CONSIDER YOU AN ALLY.
IF YOU'D EVER WANTED IT, I WOULD HAVE GLADLY WELCOMED YOU TO MY X-MEN.
NON, YOU DO NOT KNOW ME, PROFESSEUR. IF I DO GOOD, IT IS BECAUSE, IN THE END, IT IS GOOD FOR ME.
AH, YES. THE DELIGHTFUL IDENTITY THEY CODED INTO YOUR MIND WHEN THEY BUILT YOU AT WEAPON PLUS.
A THIEF WITH A HEART OF COAL.
NOT JUST A THIEF, MON AMI! A CRIMINAL THROUGH AND THROUGH. A KILLER, EVEN.

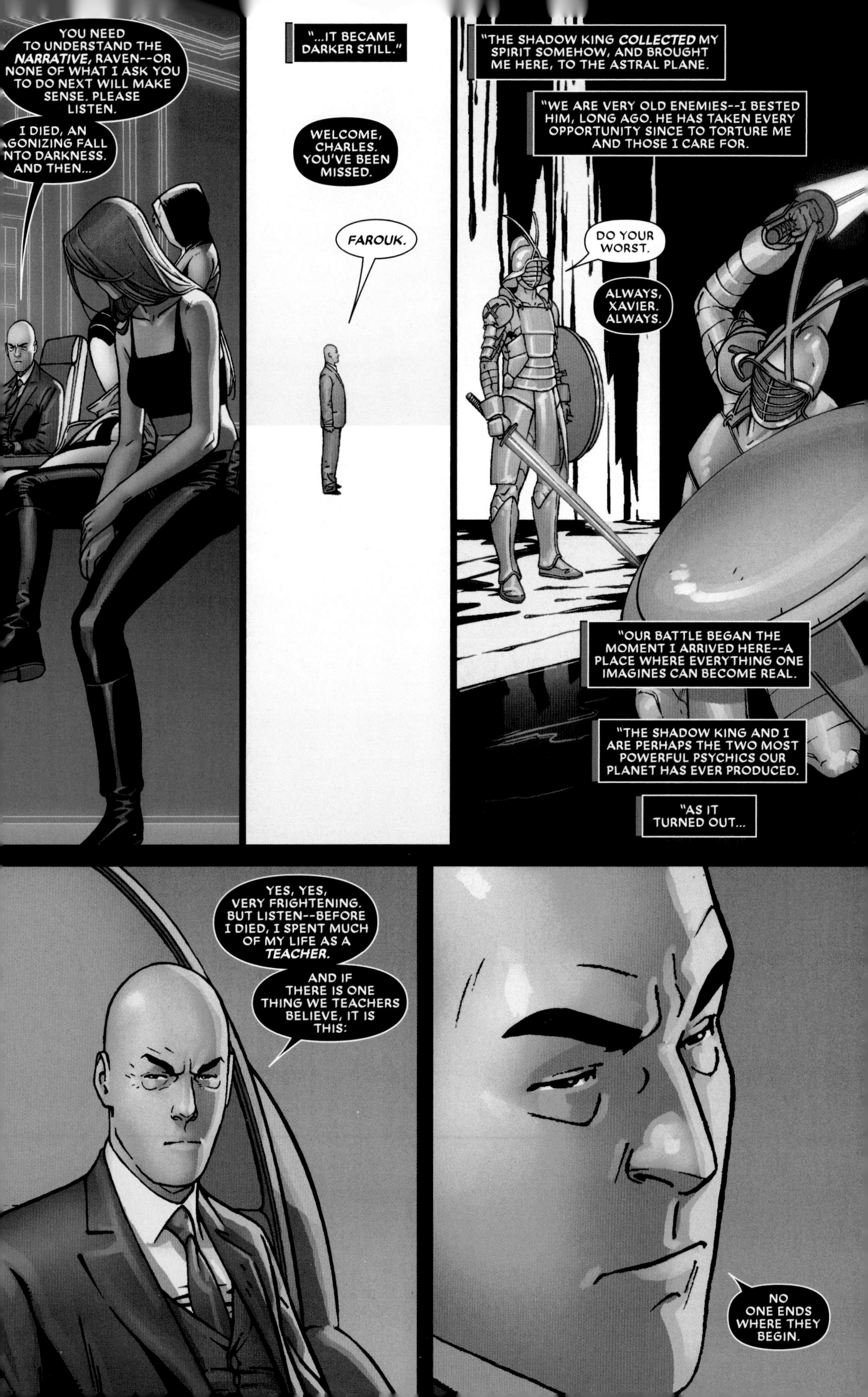

YOU NEED TO UNDERSTAND THE *NARRATIVE,* RAVEN--OR NONE OF WHAT I ASK YOU TO DO NEXT WILL MAKE SENSE. PLEASE LISTEN.
I DIED, AN AGONIZING FALL INTO DARKNESS. AND THEN...
"...IT BECAME DARKER STILL."
WELCOME, CHARLES. YOU'VE BEEN MISSED.
FAROUK.
"THE SHADOW KING *COLLECTED* MY SPIRIT SOMEHOW, AND BROUGHT ME HERE, TO THE ASTRAL PLANE.
"WE ARE VERY OLD ENEMIES--I BESTED HIM, LONG AGO. HE HAS TAKEN EVERY OPPORTUNITY SINCE TO TORTURE ME AND THOSE I CARE FOR.
DO YOUR WORST.
ALWAYS, XAVIER. ALWAYS.
"OUR BATTLE BEGAN THE MOMENT I ARRIVED HERE--A PLACE WHERE EVERYTHING ONE IMAGINES CAN BECOME REAL.
"THE SHADOW KING AND I ARE PERHAPS THE TWO MOST POWERFUL PSYCHICS OUR PLANET HAS EVER PRODUCED.
"AS IT TURNED OUT...
YES, YES, VERY FRIGHTENING. BUT LISTEN--BEFORE I DIED, I SPENT MUCH OF MY LIFE AS A *TEACHER.*
AND IF THERE IS ONE THING WE TEACHERS BELIEVE, IT IS THIS:
NO ONE ENDS WHERE THEY BEGIN.

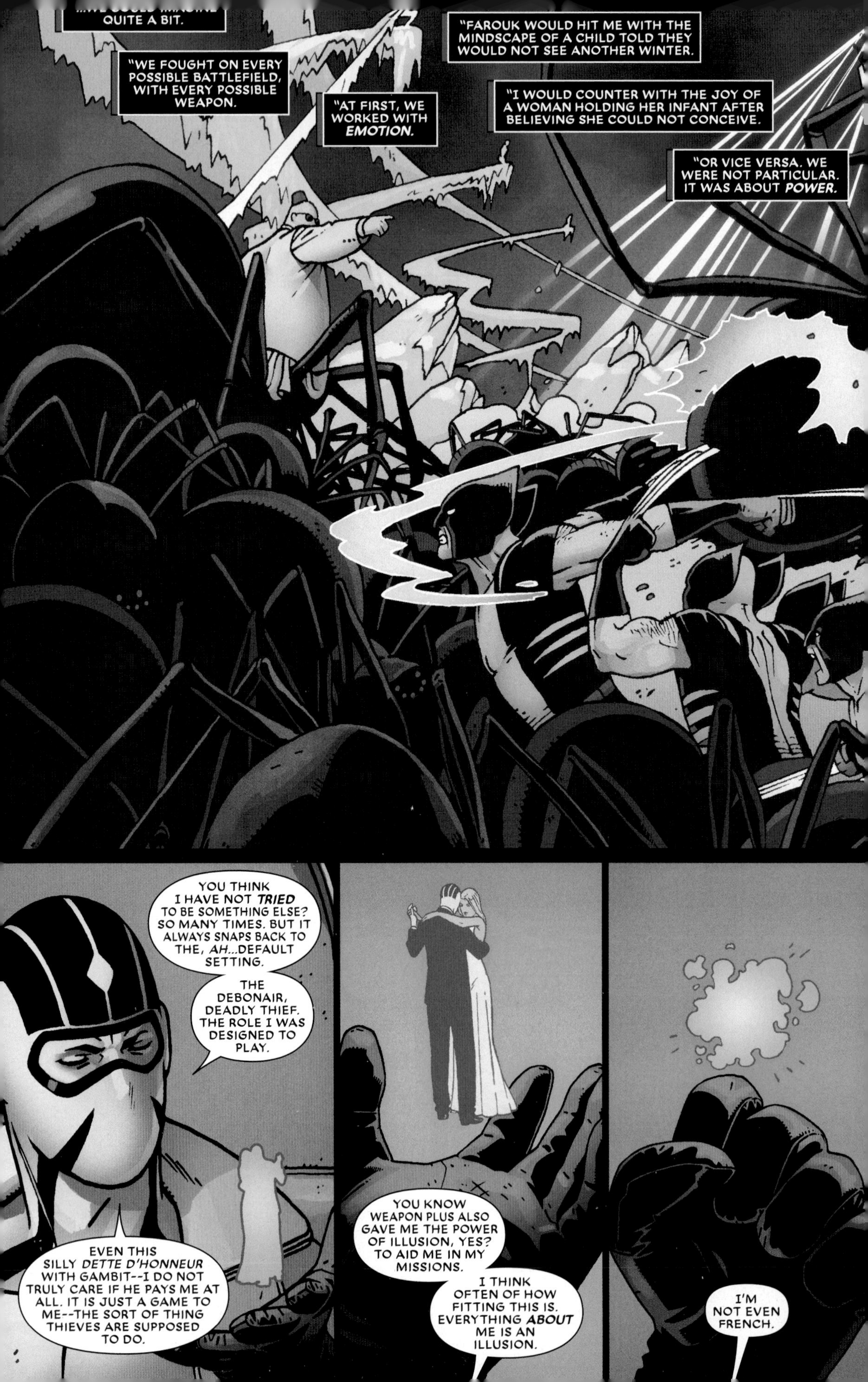
QUITE A BIT.
"WE FOUGHT ON EVERY POSSIBLE BATTLEFIELD, WITH EVERY POSSIBLE WEAPON.
"AT FIRST, WE WORKED WITH *EMOTION.*
"FAROUK WOULD HIT ME WITH THE MINDSCAPE OF A CHILD TOLD THEY WOULD NOT SEE ANOTHER WINTER.
"I WOULD COUNTER WITH THE JOY OF A WOMAN HOLDING HER INFANT AFTER BELIEVING SHE COULD NOT CONCEIVE.
"OR VICE VERSA. WE WERE NOT PARTICULAR. IT WAS ABOUT *POWER.*
YOU THINK I HAVE NOT *TRIED* TO BE SOMETHING ELSE? SO MANY TIMES. BUT IT ALWAYS SNAPS BACK TO THE, *AH...*DEFAULT SETTING.
THE DEBONAIR, DEADLY THIEF. THE ROLE I WAS DESIGNED TO PLAY.
EVEN THIS SILLY *DETTE D'HONNEUR* WITH GAMBIT--I DO NOT TRULY CARE IF HE PAYS ME AT ALL. IT IS JUST A GAME TO ME--THE SORT OF THING THIEVES ARE SUPPOSED TO DO.
YOU KNOW WEAPON PLUS ALSO GAVE ME THE POWER OF ILLUSION, YES? TO AID ME IN MY MISSIONS.
I THINK OFTEN OF HOW FITTING THIS IS. EVERYTHING *ABOUT* ME IS AN ILLUSION.
I'M NOT EVEN FRENCH.

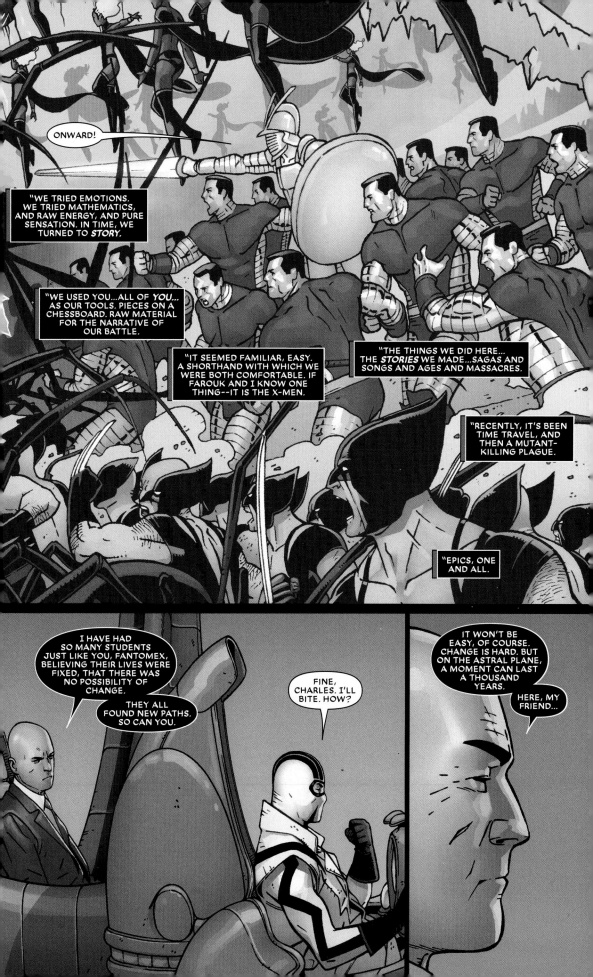

ONWARD!

"WE TRIED EMOTIONS. WE TRIED MATHEMATICS, AND RAW ENERGY, AND PURE SENSATION. IN TIME, WE TURNED TO *STORY*.

"WE USED YOU...ALL OF *YOU*... AS OUR TOOLS. PIECES ON A CHESSBOARD. RAW MATERIAL FOR THE NARRATIVE OF OUR BATTLE.

"IT SEEMED FAMILIAR, EASY. A SHORTHAND WITH WHICH WE WERE BOTH COMFORTABLE. IF FAROUK AND I KNOW ONE THING--IT IS THE X-MEN.

"THE THINGS WE DID HERE... THE *STORIES* WE MADE...SAGAS AND SONGS AND AGES AND MASSACRES.

"RECENTLY, IT'S BEEN TIME TRAVEL, AND THEN A MUTANT- KILLING PLAGUE.

"EPICS, ONE AND ALL.

I HAVE HAD SO MANY STUDENTS JUST LIKE YOU, FANTOMEX, BELIEVING THEIR LIVES WERE FIXED, THAT THERE WAS NO POSSIBILITY OF CHANGE.

THEY ALL FOUND NEW PATHS. SO CAN YOU.

FINE, CHARLES. I'LL BITE. HOW?

IT WON'T BE EASY, OF COURSE. CHANGE IS HARD. BUT ON THE ASTRAL PLANE, A MOMENT CAN LAST A THOUSAND YEARS.

HERE, MY FRIEND...

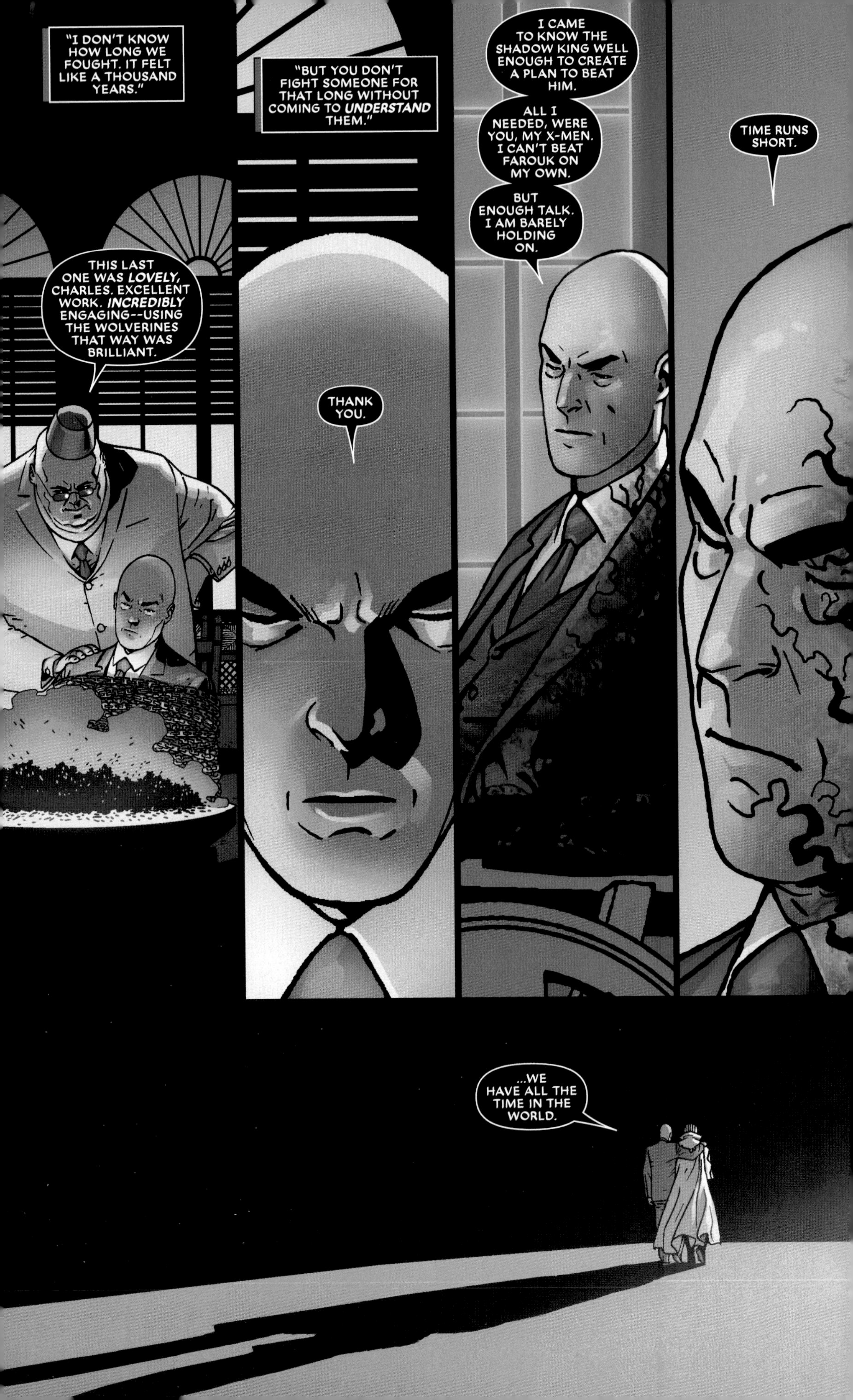
"I DON'T KNOW HOW LONG WE FOUGHT. IT FELT LIKE A THOUSAND YEARS."
THIS LAST ONE WAS *LOVELY,* CHARLES. EXCELLENT WORK. *INCREDIBLY* ENGAGING--USING THE WOLVERINES THAT WAY WAS BRILLIANT.
"BUT YOU DON'T FIGHT SOMEONE FOR THAT LONG WITHOUT COMING TO *UNDERSTAND* THEM."
THANK YOU.
I CAME TO KNOW THE SHADOW KING WELL ENOUGH TO CREATE A PLAN TO BEAT HIM.
ALL I NEEDED, WERE YOU, MY X-MEN. I CAN'T BEAT FAROUK ON MY OWN.
BUT ENOUGH TALK. I AM BARELY HOLDING ON.
TIME RUNS SHORT.
...WE HAVE ALL THE TIME IN THE WORLD.

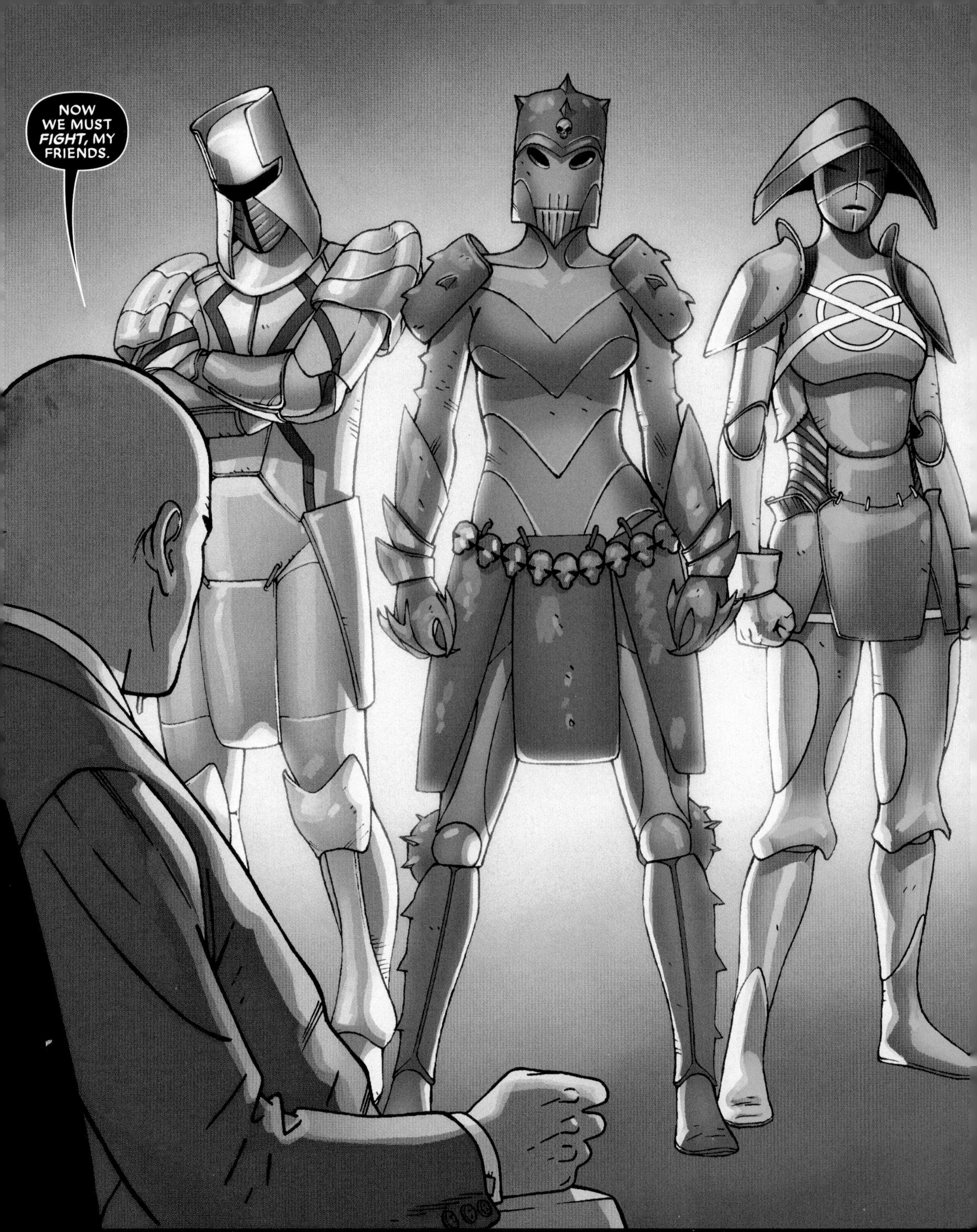
NOW WE MUST *FIGHT,* MY FRIENDS.

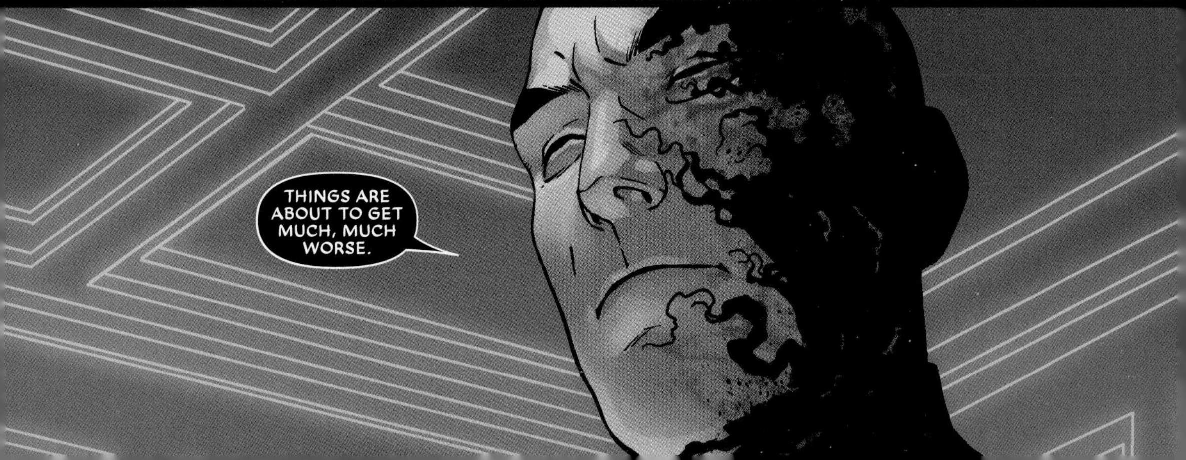
THINGS ARE ABOUT TO GET MUCH, MUCH WORSE.

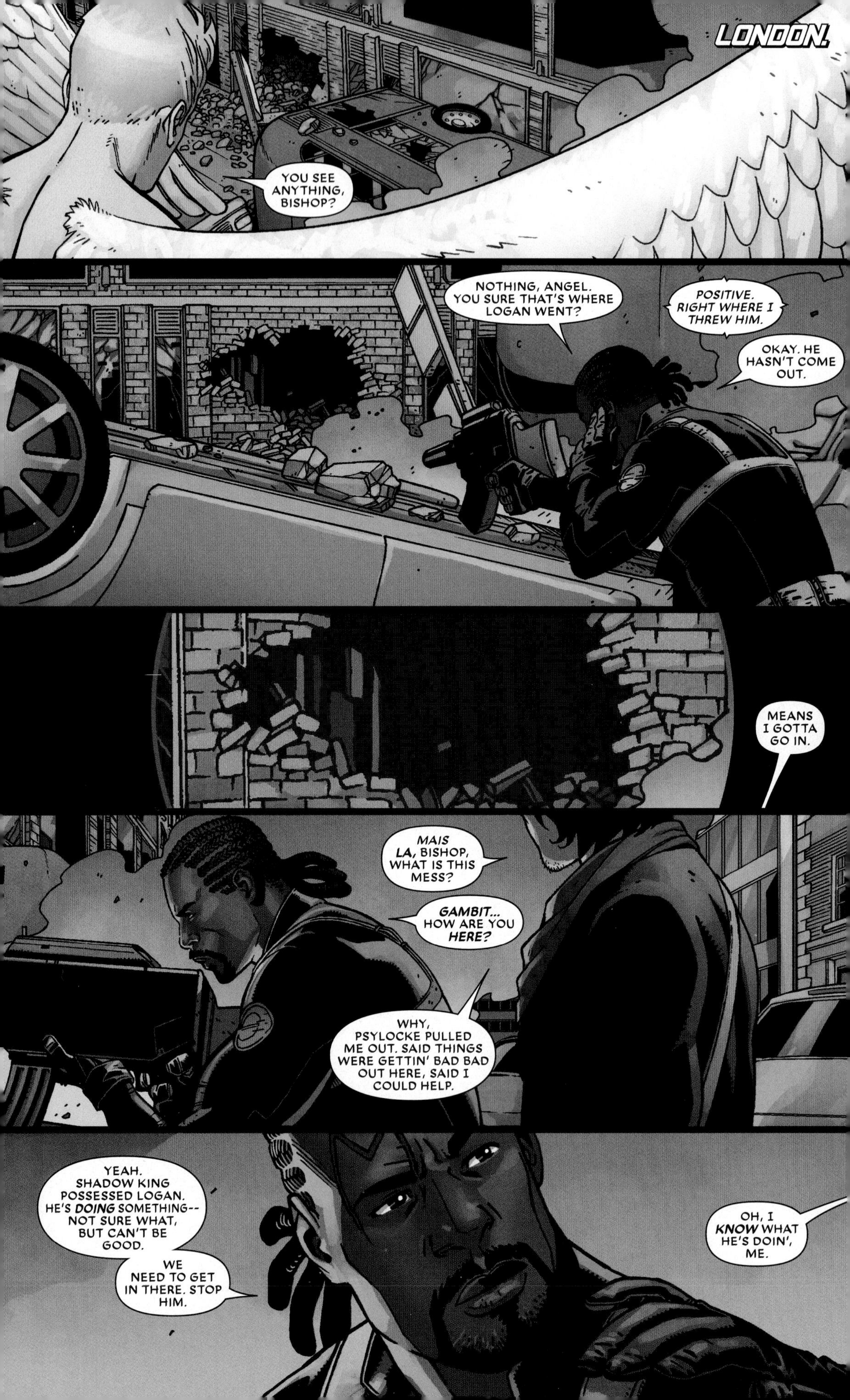
LONDON.
YOU SEE ANYTHING, BISHOP?
NOTHING, ANGEL. YOU SURE THAT'S WHERE LOGAN WENT?
POSITIVE. RIGHT WHERE I THREW HIM.
OKAY. HE HASN'T COME OUT.
MEANS I GOTTA GO IN.
MAIS LA, BISHOP, WHAT IS THIS MESS?
GAMBIT... HOW ARE YOU HERE?
WHY, PSYLOCKE PULLED ME OUT. SAID THINGS WERE GETTIN' BAD BAD OUT HERE, SAID I COULD HELP.
YEAH. SHADOW KING POSSESSED LOGAN. HE'S DOING SOMETHING-- NOT SURE WHAT, BUT CAN'T BE GOOD.
WE NEED TO GET IN THERE. STOP HIM.
OH, I KNOW WHAT HE'S DOIN', ME.

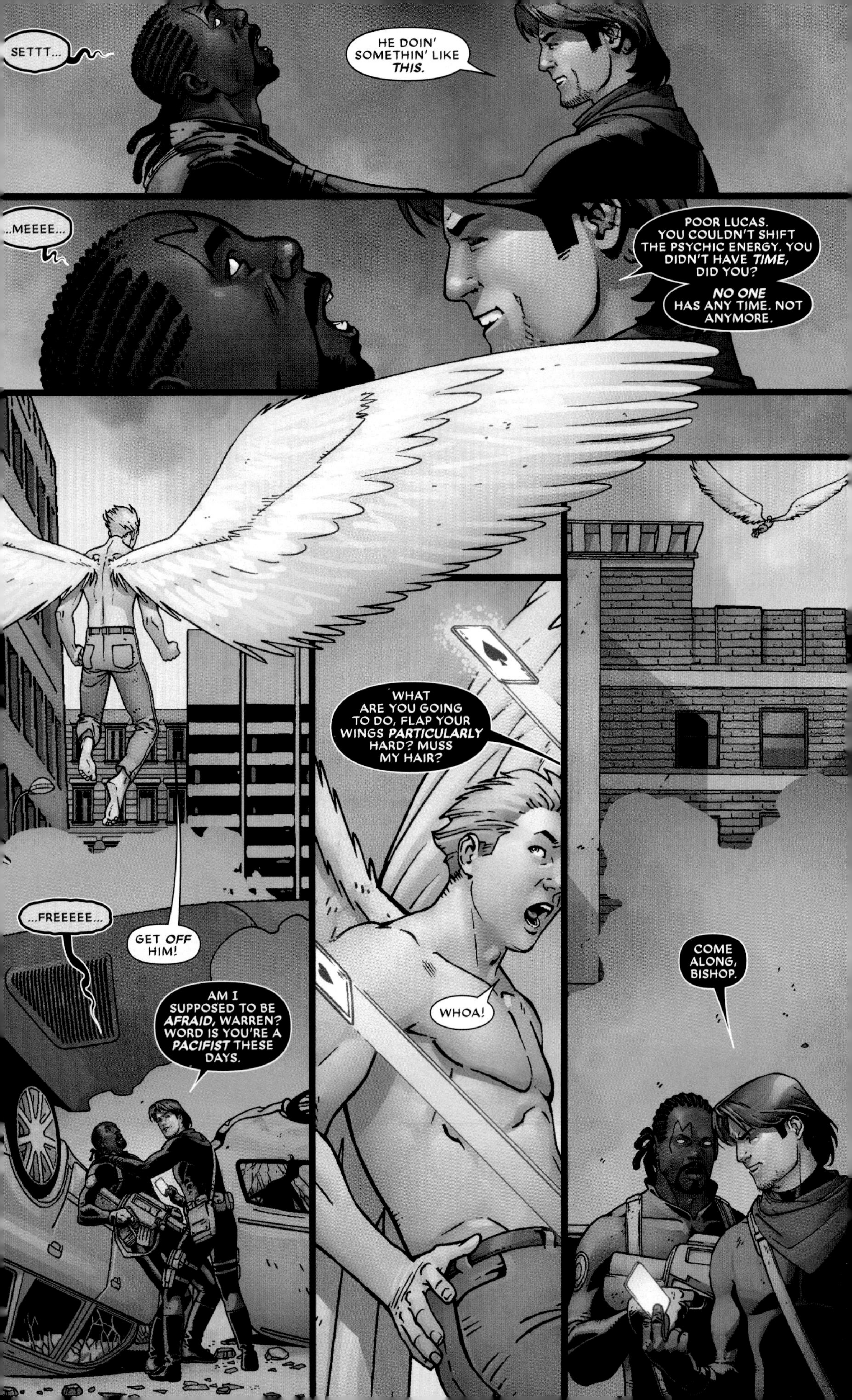
SETTT...
HE DOIN' SOMETHIN' LIKE THIS.
...MEEEE...
POOR LUCAS. YOU COULDN'T SHIFT THE PSYCHIC ENERGY. YOU DIDN'T HAVE TIME, DID YOU?
NO ONE HAS ANY TIME. NOT ANYMORE.
...FREEEEE...
GET OFF HIM!
AM I SUPPOSED TO BE AFRAID, WARREN? WORD IS YOU'RE A PACIFIST THESE DAYS.
WHAT ARE YOU GOING TO DO, FLAP YOUR WINGS PARTICULARLY HARD? MUSS MY HAIR?
WHOA!
COME ALONG, BISHOP.

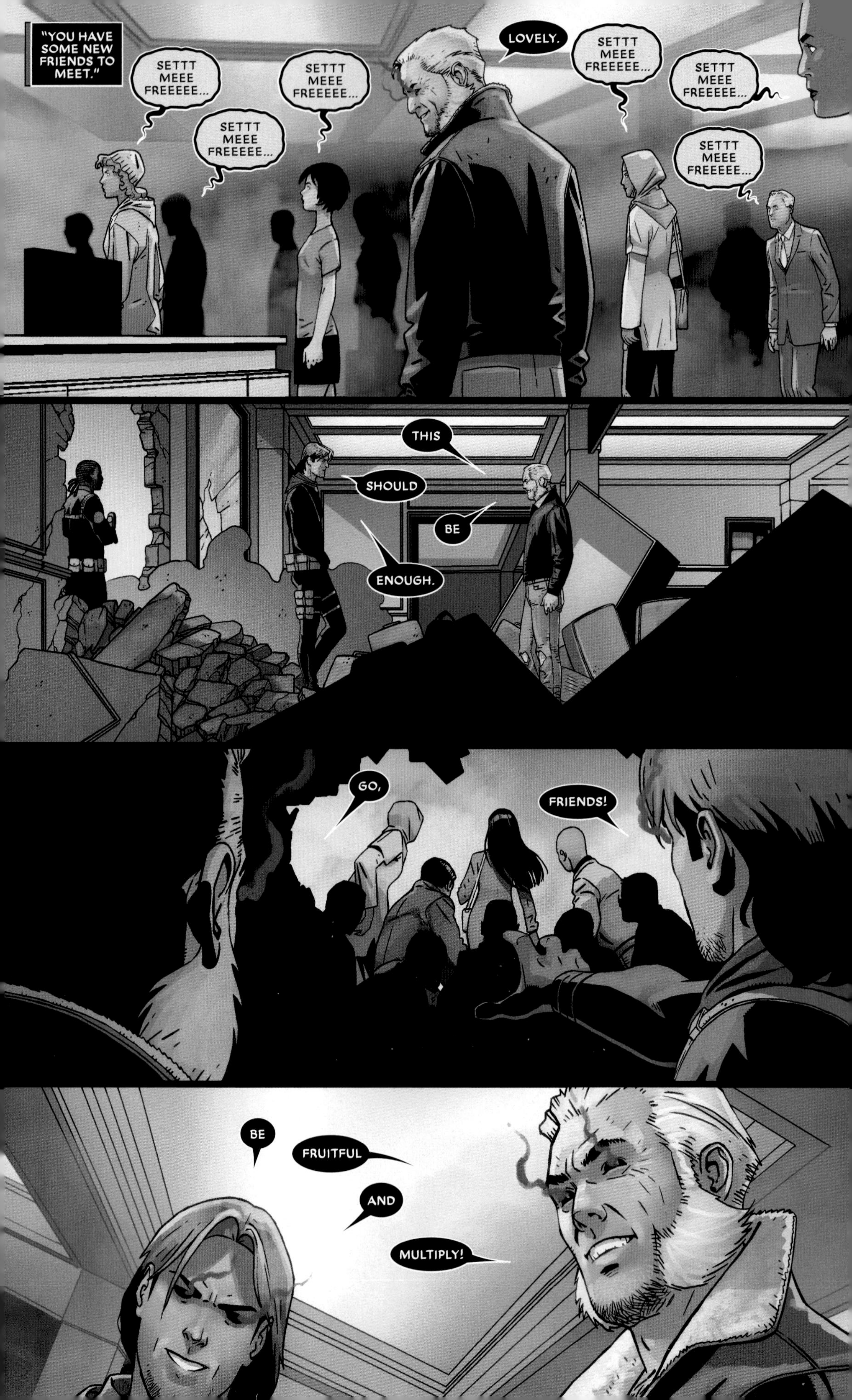
"YOU HAVE SOME NEW FRIENDS TO MEET."
SETTT MEEE FREEEEE...
SETTT MEEE FREEEEE...
SETTT MEEE FREEEEE...
LOVELY.
SETTT MEEE FREEEEE...
SETTT MEEE FREEEEE...
SETTT MEEE FREEEEE...
THIS
SHOULD
BE
ENOUGH.
GO,
FRIENDS!
BE
FRUITFUL
AND
MULTIPLY!

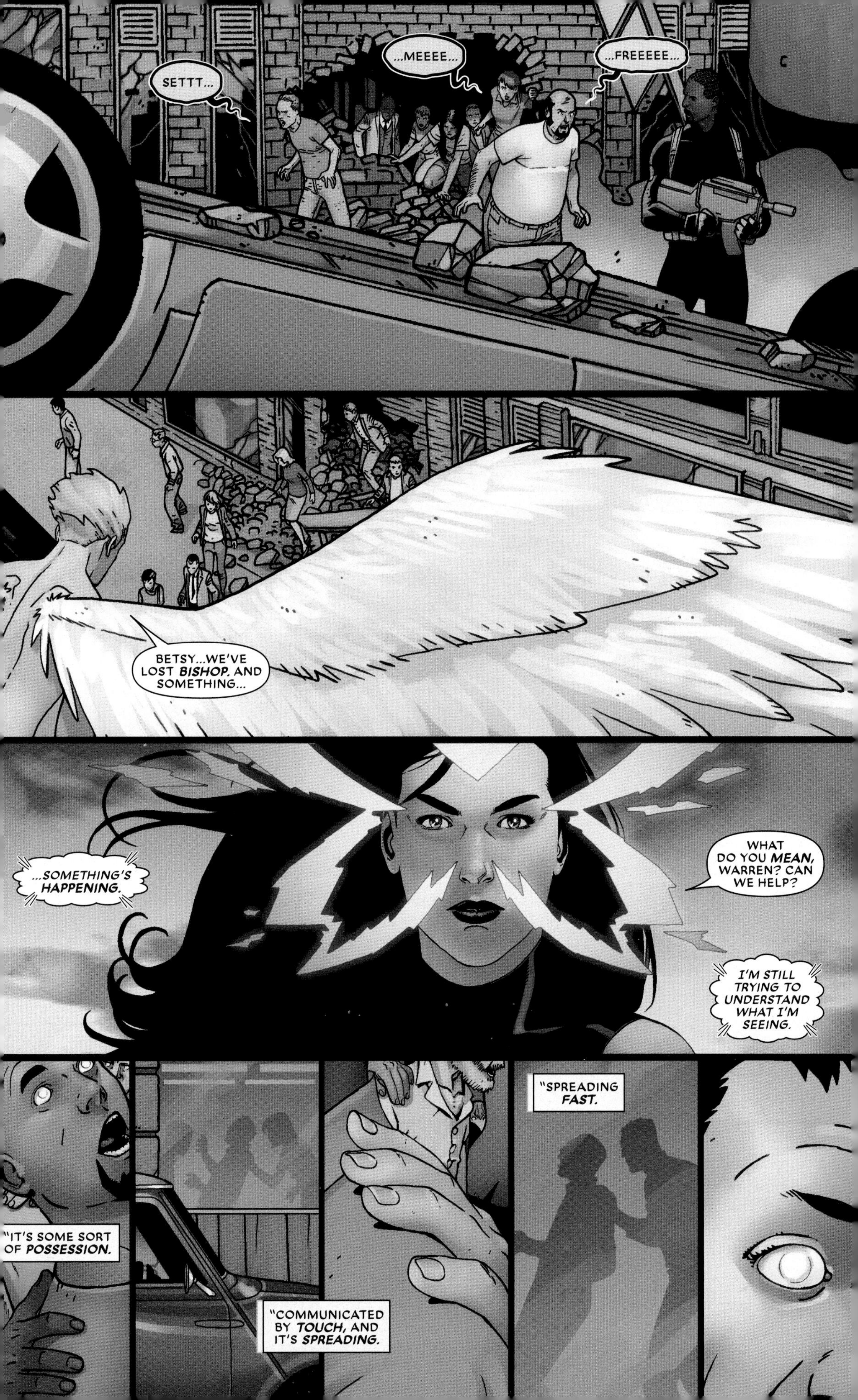
SETTT...
...MEEEE...
...FREEEEE...
BETSY...WE'VE LOST BISHOP. AND SOMETHING...
...SOMETHING'S HAPPENING.
WHAT DO YOU MEAN, WARREN? CAN WE HELP?
I'M STILL TRYING TO UNDERSTAND WHAT I'M SEEING.
"IT'S SOME SORT OF POSSESSION.
"COMMUNICATED BY TOUCH, AND IT'S SPREADING.
"SPREADING FAST.

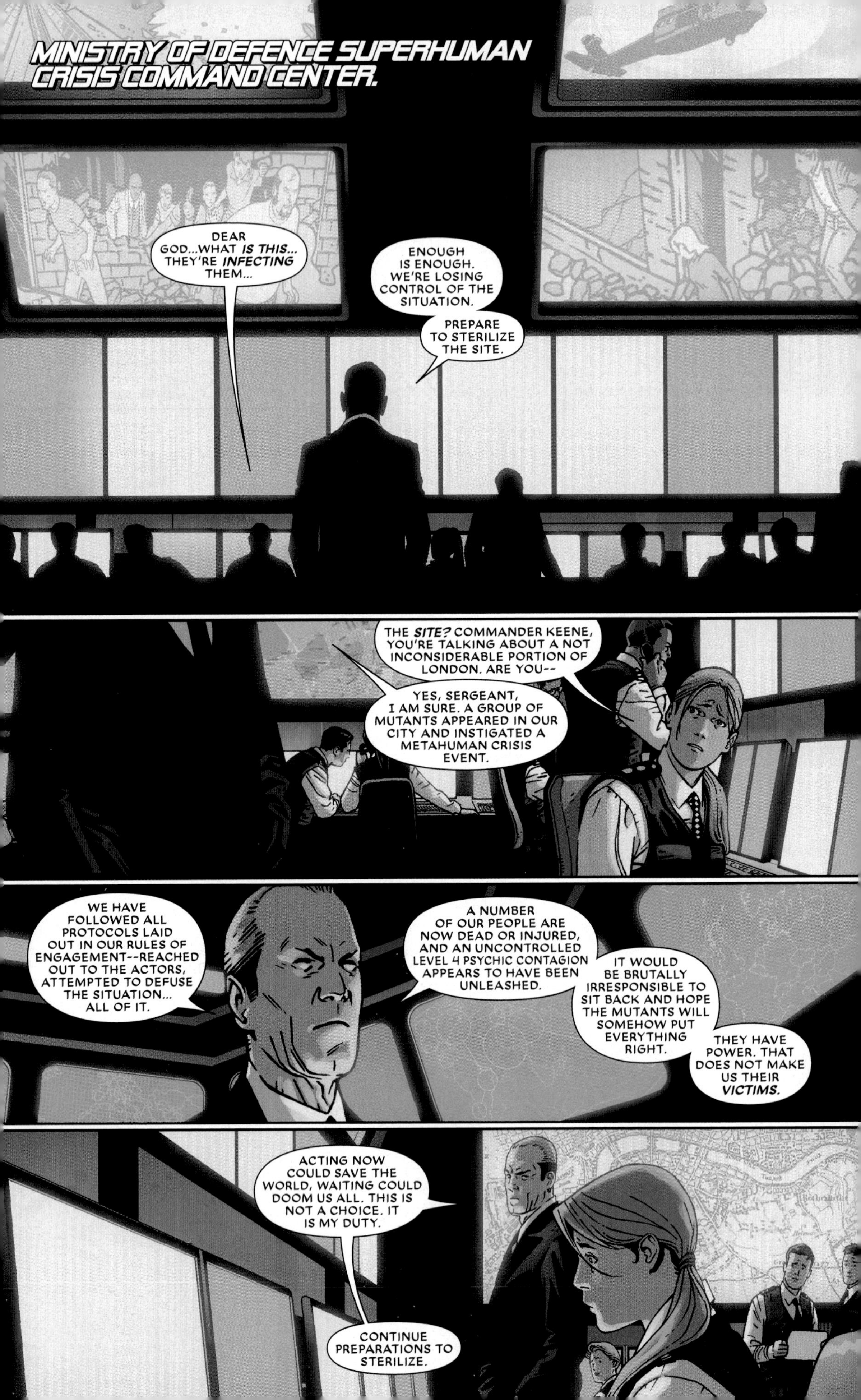
MINISTRY OF DEFENCE SUPERHUMAN CRISIS COMMAND CENTER.
DEAR GOD...WHAT IS THIS... THEY'RE INFECTING THEM...
ENOUGH IS ENOUGH. WE'RE LOSING CONTROL OF THE SITUATION.
PREPARE TO STERILIZE THE SITE.
THE SITE? COMMANDER KEENE, YOU'RE TALKING ABOUT A NOT INCONSIDERABLE PORTION OF LONDON. ARE YOU--
YES, SERGEANT, I AM SURE. A GROUP OF MUTANTS APPEARED IN OUR CITY AND INSTIGATED A METAHUMAN CRISIS EVENT.
WE HAVE FOLLOWED ALL PROTOCOLS LAID OUT IN OUR RULES OF ENGAGEMENT--REACHED OUT TO THE ACTORS, ATTEMPTED TO DEFUSE THE SITUATION... ALL OF IT.
A NUMBER OF OUR PEOPLE ARE NOW DEAD OR INJURED, AND AN UNCONTROLLED LEVEL 4 PSYCHIC CONTAGION APPEARS TO HAVE BEEN UNLEASHED.
IT WOULD BE BRUTALLY IRRESPONSIBLE TO SIT BACK AND HOPE THE MUTANTS WILL SOMEHOW PUT EVERYTHING RIGHT.
THEY HAVE POWER. THAT DOES NOT MAKE US THEIR VICTIMS.
ACTING NOW COULD SAVE THE WORLD, WAITING COULD DOOM US ALL. THIS IS NOT A CHOICE. IT IS MY DUTY.
CONTINUE PREPARATIONS TO STERILIZE.

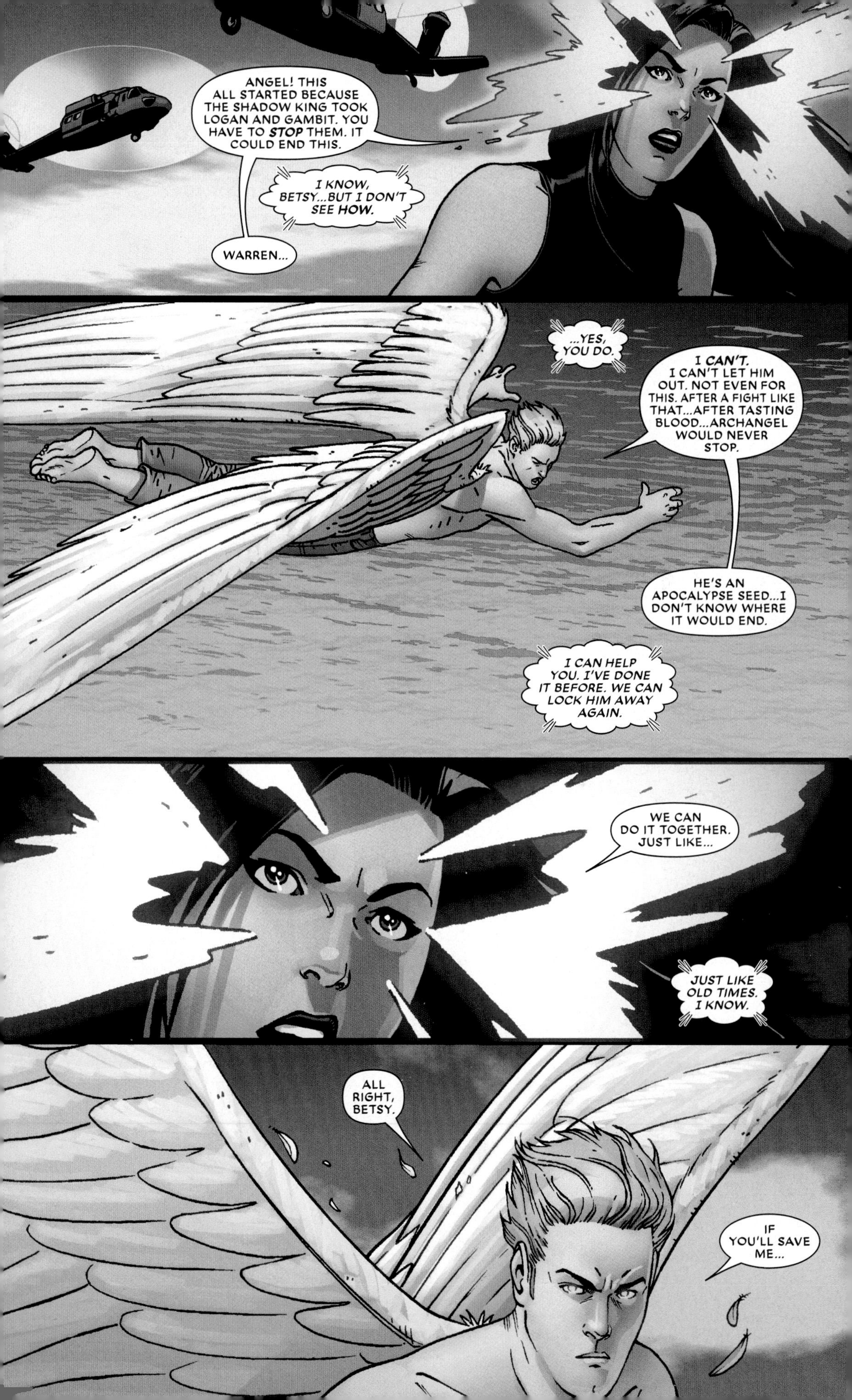
ANGEL! THIS ALL STARTED BECAUSE THE SHADOW KING TOOK LOGAN AND GAMBIT. YOU HAVE TO **STOP** THEM. IT COULD END THIS.
I KNOW, BETSY...BUT I DON'T SEE **HOW.**
WARREN...
...YES, YOU DO.
I **CAN'T.** I CAN'T LET HIM OUT. NOT EVEN FOR THIS. AFTER A FIGHT LIKE THAT...AFTER TASTING BLOOD...ARCHANGEL WOULD NEVER STOP.
HE'S AN APOCALYPSE SEED...I DON'T KNOW WHERE IT WOULD END.
I CAN HELP YOU. I'VE DONE IT BEFORE. WE CAN LOCK HIM AWAY AGAIN.
WE CAN DO IT TOGETHER. JUST LIKE...
JUST LIKE OLD TIMES. I KNOW.
ALL RIGHT, BETSY.
IF YOU'LL SAVE ME...

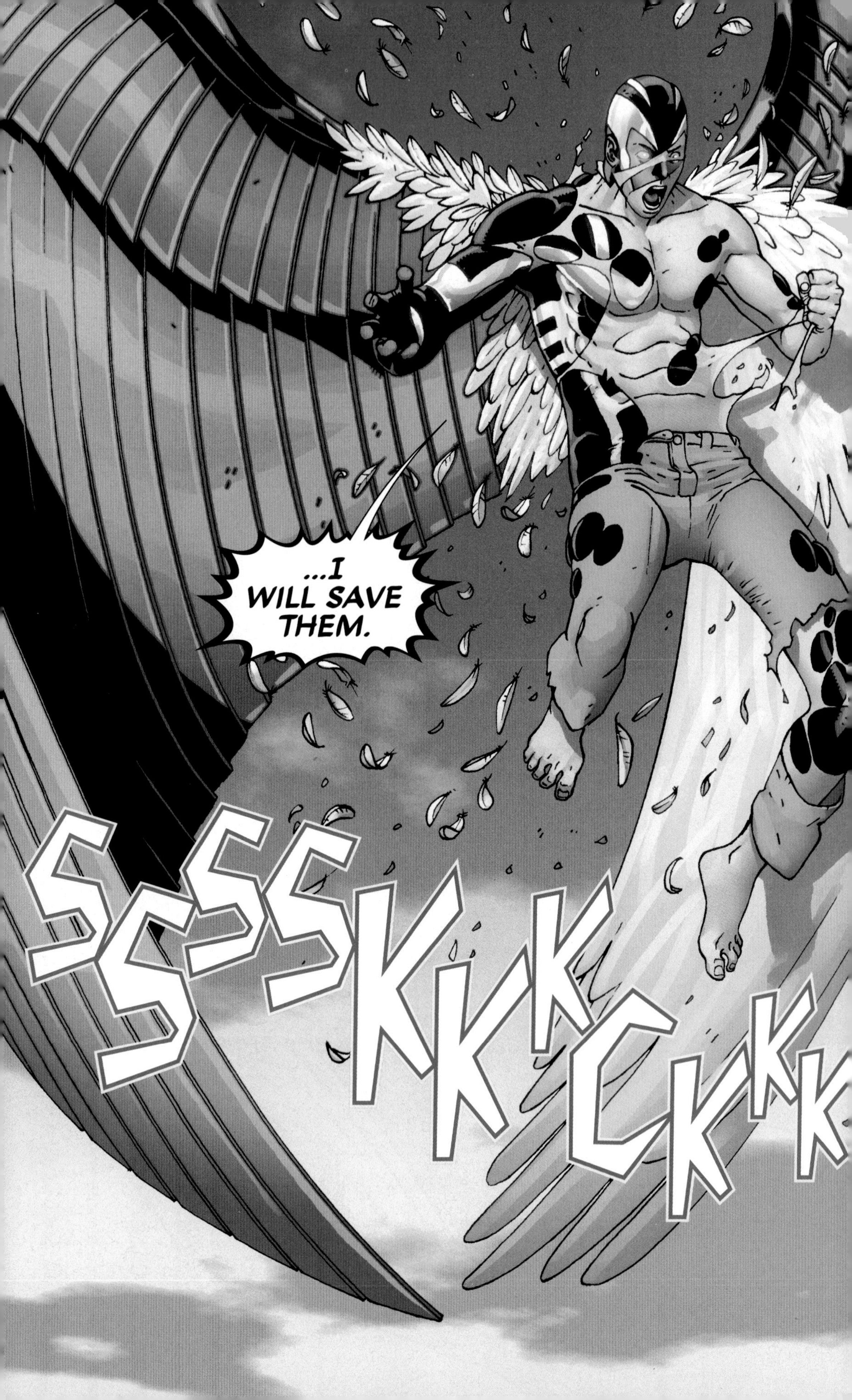
...I WILL SAVE THEM.
SSSSSKKKCKKK

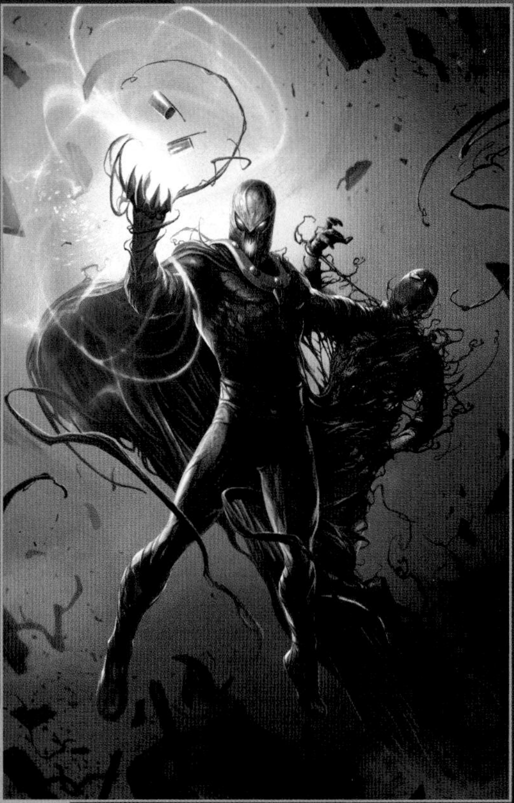

#3 VENOMIZED VILLAINS VARIANT
BY **FRANCESCO MATTINA**

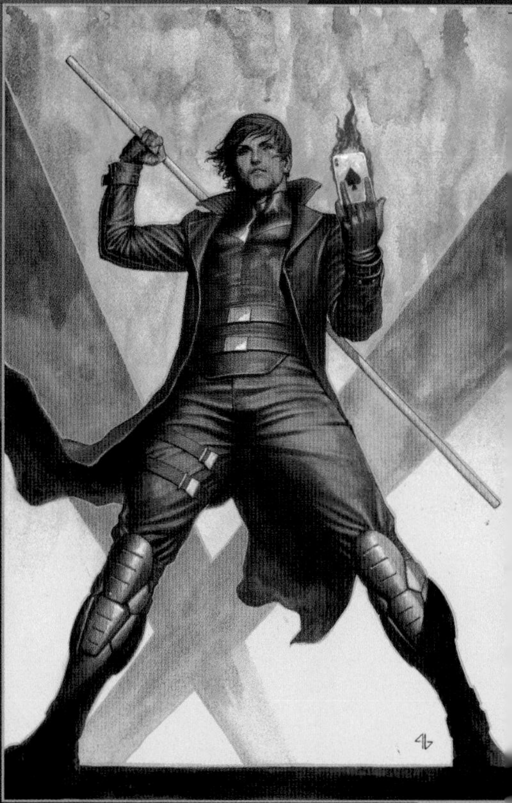

#4 VARIANT
BY **ADI GRANOV**

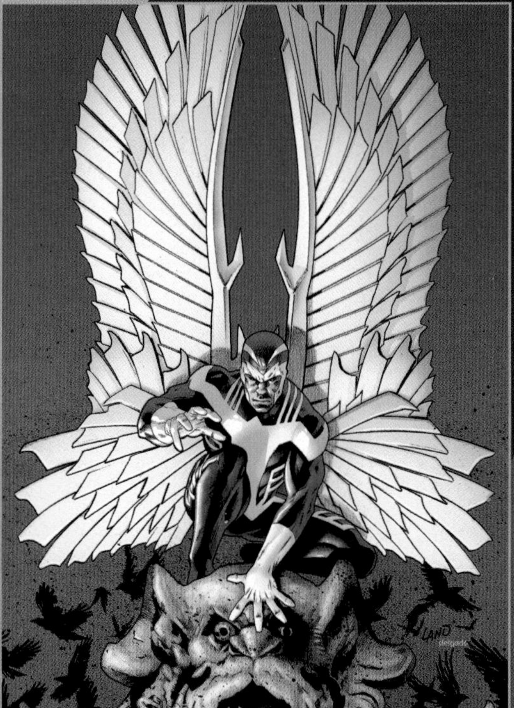

#5 VARIANT
BY **GREG LAND**
& **EDGAR DELGADO**

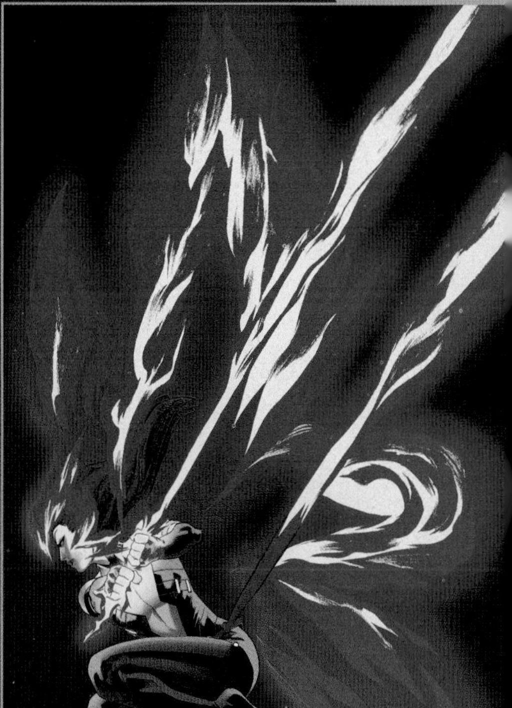

#6 PHOENIX VARIANT
BY **KRIS ANKA**

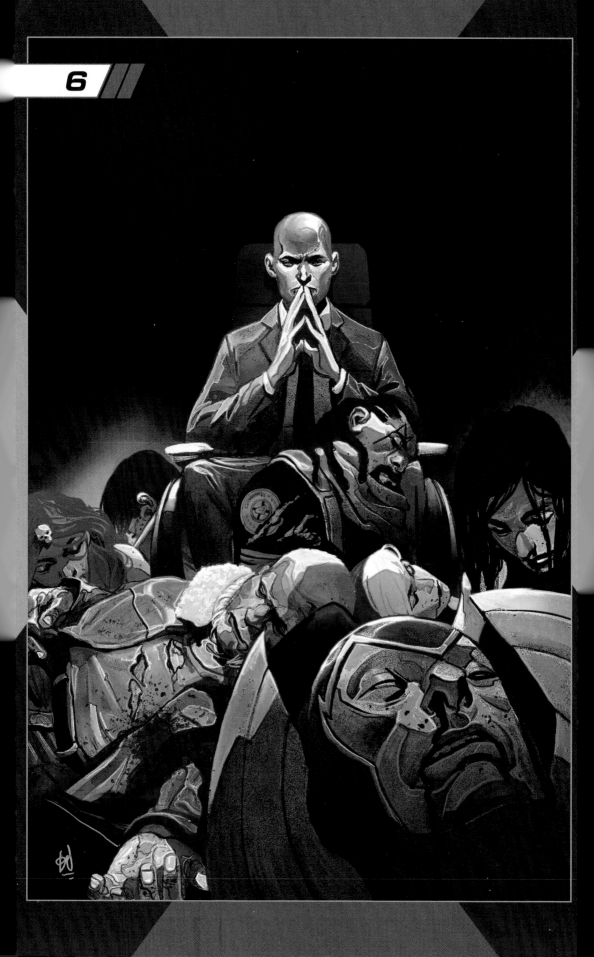

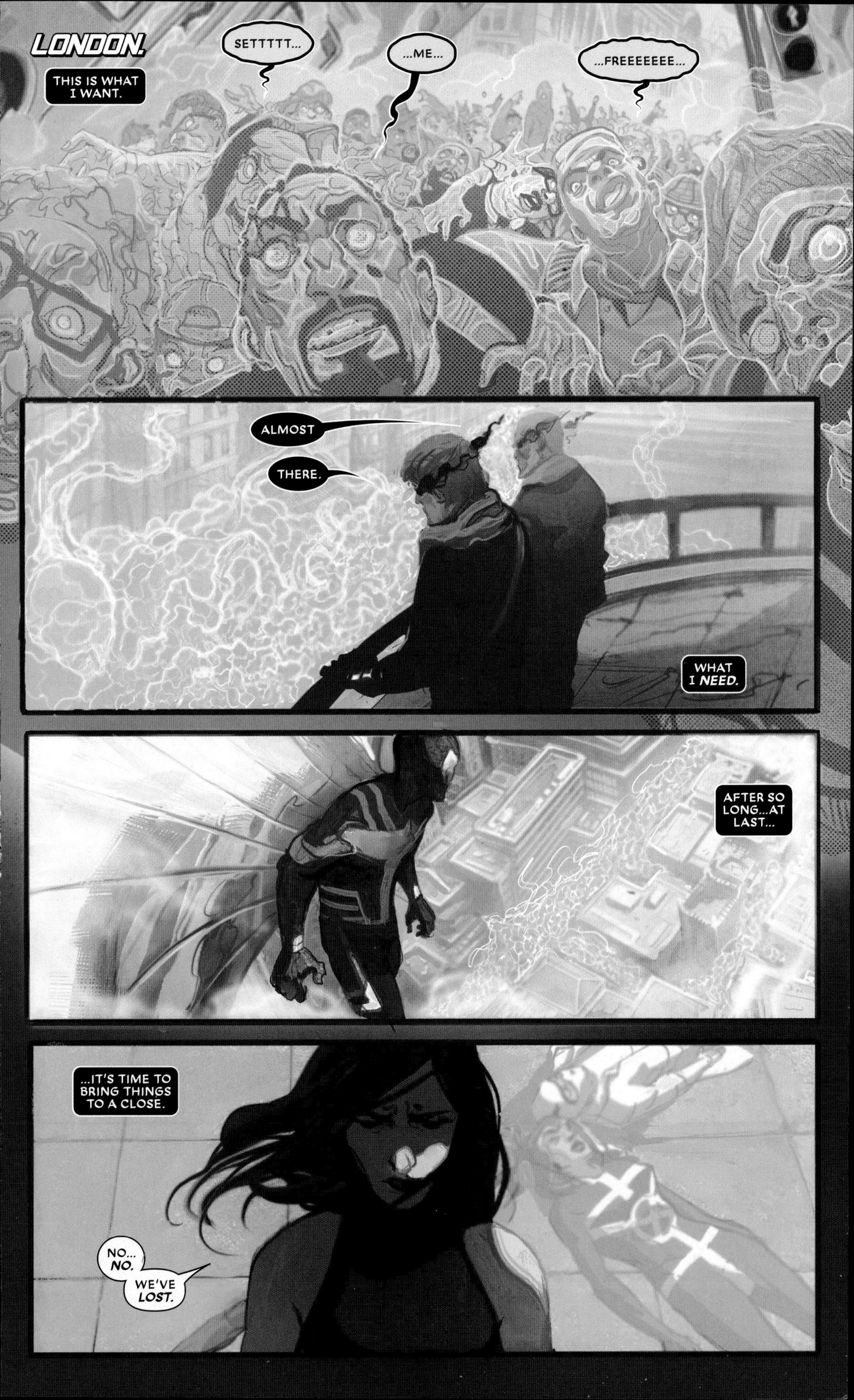
LONDON.
THIS IS WHAT I WANT.
SETTTTT...
...ME...
...FREEEEEEE...
ALMOST
THERE.
WHAT I NEED.
AFTER SO LONG...AT LAST...
...IT'S TIME TO BRING THINGS TO A CLOSE.
NO... NO.
WE'VE LOST.

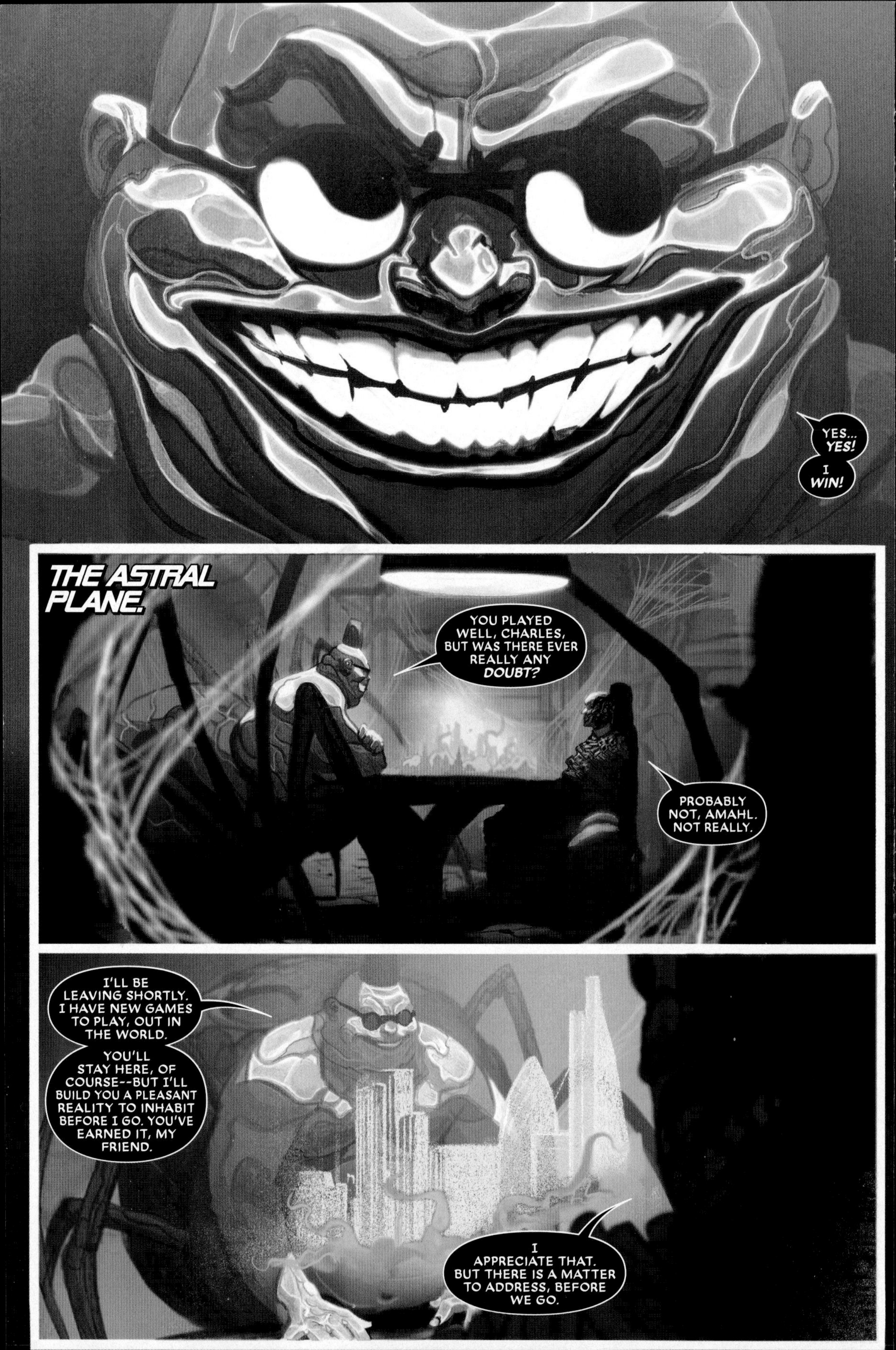
YES... YES!
I WIN!
THE ASTRAL PLANE.
YOU PLAYED WELL, CHARLES, BUT WAS THERE EVER REALLY ANY DOUBT?
PROBABLY NOT, AMAHL. NOT REALLY.
I'LL BE LEAVING SHORTLY. I HAVE NEW GAMES TO PLAY, OUT IN THE WORLD.
YOU'LL STAY HERE, OF COURSE--BUT I'LL BUILD YOU A PLEASANT REALITY TO INHABIT BEFORE I GO. YOU'VE EARNED IT, MY FRIEND.
I APPRECIATE THAT. BUT THERE IS A MATTER TO ADDRESS, BEFORE WE GO.

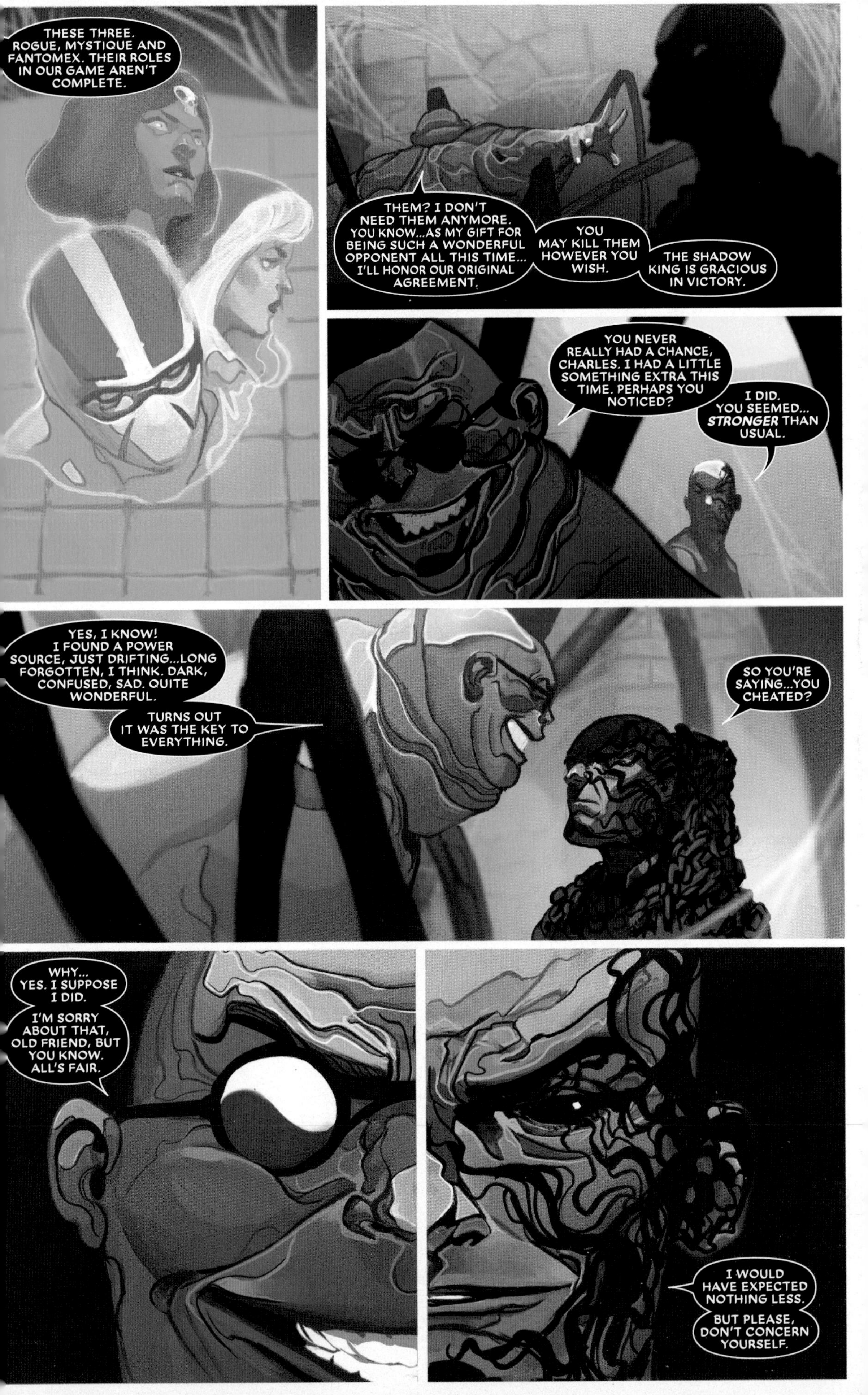
THESE THREE. ROGUE, MYSTIQUE AND FANTOMEX. THEIR ROLES IN OUR GAME AREN'T COMPLETE.
THEM? I DON'T NEED THEM ANYMORE. YOU KNOW...AS MY GIFT FOR BEING SUCH A WONDERFUL OPPONENT ALL THIS TIME... I'LL HONOR OUR ORIGINAL AGREEMENT.
YOU MAY KILL THEM HOWEVER YOU WISH.
THE SHADOW KING IS GRACIOUS IN VICTORY.
YOU NEVER REALLY HAD A CHANCE, CHARLES. I HAD A LITTLE SOMETHING EXTRA THIS TIME. PERHAPS YOU NOTICED?
I DID. YOU SEEMED... STRONGER THAN USUAL.
YES, I KNOW! I FOUND A POWER SOURCE, JUST DRIFTING...LONG FORGOTTEN, I THINK. DARK, CONFUSED, SAD. QUITE WONDERFUL.
TURNS OUT IT WAS THE KEY TO EVERYTHING.
SO YOU'RE SAYING...YOU CHEATED?
WHY... YES. I SUPPOSE I DID.
I'M SORRY ABOUT THAT, OLD FRIEND, BUT YOU KNOW. ALL'S FAIR.
I WOULD HAVE EXPECTED NOTHING LESS.
BUT PLEASE, DON'T CONCERN YOURSELF.

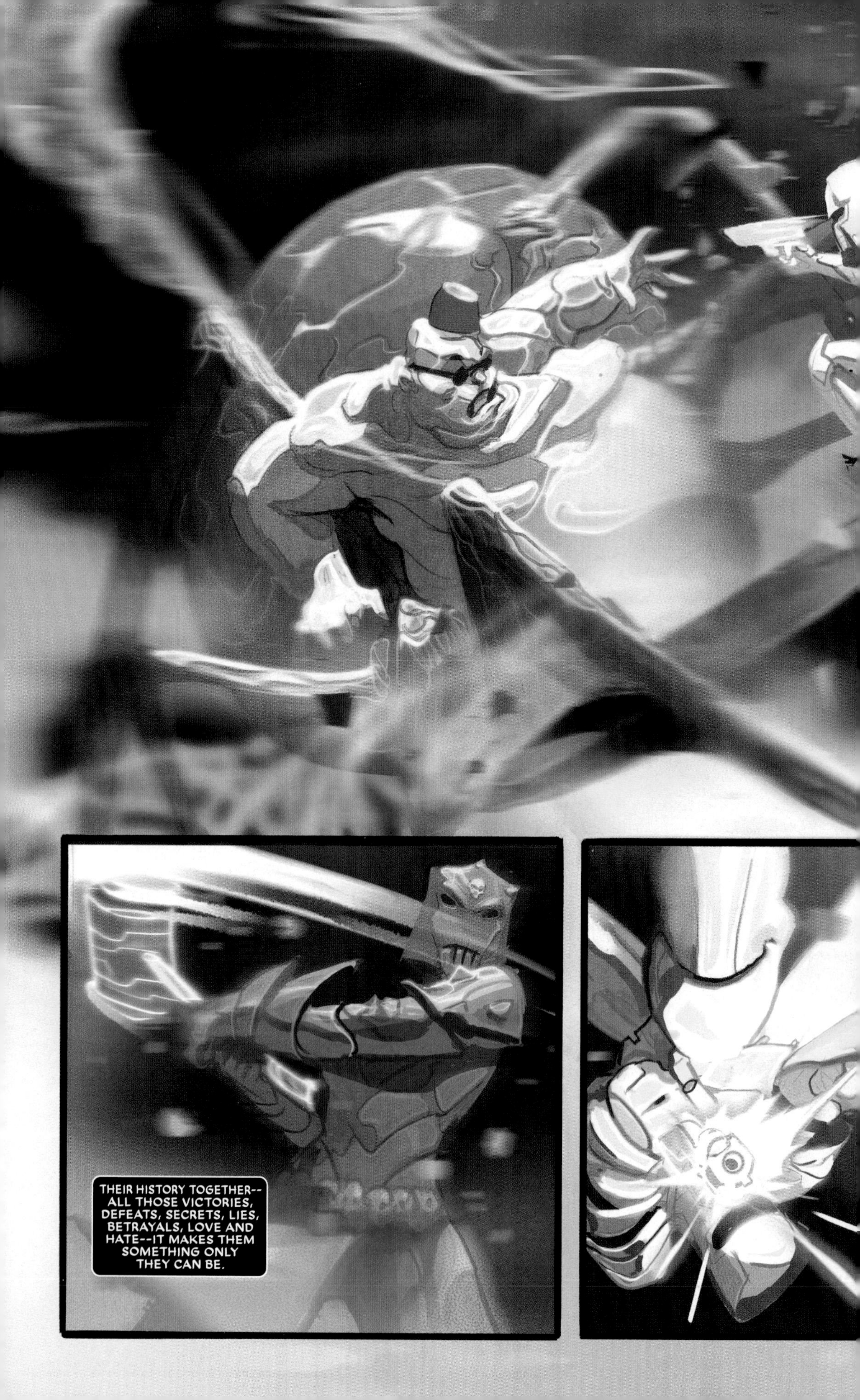
THEIR HISTORY TOGETHER--
ALL THOSE VICTORIES,
DEFEATS, SECRETS, LIES,
BETRAYALS, LOVE AND
HATE--IT MAKES THEM
SOMETHING ONLY
THEY CAN BE.

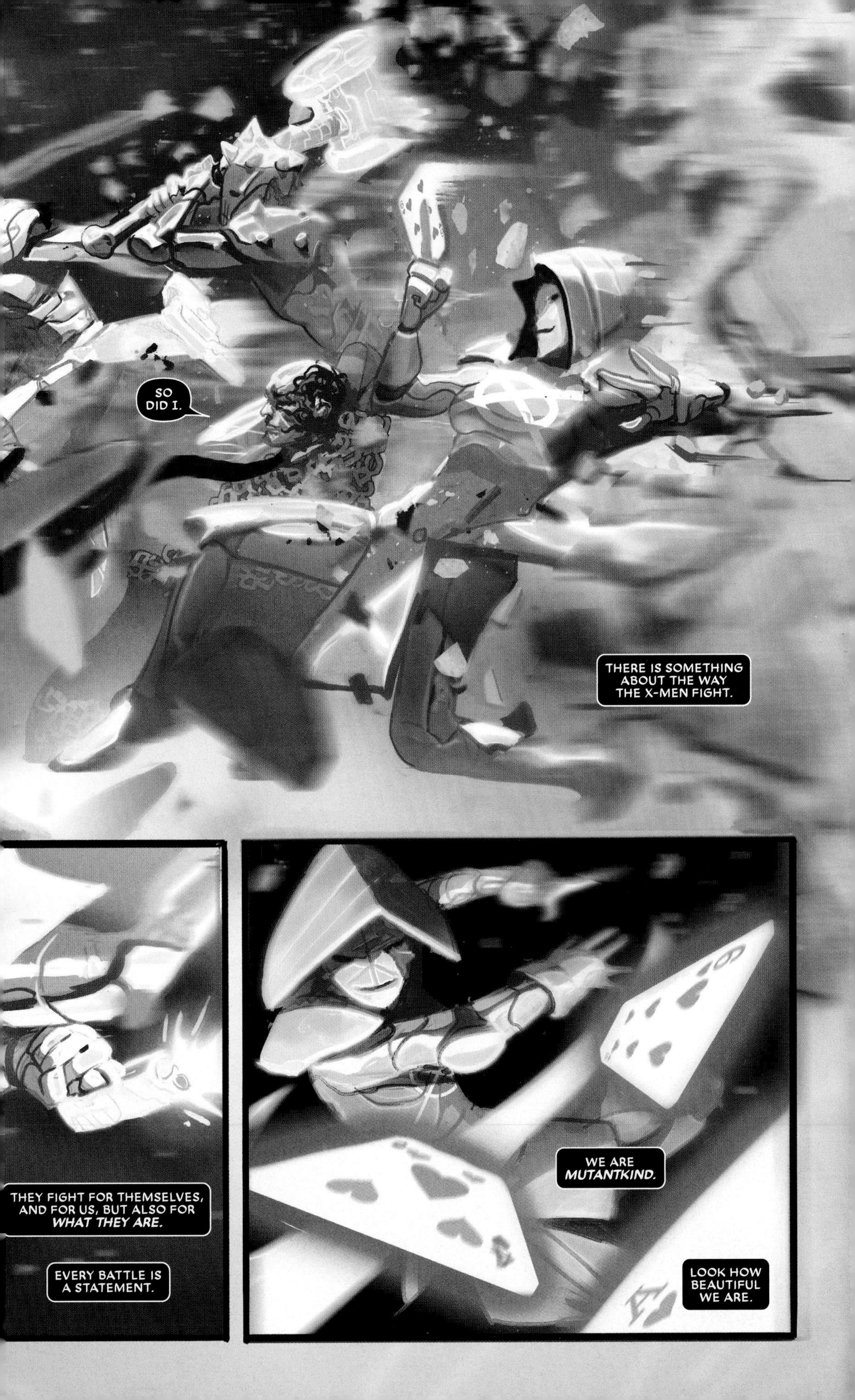
SO DID I.
THERE IS SOMETHING ABOUT THE WAY THE X-MEN FIGHT.
THEY FIGHT FOR THEMSELVES, AND FOR US, BUT ALSO FOR *WHAT THEY ARE.*
EVERY BATTLE IS A STATEMENT.
WE ARE *MUTANTKIND.*
LOOK HOW BEAUTIFUL WE ARE.

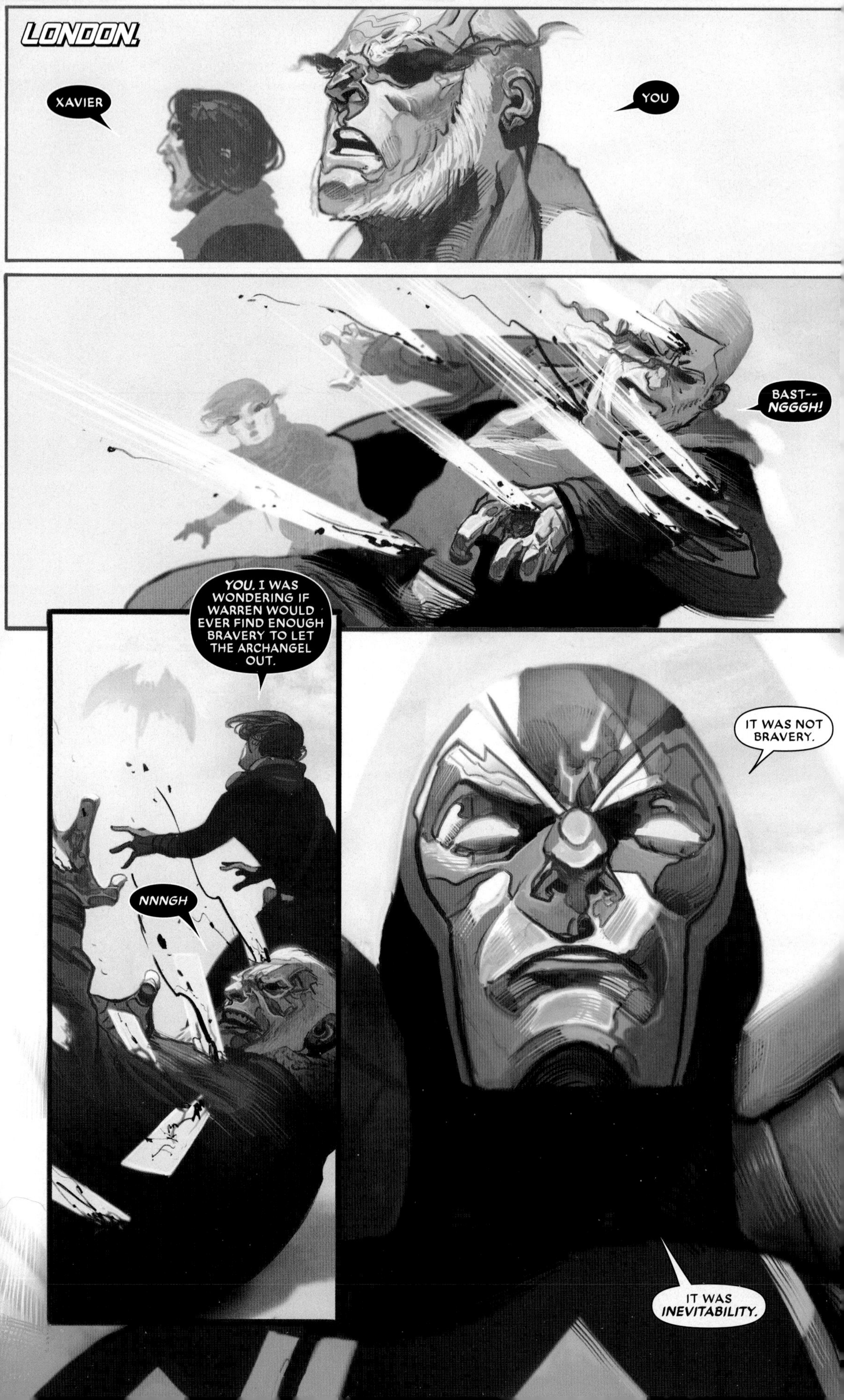
LONDON.
XAVIER
YOU
BAST--
NGGGH!
YOU. I WAS WONDERING IF WARREN WOULD EVER FIND ENOUGH BRAVERY TO LET THE ARCHANGEL OUT.
NNNGH
IT WAS NOT BRAVERY.
IT WAS INEVITABILITY.

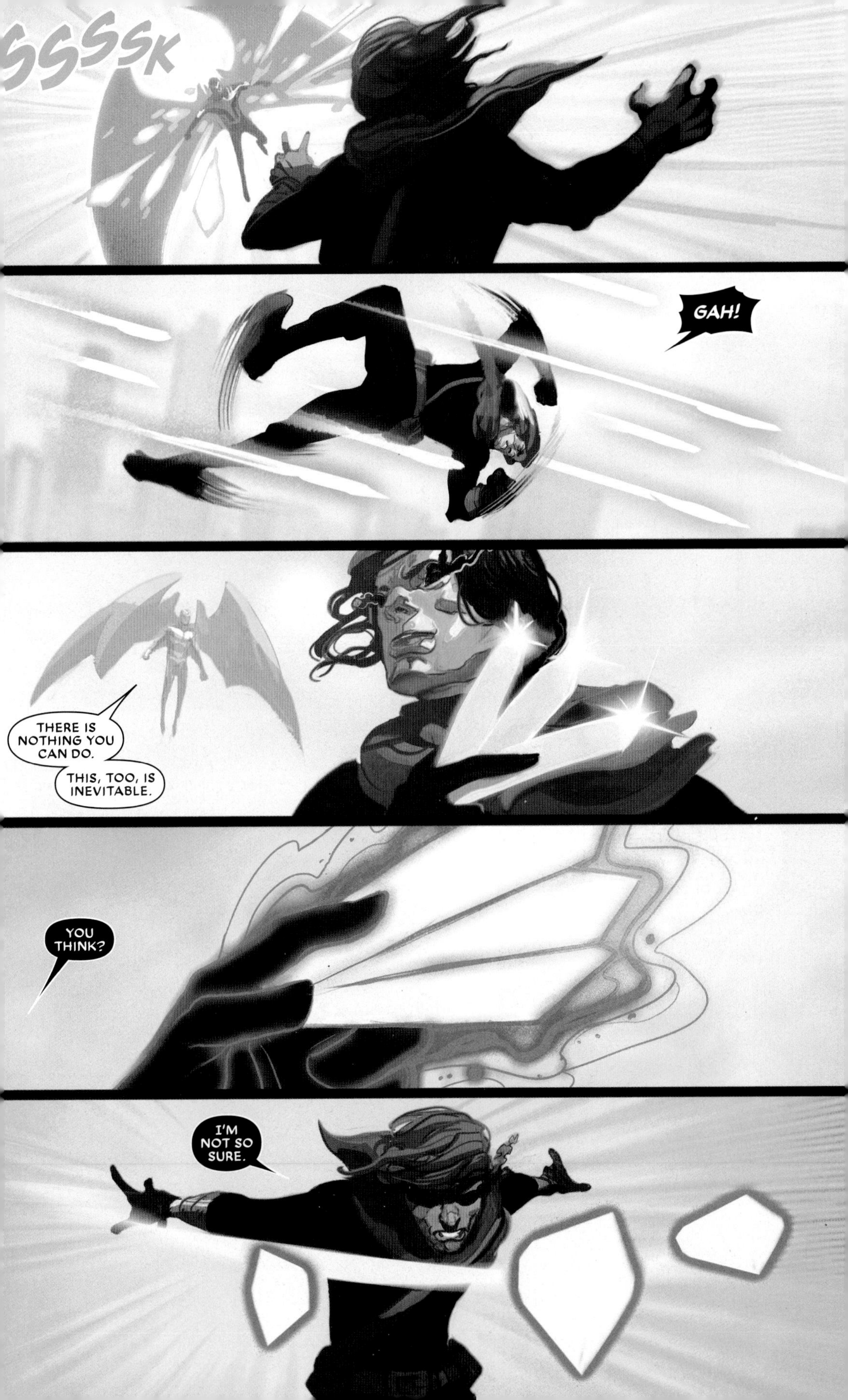
SSSSK
GAH!
THERE IS NOTHING YOU CAN DO.
THIS, TOO, IS INEVITABLE.
YOU THINK?
I'M NOT SO SURE.

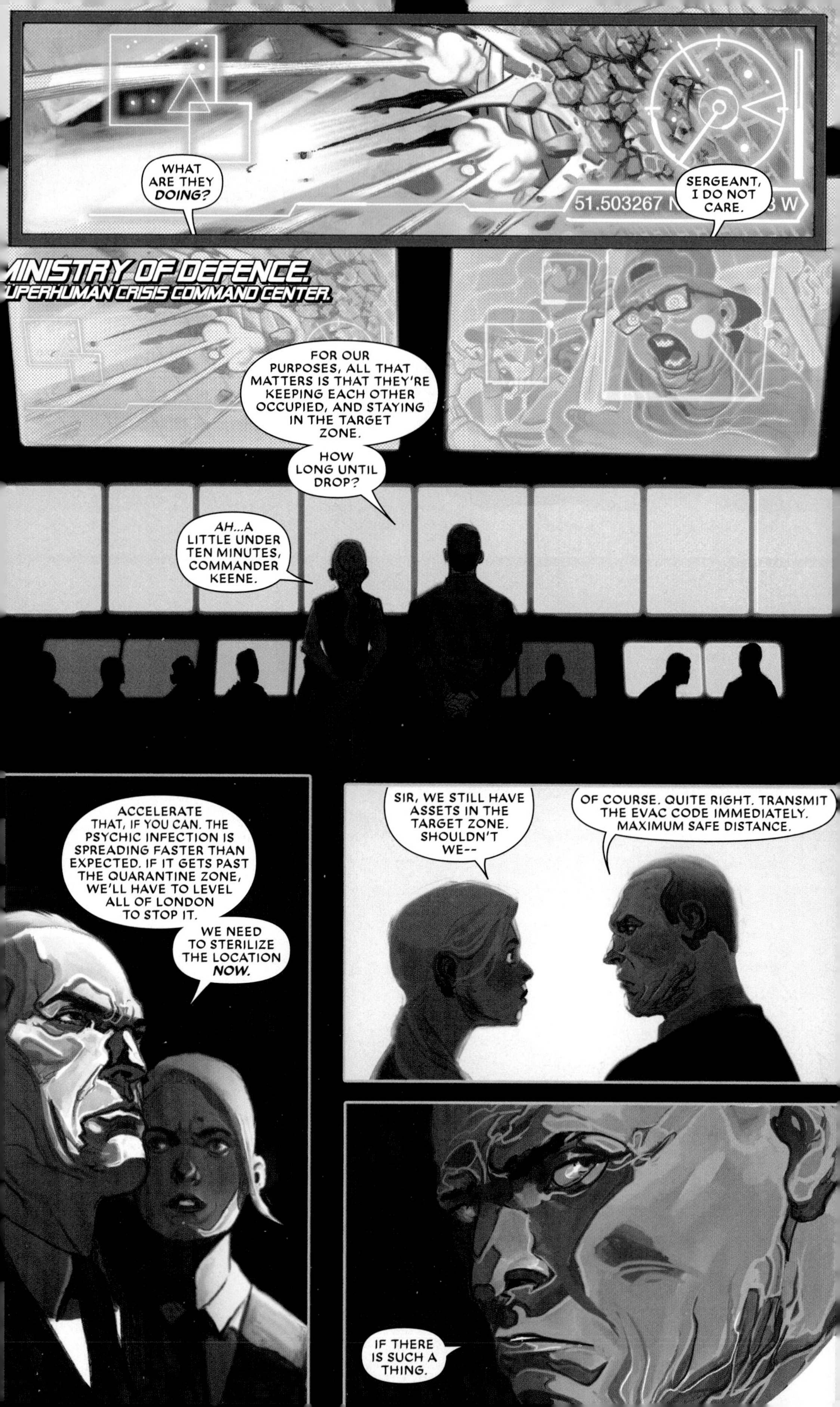

WHAT ARE THEY DOING?
51.503267 N
SERGEANT, I DO NOT CARE.
MINISTRY OF DEFENCE.
UPERHUMAN CRISIS COMMAND CENTER.
FOR OUR PURPOSES, ALL THAT MATTERS IS THAT THEY'RE KEEPING EACH OTHER OCCUPIED, AND STAYING IN THE TARGET ZONE.
HOW LONG UNTIL DROP?
AH...A LITTLE UNDER TEN MINUTES, COMMANDER KEENE.
ACCELERATE THAT, IF YOU CAN. THE PSYCHIC INFECTION IS SPREADING FASTER THAN EXPECTED. IF IT GETS PAST THE QUARANTINE ZONE, WE'LL HAVE TO LEVEL ALL OF LONDON TO STOP IT.
WE NEED TO STERILIZE THE LOCATION NOW.
SIR, WE STILL HAVE ASSETS IN THE TARGET ZONE. SHOULDN'T WE--
OF COURSE. QUITE RIGHT. TRANSMIT THE EVAC CODE IMMEDIATELY. MAXIMUM SAFE DISTANCE.
IF THERE IS SUCH A THING.

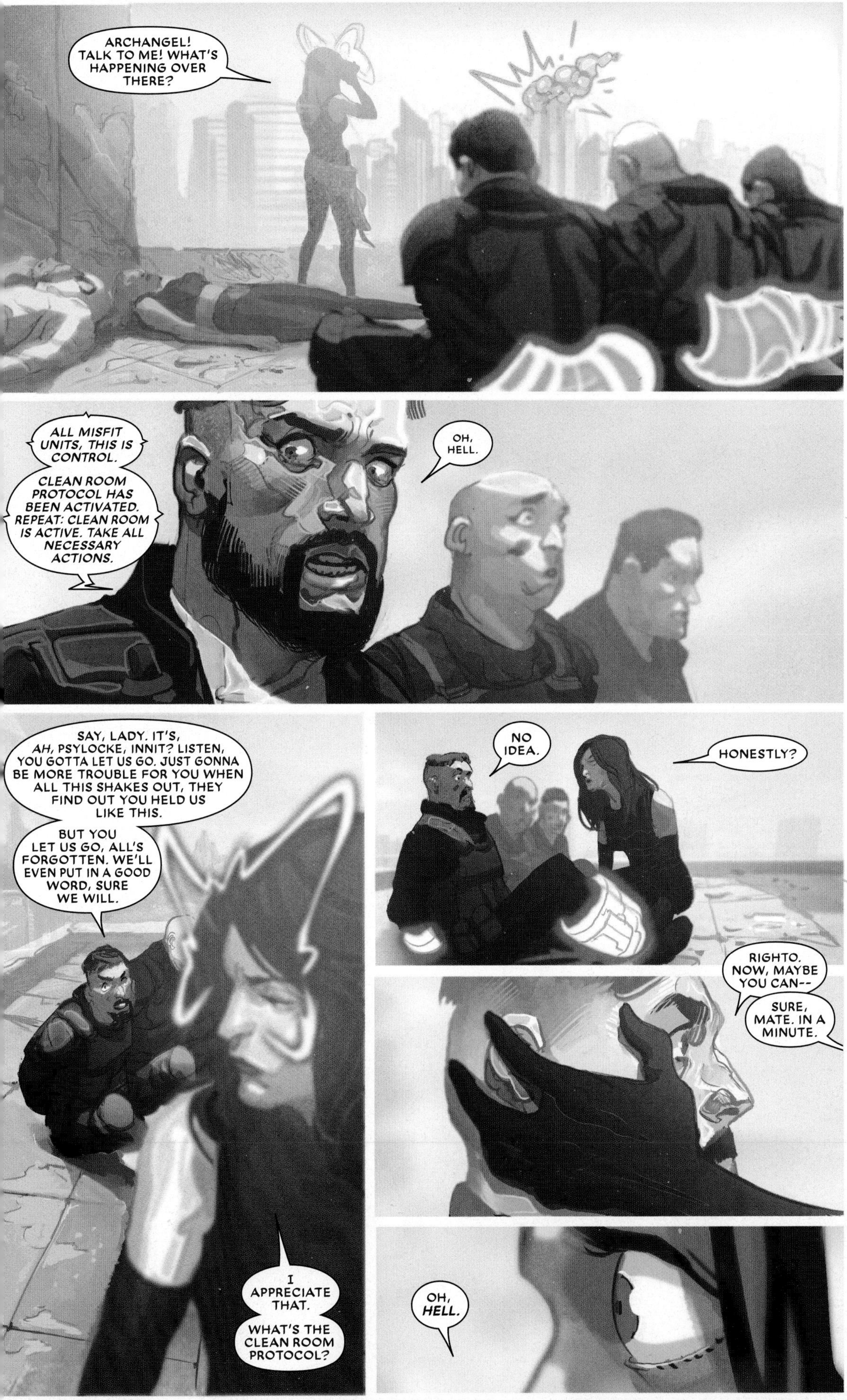
ARCHANGEL! TALK TO ME! WHAT'S HAPPENING OVER THERE?
ALL MISFIT UNITS, THIS IS CONTROL.
CLEAN ROOM PROTOCOL HAS BEEN ACTIVATED. REPEAT: CLEAN ROOM IS ACTIVE. TAKE ALL NECESSARY ACTIONS.
OH, HELL.
SAY, LADY. IT'S, AH, PSYLOCKE, INNIT? LISTEN, YOU GOTTA LET US GO. JUST GONNA BE MORE TROUBLE FOR YOU WHEN ALL THIS SHAKES OUT, THEY FIND OUT YOU HELD US LIKE THIS.
BUT YOU LET US GO, ALL'S FORGOTTEN. WE'LL EVEN PUT IN A GOOD WORD, SURE WE WILL.
I APPRECIATE THAT.
WHAT'S THE CLEAN ROOM PROTOCOL?
HONESTLY?
NO IDEA.
RIGHTO. NOW, MAYBE YOU CAN--
SURE, MATE. IN A MINUTE.
OH, HELL.

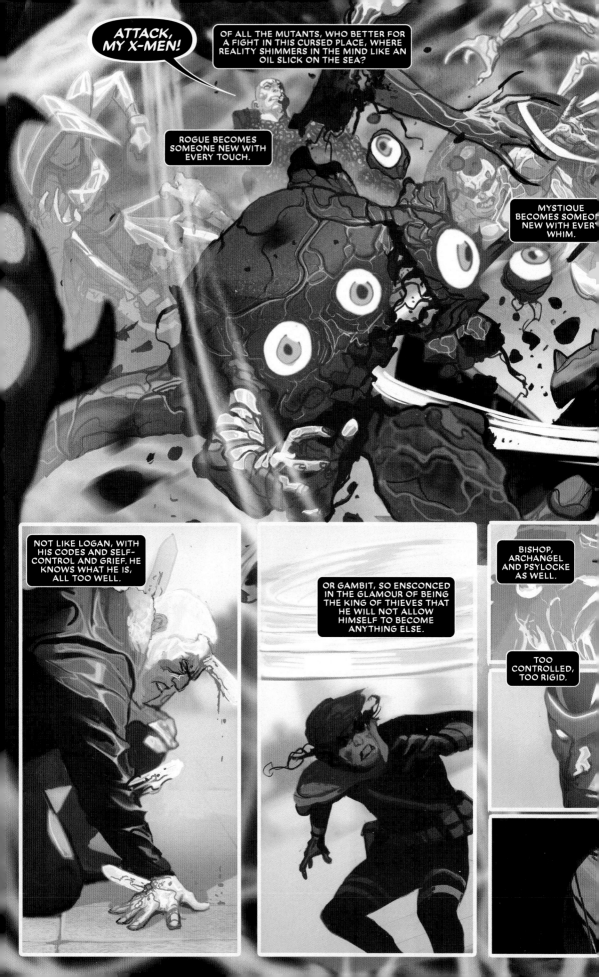

ATTACK, MY X-MEN!

OF ALL THE MUTANTS, WHO BETTER FOR A FIGHT IN THIS CURSED PLACE, WHERE REALITY SHIMMERS IN THE MIND LIKE AN OIL SLICK ON THE SEA?

ROGUE BECOMES SOMEONE NEW WITH EVERY TOUCH.

MYSTIQUE BECOMES SOMEONE NEW WITH EVERY WHIM.

NOT LIKE LOGAN, WITH HIS CODES AND SELF-CONTROL AND GRIEF. HE KNOWS WHAT HE IS, ALL TOO WELL.

OR GAMBIT, SO ENSCONCED IN THE GLAMOUR OF BEING THE KING OF THIEVES THAT HE WILL NOT ALLOW HIMSELF TO BECOME ANYTHING ELSE.

BISHOP, ARCHANGEL AND PSYLOCKE AS WELL.

TOO CONTROLLED, TOO RIGID.

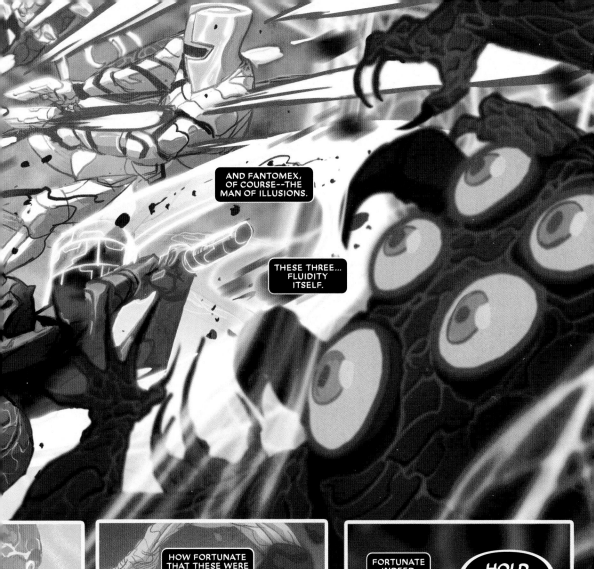

AND FANTOMEX, OF COURSE--THE MAN OF ILLUSIONS.

THESE THREE... FLUIDITY ITSELF.

THEY COULD NOT FIGHT THE SHADOW KING HERE.

BUT ALL HAVE THEIR ROLES.

HOW FORTUNATE THAT THESE WERE THE ONES WHO WERE CALLED.

FORTUNATE INDEED.

HOLD NOTHING BACK!

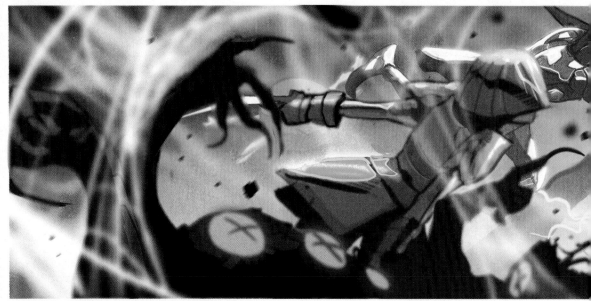

FAROUK'S MIND IS FRACTURED BETWEEN DEFENDING HIMSELF ON THE ASTRAL PLANE...

...SPREADING HIS FILTH THROUGH THE PEOPLE OF LONDON, TRYING TO BUILD A LARGE ENOUGH PSYCHIC PRESENCE IN THE REAL WORLD TO ESCAPE...

...KEEPING ME CHAINED.

OF THESE, THE LEAST OF HIS ATTENTION IS FOCUSED ON ME. AND WHY NOT?

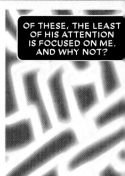

NOT WITHOUT MY X-MEN.

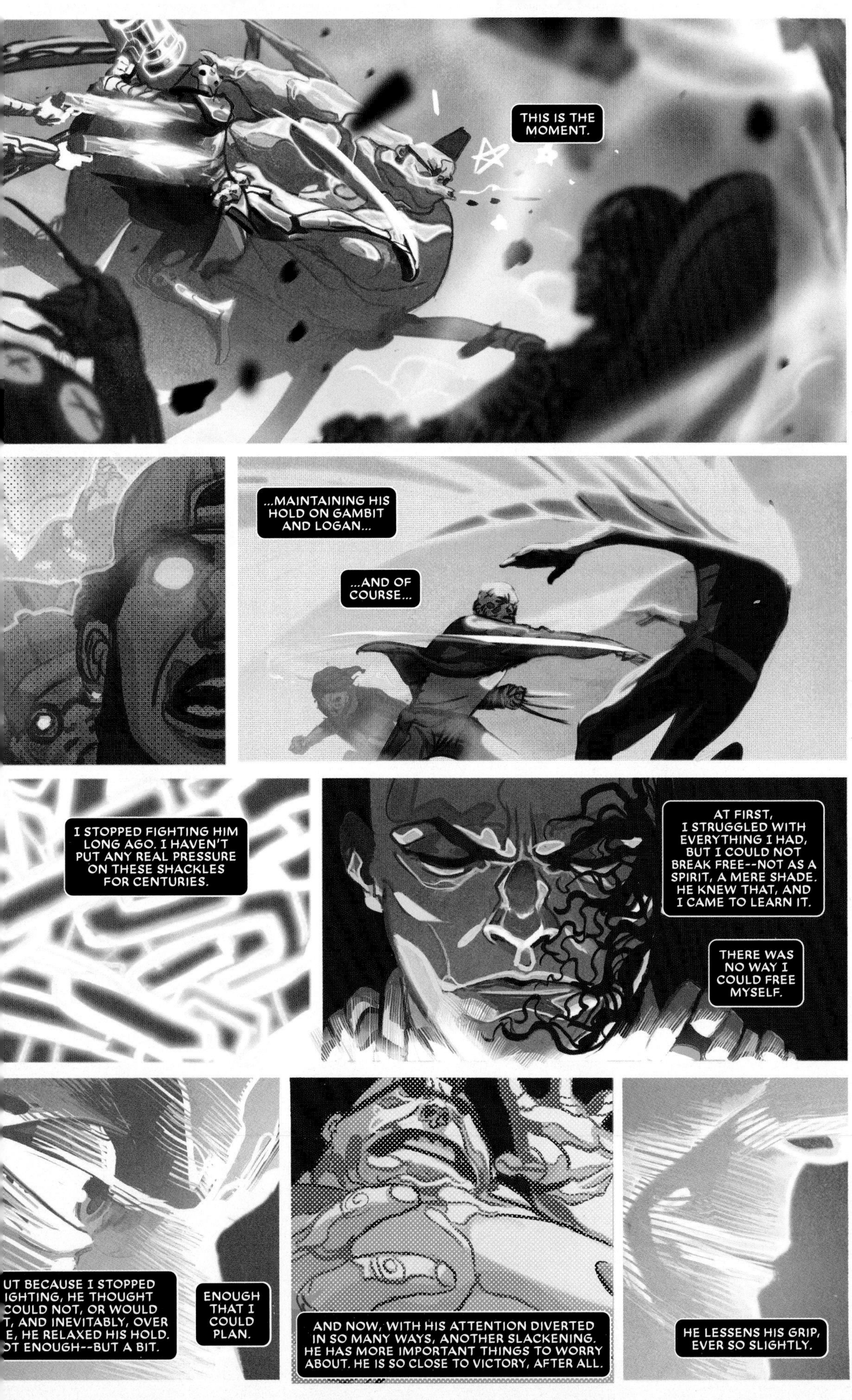
THIS IS THE MOMENT.
...MAINTAINING HIS HOLD ON GAMBIT AND LOGAN...
...AND OF COURSE...
I STOPPED FIGHTING HIM LONG AGO. I HAVEN'T PUT ANY REAL PRESSURE ON THESE SHACKLES FOR CENTURIES.
AT FIRST, I STRUGGLED WITH EVERYTHING I HAD, BUT I COULD NOT BREAK FREE--NOT AS A SPIRIT, A MERE SHADE. HE KNEW THAT, AND I CAME TO LEARN IT.
THERE WAS NO WAY I COULD FREE MYSELF.
UT BECAUSE I STOPPED IGHTING, HE THOUGHT COULD NOT, OR WOULD T, AND INEVITABLY, OVER E, HE RELAXED HIS HOLD. OT ENOUGH--BUT A BIT.
ENOUGH THAT I COULD PLAN.
AND NOW, WITH HIS ATTENTION DIVERTED IN SO MANY WAYS, ANOTHER SLACKENING. HE HAS MORE IMPORTANT THINGS TO WORRY ABOUT. HE IS SO CLOSE TO VICTORY, AFTER ALL.
HE LESSENS HIS GRIP, EVER SO SLIGHTLY.

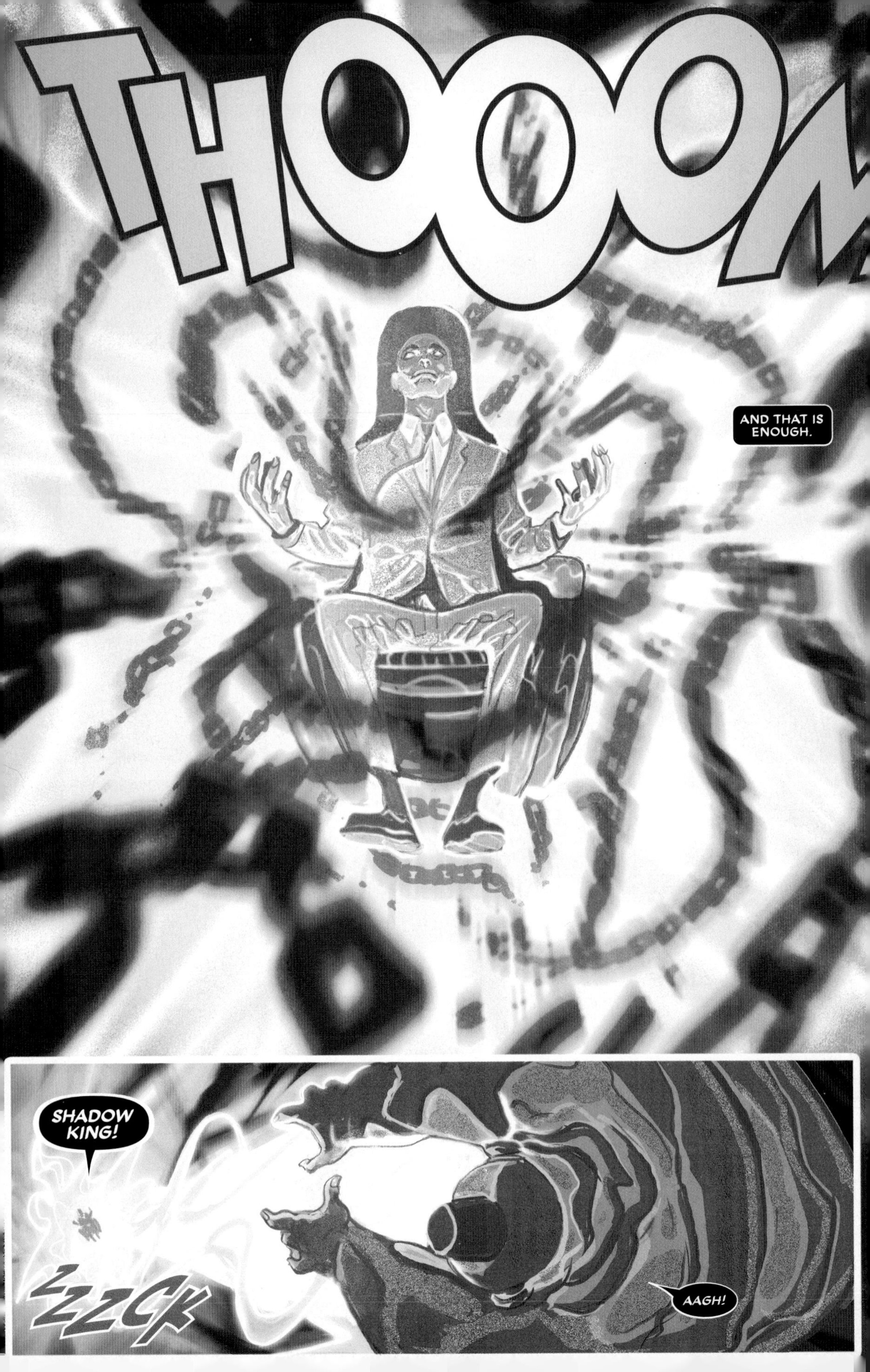
THOOOM
AND THAT IS ENOUGH.
SHADOW KING!
ZZZCK
AAGH!

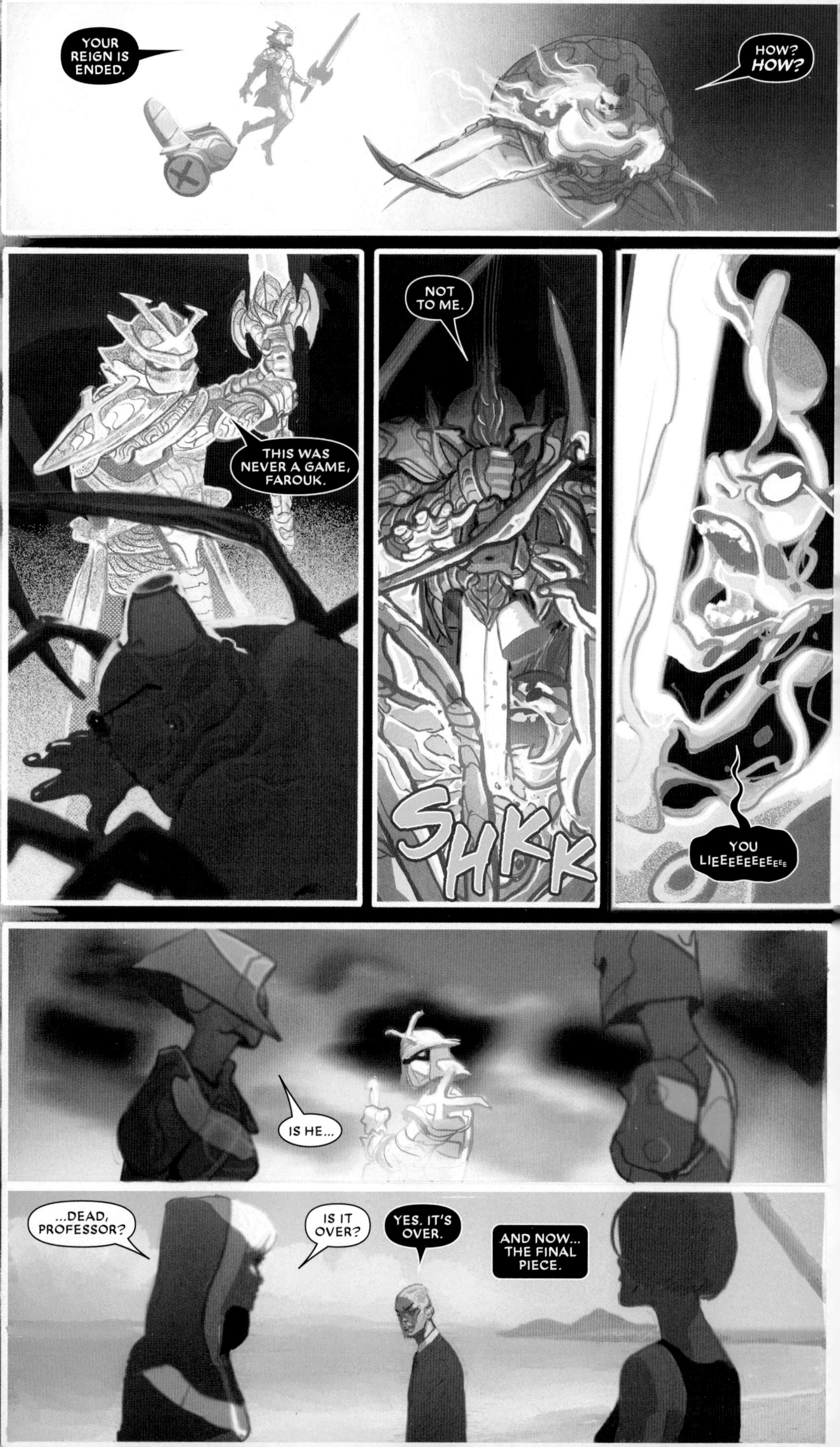
YOUR REIGN IS ENDED.
HOW? HOW?
THIS WAS NEVER A GAME, FAROUK.
NOT TO ME.
SHKK
YOU LIEEEEEEEEEEE
IS HE...
...DEAD, PROFESSOR?
IS IT OVER?
YES. IT'S OVER.
AND NOW... THE FINAL PIECE.

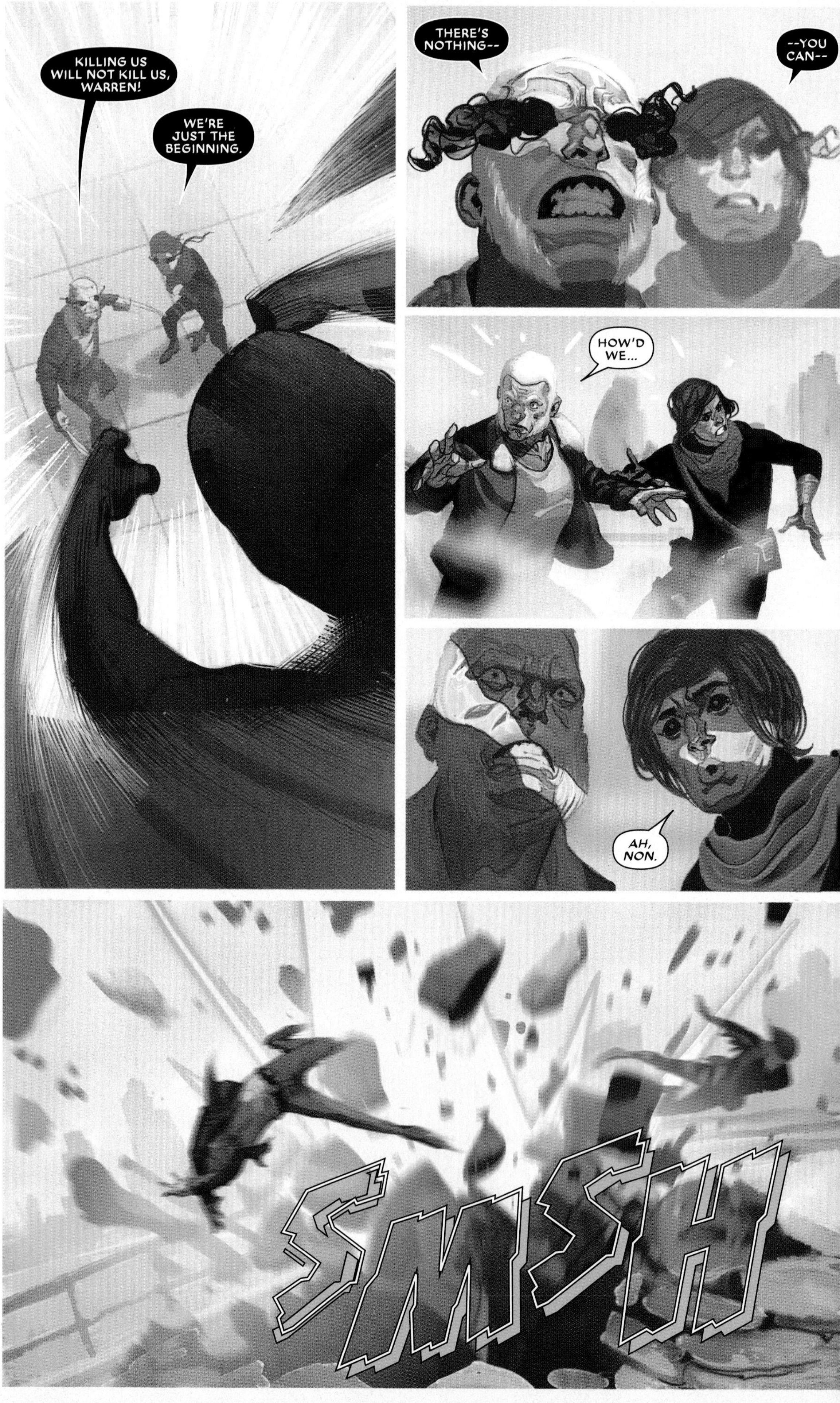
KILLING US WILL NOT KILL US, WARREN!
WE'RE JUST THE BEGINNING.
THERE'S NOTHING--
--YOU CAN--
HOW'D WE...
AH, NON.
SMSH

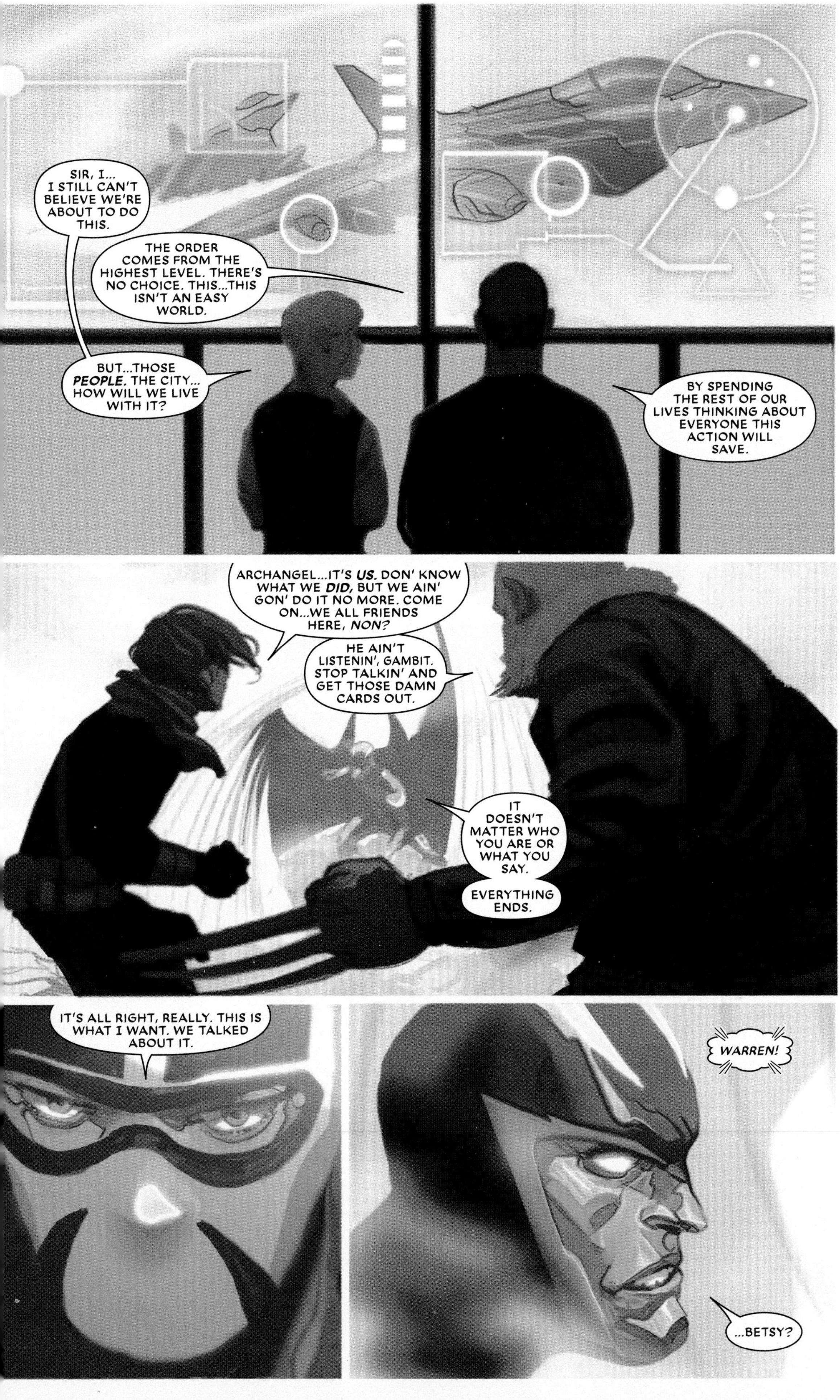

SIR, I... I STILL CAN'T BELIEVE WE'RE ABOUT TO DO THIS.
THE ORDER COMES FROM THE HIGHEST LEVEL. THERE'S NO CHOICE. THIS...THIS ISN'T AN EASY WORLD.
BUT...THOSE *PEOPLE.* THE CITY... HOW WILL WE LIVE WITH IT?
BY SPENDING THE REST OF OUR LIVES THINKING ABOUT EVERYONE THIS ACTION WILL SAVE.
ARCHANGEL...IT'S *US.* DON' KNOW WHAT WE *DID,* BUT WE AIN' GON' DO IT NO MORE. COME ON...WE ALL FRIENDS HERE, *NON?*
HE AIN'T LISTENIN', GAMBIT. STOP TALKIN' AND GET THOSE DAMN CARDS OUT.
IT DOESN'T MATTER WHO YOU ARE OR WHAT YOU SAY.
EVERYTHING ENDS.
IT'S ALL RIGHT, REALLY. THIS IS WHAT I WANT. WE TALKED ABOUT IT.
WARREN!
...BETSY?

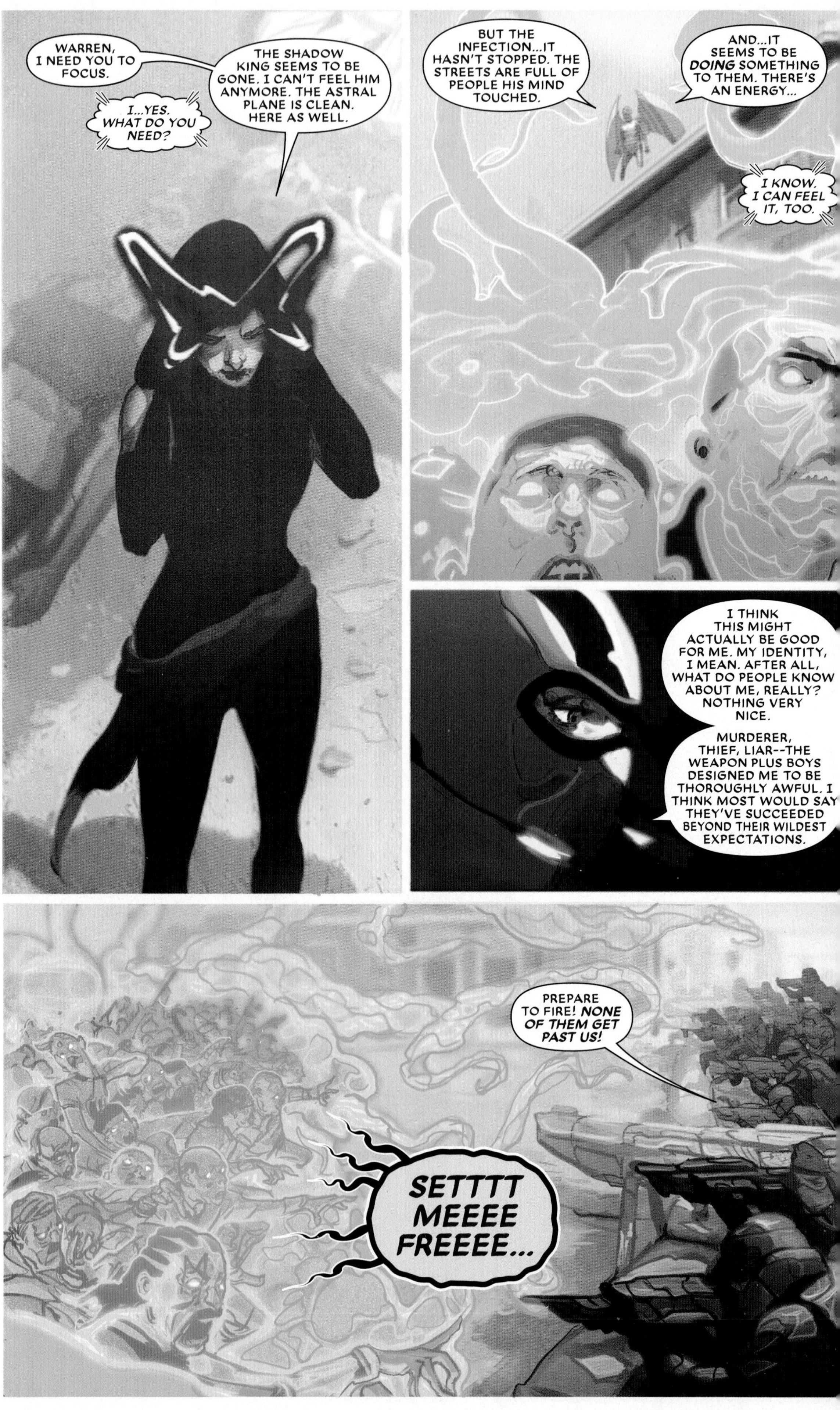

WARREN, I NEED YOU TO FOCUS.
I...YES. WHAT DO YOU NEED?
THE SHADOW KING SEEMS TO BE GONE. I CAN'T FEEL HIM ANYMORE. THE ASTRAL PLANE IS CLEAN. HERE AS WELL.
BUT THE INFECTION...IT HASN'T STOPPED. THE STREETS ARE FULL OF PEOPLE HIS MIND TOUCHED.
AND...IT SEEMS TO BE DOING SOMETHING TO THEM. THERE'S AN ENERGY...
I KNOW. I CAN FEEL IT, TOO.
I THINK THIS MIGHT ACTUALLY BE GOOD FOR ME. MY IDENTITY, I MEAN. AFTER ALL, WHAT DO PEOPLE KNOW ABOUT ME, REALLY? NOTHING VERY NICE.
MURDERER, THIEF, LIAR--THE WEAPON PLUS BOYS DESIGNED ME TO BE THOROUGHLY AWFUL. I THINK MOST WOULD SAY THEY'VE SUCCEEDED BEYOND THEIR WILDEST EXPECTATIONS.
PREPARE TO FIRE! NONE OF THEM GET PAST US!
SETTTT MEEEE FREEEE...

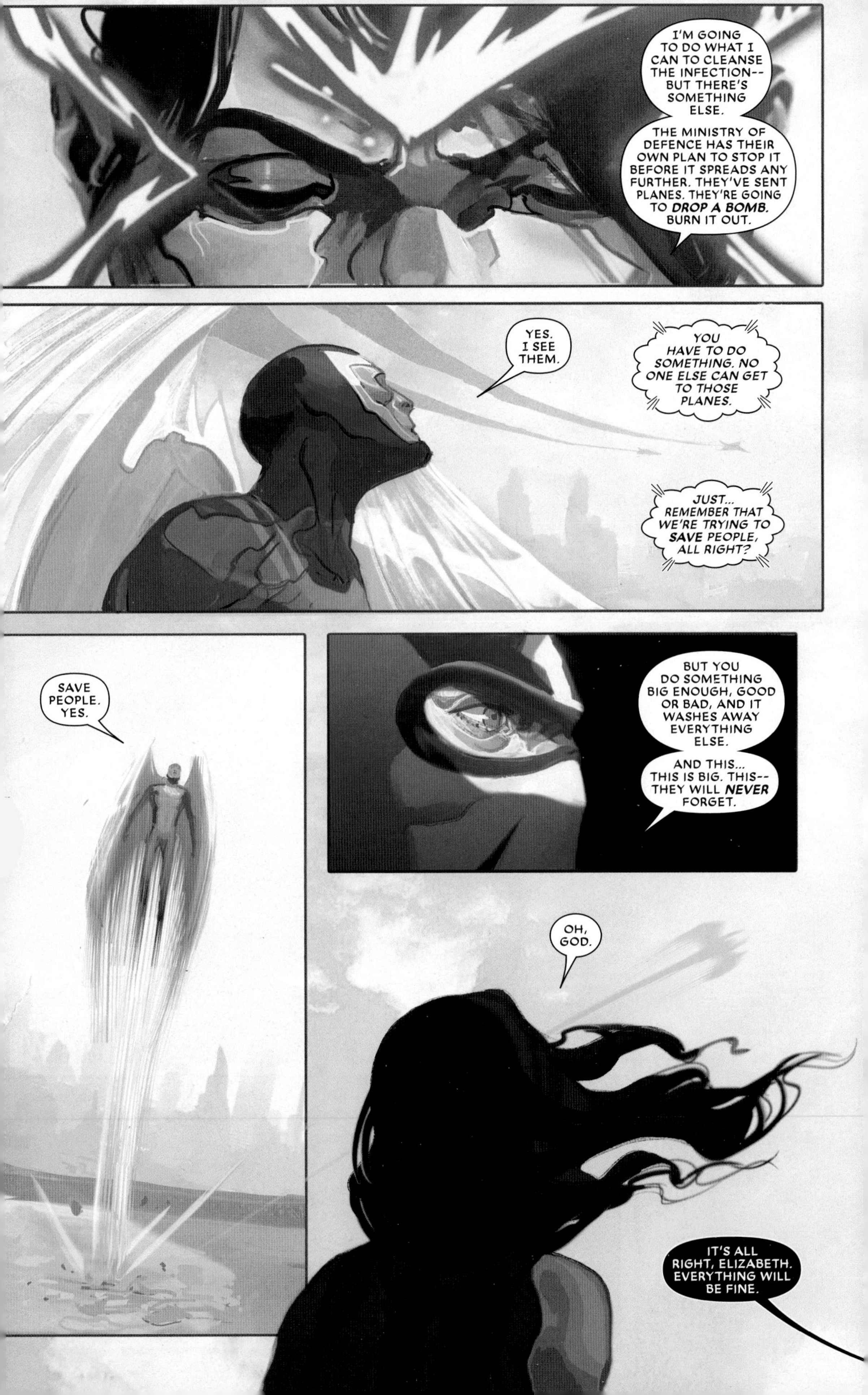

I'M GOING TO DO WHAT I CAN TO CLEANSE THE INFECTION-- BUT THERE'S SOMETHING ELSE.
THE MINISTRY OF DEFENCE HAS THEIR OWN PLAN TO STOP IT BEFORE IT SPREADS ANY FURTHER. THEY'VE SENT PLANES. THEY'RE GOING TO ***DROP A BOMB.*** BURN IT OUT.
YES. I SEE THEM.
YOU HAVE TO DO SOMETHING. NO ONE ELSE CAN GET TO THOSE PLANES.
*JUST... REMEMBER THAT WE'RE TRYING TO **SAVE** PEOPLE, ALL RIGHT?*
SAVE PEOPLE. YES.
BUT YOU DO SOMETHING BIG ENOUGH, GOOD OR BAD, AND IT WASHES AWAY EVERYTHING ELSE.
AND THIS... THIS IS BIG. THIS-- THEY WILL ***NEVER*** FORGET.
OH, GOD.
IT'S ALL RIGHT, ELIZABETH. EVERYTHING WILL BE FINE.

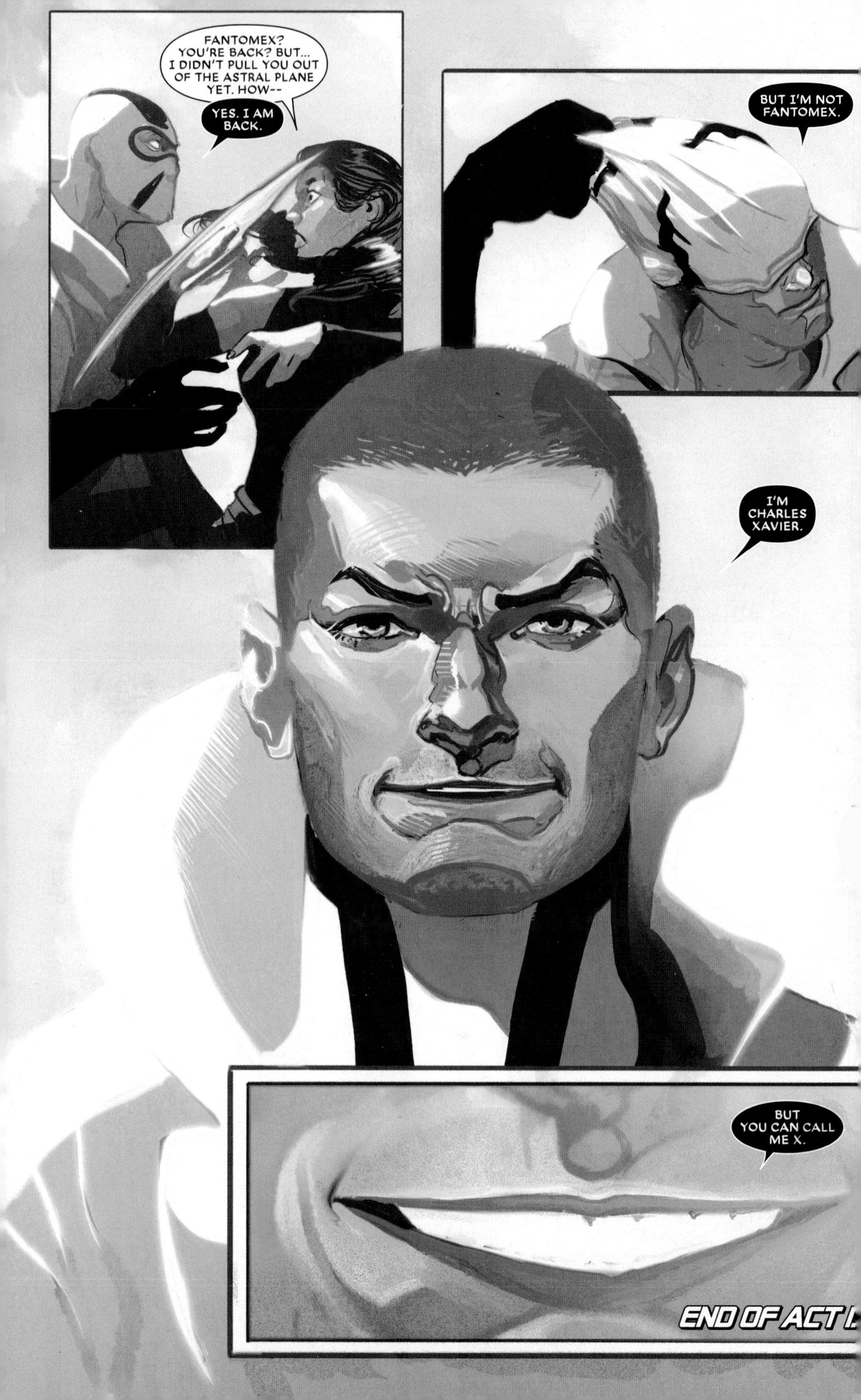
FANTOMEX? YOU'RE BACK? BUT... I DIDN'T PULL YOU OUT OF THE ASTRAL PLANE YET. HOW--
YES. I AM BACK.
BUT I'M NOT FANTOMEX.
I'M CHARLES XAVIER.
BUT YOU CAN CALL ME X.
END OF ACT I.